Developing Core Literacy Proficiencies

GRADE 9

Student Edition

GRADE
9

STUDENT EDITION

Developing
Core Literacy
Proficiencies

ODELL
EDUCATION

JB JOSSEY-BASS™
A Wiley Brand

Published by Jossey-Bass

A Wiley Brand

One Montgomery Street, Suite 1000, San Francisco, CA 94104-4594—www.josseybass.com

Jossey-Bass books and products are available through most bookstores. To contact Jossey-Bass directly call our Customer Care Department within the U.S. at 800-956-7739, outside the U.S. at 317-572-3986, or fax 317-572-4002.

Wiley publishes in a variety of print and electronic formats and by print-on-demand. Some material included with standard print versions of this book may not be included in e-books or in print-on-demand. If this book refers to media such as a CD or DVD that is not included in the version you purchased, you may download this material at www.wiley.com/go/coreliteracy (use the following password: odell2016). For more information about Wiley products, visit www.wiley.com.

Library of Congress Cataloging-in-Publication Data

Names: Odell Education, author.
Title: Developing core literacy proficiencies. Grade 9 / Odell Education.
Description: Student edition. | 1 | San Francisco, CA : Jossey-Bass, 2016.
Identifiers: LCCN 2016007130 (print) | LCCN 2016017226 (ebook) | ISBN
  9781119192923 (paperback)| ISBN 9781119192930 (pdf) | ISBN 9781119192947
  (epub)
Subjects: LCSH: Language arts (Secondary)—Curricula—United States. | Common
  Core State Standards (Education)
Classification: LCC LB1631 .O39 2016b (print) | LCC LB1631 (ebook) | DDC
  428.0071/2—dc23
LC record available at https://lccn.loc.gov/2016007130

Cover Design: Wiley
Cover Image: ©Alfredo Dagli Orti/The Art Archive/Corbis Images

Printed in the United States of America

FIRST EDITION

PB Printing   10 9 8 7 6 5 4 3 2 1

ACKNOWLEDGMENTS

Project director: Stephanie Smythe

Primary program designers:

- Rick Dills, EdD
- Judson Odell
- Ioana Radoi
- Daniel Fennessy

Curriculum consultant: Nemeesha Brown

Contributing text specialist: Rosemarie Heinegg, PhD

Unit developers—Texts, notes, and questions:

- Reading Closely for Textual Details: "Education is the new currency": Luke Bauer
- Making Evidence-Based Claims: "The unexamined life is not worth living.": Mary Catherine Youmell, PhD, and Judson Odell
- Making Evidence-Based Claims about Literary Technique: "Macomber laughed, a very natural hearty laugh.": Judson Odell
- Researching to Deepen Understanding: Music: What role does it play in our lives?: Facundo Gomez and Keeva Kase
- Building Evidence-Based Arguments: "What is the virtue of a proportional response?": Judson Odell and Daniel Fennessy

We are grateful for feedback we received on early versions of units from Achieve's EQuIP Review Process, under the direction of Christine Tell, Alissa Peltzman, and Cristina Marks.

We are also grateful for the students and teachers of the Bay Shore Schools who collaborated with us to pilot the curriculum. Thanks especially to LaQuita Outlaw, Elizabeth Galarza, Caitlin Moreira, and Jen Ritter (who personally renamed the **Supporting Evidence-Based Claims Tool**).

We are especially grateful for New York State and the Regents Research Fund for funding the development of the earlier Open Educational Resource version of this curriculum. Without the support we received from Kristen Huff, David Abel, and Kate Gerson, none of this work would have been possible.

CONTENTS

Contents

INTRODUCTION TO THE CORE LITERACY PROFICIENCIES: BECOMING A LITERATE PERSON

"Literacy is the ability to use printed and written information to function in society, to achieve one's goals, and to develop one's knowledge and potential."

—*Definition from the National Assessment of Adult Literacy*

Becoming a Literate Person: Your school and teachers are trying to help you succeed in life—and to be the best you can be at whatever you choose to do. One of the ways they are doing this is by developing your *literacy*—but what do we mean when we talk about your literacy? A dictionary might simply tell us that developing literacy means building your *skills* as a reader, thinker, and writer—but it also might tell us that literacy is *knowledge* in an area of learning that is important to you. In addition, being literate involves ways of thinking and doing things—*habits*—that a person develops over time.

Being a literate person is even more important today—in our computer-driven world—than it was in the past, no matter what you want to do:

- Go to college and become a scientist
- Be a designer, artist, musician, or chef
- Own your own business
- Develop computer applications or video games
- Work in an industry or a construction field
- Seek a career in the military
- Just keep up with the news of the world

You will need to be literate whatever path in school and life you choose to follow. A recent study of the reading challenges faced by people in the United States found out that the textbooks students see in their first two years of college are much more challenging than the ones they use in high school—one reason so many new college students struggle. But the study also found that technical manuals, informational websites, and even newspapers demand a high level of reading and thinking skills as well as specialized knowledge and strategic habits—they demand literacy.

Core Literacy Proficiencies: The learning experiences you will discover in the Odell Education Program are designed to help you take control of your own literacy development and build the skills, knowledge, and habits you will need to be successful in life. They are also designed to excite your imagination and engage you in activities that are interesting and challenging.

The learning activities you will encounter will help you develop four key core literacy proficiencies. What do we mean by this term? We've already discussed the importance of *literacy. Core* suggests that what you will be learning is at the center—of your literacy development, your overall success in school, and your future life. The word *proficiency* is also important, because being "proficient" at something means you can do it well, can do it on your own, and have the confidence that comes with being good at something. Developing proficiency takes time, practice, and determination. However, becoming proficient is one of the great rewards of learning—whether you are learning to read closely, to play a musical instrument, or to do a difficult skateboard trick.

Literacy Proficiency Units: The Core Literacy Proficiencies you will develop in each of five units are as follows:

1. *Reading Closely for Textual Details:* In this unit you will develop your proficiency as an *investigator of texts.* You will learn how to do the following:

- Examine things closely (images, videos, websites, and texts)
- Ask and use questions to guide your close examination
- Find the key details—clues—that tell you something
- Make connections among those details
- Use those connections to develop an observation or conclusion

2. *Making Evidence-Based Claims:* In this unit you will develop your proficiency as a *maker and prover of claims.* You will learn how to do the following:

- Use the details, connections, and evidence you find in a text to form a claim—a stated conclusion—about something you have discovered
- Organize evidence from the text to support your claim and make your case
- Express and explain your claim in writing
- Improve your writing so that others will clearly understand and appreciate your evidence-based claim—and think about the case you have made for it

3. *Making Evidence-Based Claims about Literary Technique:* In this unit you will further develop your proficiency as a maker and prover of claims but now with a work of fiction. As you read and analyze Ernest Hemingway's short story, "The Short Happy Life of Francis Macomber," you will:

- Make claims about specific literary techniques he uses, including character development, focus of narration, and narrative structure. Similar to the prior Evidence-Based Claims unit.
- You will learn how to use details to form a claim about something you have discovered about the text.
- You will also strengthen your abilities to organize evidence to support your claim, express your claim in writing, and further improve the clarity of your writing to effectively communicate your claim.

4. *Researching to Deepen Understanding:* In this unit you will develop your proficiency as a *finder and user of information.* You will learn how to do the following:

- Have an inquiring mind and ask good questions
- Search for information—in texts, interviews, and on the Internet—that can help you answer your questions
- Record and organize the information you find
- Decide what is relevant and trustworthy in the sources of your information
- Come to a research-based position or solution to a problem
- Clearly communicate what you have learned

5. *Building Evidence-Based Arguments:* In this unit you will develop your proficiency as a *presenter of reasoned arguments.* You will learn how to do the following:

- Understand the background and key aspects of an important issue
- Look at various viewpoints on the issue
- Read the arguments of others closely and thoughtfully
- Develop your own view of the issue and take a stand about it
- Make and prove your case by using sound evidence and reasoning to support it
- Improve your writing so that others will clearly understand and appreciate your evidence-based argument—and think about the case you have made for it

Materials to Develop Literacy Proficiency

In each of the units, you will use the supporting materials organized in this Student Edition:

Texts

Each unit includes a set of relatively short but challenging texts, which you will read, examine, and discuss.

Tools

Each unit has its own *toolbox*—a set of graphic organizers that help you think about what you are reading or writing and record your thinking so you can discuss it with others and come back to it later.

Handouts

Each unit has a set of handouts, some of which will help you understand important things you are learning and some of which will help you be successful in completing the assignments in the unit.

Literacy Skills and Academic Habits

Throughout the units you will be developing Literacy Skills and Academic Habits. You will use these skills and habits to monitor your own growth and give feedback to other students when reading, discussing, and writing. Your teacher may use them to let you know about your areas of strength and areas in which you need to improve. The skills and habits you will develop are listed and described in the following two tables:

LITERACY SKILLS	DESCRIPTORS
Attending to Details	Identifies words, details, or quotations that are important to understanding the text
Deciphering Words	Uses context and vocabulary to define unknown words and phrases
Comprehending Syntax	Recognizes and uses sentence structures to help understand the text
Interpreting Language	Understands how words are used to express ideas and perspectives
Identifying Relationships	Notices important connections among details, ideas, or texts
Making Inferences	Draws sound conclusions from reading and examining the text closely
Summarizing	Correctly explains what the text says about the topic
Questioning	Writes questions that help identify important ideas, connections, and perspectives in a text
Recognizing Perspective	Identifies and explains the author's view of the text's topic
Evaluating Information	Assesses the relevance and credibility of information in texts
Delineating Argumentation	Identifies and analyzes the claims, evidence, and reasoning in arguments
Forming Claims	States a meaningful conclusion that is well supported by evidence from the text
Using Evidence	Uses well-chosen details from the text to support explanations; accurately paraphrases or quotes
Using Logic	Supports a position through a logical sequence of related claims, premises, and supporting evidence
Using Language	Writes and speaks clearly so others can understand claims and ideas
Presenting Details	Inserts details and quotations effectively into written or spoken explanations
Organizing Ideas	Organizes claims, supporting ideas, and evidence in a logical order
Using Conventions	Correctly uses sentence elements, punctuation, and spelling to produce clear writing
Publishing	Correctly uses, formats, and cites textual evidence to support claims
Reflecting Critically	Uses literacy concepts to discuss and evaluate personal and peer learning

ACADEMIC HABITS	DESCRIPTORS
Preparing	Reads the text(s) closely and thinks about the questions to prepare for tasks
Engaging Actively	Focuses attention on the task when working individually and with others
Collaborating	Works well with others while participating in text-centered discussions and group activities
Communicating Clearly	Presents ideas and supporting evidence so others can understand them
Listening	Pays attention to ideas from others and takes time to think about them
Generating Ideas	Generates and develops ideas, positions, products, and solutions to problems
Organizing Work	Maintains materials so that they can be used effectively and efficiently
Completing Tasks	Finishes short and extended tasks by established deadlines
Revising	Rethinks ideas and refines work based on feedback from others
Understanding Purpose and Process	Understands why and how a task should be accomplished
Remaining Open	Asks questions of others rather than arguing for a personal idea or opinion
Qualifying Views	Modifies and further justifies ideas in response to thinking from others

Introduction to the Core Literacy Proficiencies

UNIT 1

READING CLOSELY
FOR TEXTUAL DETAILS

DEVELOPING CORE LITERACY
PROFICIENCIES

GRADE 9

"Education is the new currency"

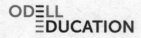

GOAL

In this unit you will develop your proficiency as an investigator of texts. You will learn how to do the following:

1. Examine things closely (images, videos, websites, and texts).
2. Ask and use questions to guide your close examination.
3. Find the key details—clues—that tell you something.
4. Make connections among those details.
5. Use those connections to develop an observation or conclusion.

TOPIC

In this unit, you will read a variety of texts related to education in the United States, specifically exploring how education has changed throughout the United States and why it continues to do so. You will examine and compare historical and modern-day photographs of classrooms and listen to arguments favoring different methods of education. You will then investigate the main ideas and purposes that drive our ever-changing educational system and the impacts these changes have on your learning environment and how you learn.

ACTIVITIES

You will start by examining two photographs to develop your skills of looking closely for key details, then work on these same skills with a video and websites. When you read, the details you look for will be things such as key information or statistics, explanations, and mental pictures the author creates through images and sentences. You'll also look for important words that you need to understand because they tell you something about the topic and how the author views it. You will learn how to use questions the way an expert investigator does—in this case to dig deeply into what you are seeing or reading. Those questions will also guide the discussions you will have with other students and your teacher. From your investigation of the texts, you will come to your own understanding of the topic of education in the United States. You will then share your understanding with others through a final written explanation and a discussion you will lead.

Developing Core Literacy Proficiencies

READING CLOSELY FOR TEXTUAL DETAILS LITERACY TOOLBOX

In *Reading Closely for Textual Details*, you will begin to build your "literacy toolbox" by learning how to use the following handouts, tools, and checklists organized in your Student Edition.

 HANDOUTS

To support your work with the texts and the tools, you will be able to use the following informational handouts:

Reading Closely Graphic

This graphic helps you understand the relationship among the various steps you will follow as you use questions to read a text closely: *approaching, questioning, analyzing, deepening,* and *extending.*

Guiding Questions Handout

This handout organizes a set of good, general questions to use when you are reading any text—called *Guiding Questions.* The questions are organized in rows that match the questioning process in the Reading Closely Graphic (*approaching, questioning, analyzing, deepening,* and *extending*) and also by four areas that we often pay attention to when we read a text.

Attending to Details Handout

This handout presents descriptions and examples of the kinds of details you might look for as you read a text, for example, facts and statistics, explanations of things, images and word pictures, technical terms, and so on.

Reading Closely Final Writing and Discussion Task Handout

This handout will explain to you what you will be doing in the two-part final assignment for this unit: (1) writing a multiparagraph explanation of an understanding you have come to about the topic and one of the texts and (2) participating in and leading a discussion of your text and how it compares to others in the unit. The handout will also help you know what your teacher will be looking for so you can be successful on the assignments.

 TOOLS

In addition to using the handouts, you will learn how to use the following tools:

Approaching the Text Tool

This two-part tool helps you prepare to read a text closely. It provides places to think about what you initially know about the text as you *approach* it—your purpose for reading, the author, publication date, and other information. It also lets you record several *questions* that you can use to do a first reading and then a rereading of the text.

Analyzing Details Tool

This four-part tool supports you in developing and using the key skills of the unit: searching for and *selecting* key details or quotations, *recording* references from the text about where you found the details and quotations, *analyzing* what those details mean to you as a reader, and *connecting* the details to form your understanding of the text.

Questioning Path Tool

This graphic organizer will provide places for you to record questions you or your teacher want to think about as you read a particular text. You will be able to record general Guiding Questions and also questions that are very specific to the text you are reading. What you record in the **Questioning Path Tool** can help you initially *approach* the text, *question* it during a first reading and investigation, *analyze* it further, *deepen* your understanding, and *extend* your reading and thinking to other questions and texts.

Model Questioning Path Tools

For each text you will read, there is a Questioning Path Tool that has been filled out for you with questions to frame and guide your reading. These model Questioning Paths are just starting points, and your teacher or you may prefer to develop your own paths and questions. The model paths are organized by the steps from the Reading Closely Graphic (*approaching, questioning, analyzing, deepening,* and *extending*) and include general Guiding Questions from the Guiding Questions Handout and some questions that are specific to each text and its content. You will use these model paths to guide your reading, frame your discussions with your teacher and other students, and help you when you are doing the final activities in the unit.

 CHECKLIST

You will also use this checklist throughout the unit to support peer- and self-review:

Reading Closely Literacy Skills and Discussion Habits Checklist

This checklist presents and briefly describes the Literacy Skills and Habits you will be working on during the unit. You can use it to remind you of what you are trying to learn; reflect on what you have done when reading, discussing, or writing; or give feedback to other students. Your teacher may use it to let you know about your areas of strength and areas in which you need to improve.

READING CLOSELY FOR TEXTUAL DETAILS UNIT TEXTS

AUTHOR	DATE	PUBLISHER	NOTES
Text 1: Classroom Pictures (Photos)			
NA	1950s and 2012	KJJS—Craig Michaels Inc.	Photos from a 1950s classroom and classrooms in 2012
Text 2: *The Story of My Life* (Personal narrative)			
Helen Keller	1905	Doubleday, Page & Co.	An excerpt of Keller talking about her teacher, Anne Sullivan
Text 3: "Changing Education Paradigms" (Video)			
Ken Robinson	2010	TED Talk	TED Talk from RSA Animate describing the changing educational landscape across the United States and world
Text 4: Only a Teacher (Website)			
NA	NA	PBS	Website for students to read and search about the history of the role of the teacher in US education
Text 5: "Kids Need Structure" (Speech)			
Colin Powell	2012	TED Talk	Excerpted text of Powell's TED Talk in which he states the importance of structure in kids' lives
Text 6: *Dr. Montessori's Own Handbook* (Informational text)			
Maria Montessori	1914	Frederick A. Stokes Co.	Descriptive text describing how children should be allowed to develop through independence and little influence from adults
Text 7: "Good Citizenship: The Purpose of Education" (Personal narrative)			
Eleanor Roosevelt	1930	Pictorial review	Abridged essay describing Roosevelt's beliefs on the purpose of education
Text 8: *Notes on the State of Virginia* (Government document)			
Thomas Jefferson	1784	University of Chicago Press	Jefferson's note on the importance of compulsory education

Text 9: "The Vision of Education Reform in the United States" (Speech)			
Arne Duncan	2010	United States Department of Education	Duncan's argument for raising educational standards in order to remain economically competitive
Extended Reading: "Lectures and Biographical Sketches" (Personal narrative)			
Ralph Waldo Emerson	1863–1864	Houghton Mifflin and Co.	Essay describing Emerson's beliefs on the purpose of education
Extended Reading: "Education and National Welfare" (Speech)			
Horace Mann	1848	Tennessee Criminal Law Resources	Report detailing how education leads to social mobility in society

TEXT 1

Classroom Pictures
1950s and 2012

(1950s CLASSROOM)

(2012 CLASSROOM)

TEXT 2

The Story of My Life
Helen Keller
Doubleday, Page & Co., 1905

Thus I learned from life itself. At the beginning I was only a little mass of possibilities. It was my **P1**
teacher who unfolded and developed them. When she came, everything about me breathed of love
and joy and was full of meaning. She has never since let pass an opportunity to point out the beauty
that is in everything, nor has she ceased trying in thought and action and example to make my life
5 sweet and useful.

It was my teacher's genius, her quick sympathy, her loving tact which made the first years of my **P2**
education so beautiful. It was because she seized the right moment to impart knowledge that made it
so pleasant and acceptable to me. She realized that a child's mind is like a shallow brook which ripples
and dances merrily over the stony course of its education and reflects here a flower, there a bush,
10 **yonder** a **fleecy** cloud; and she attempted to guide my mind on its way, knowing that like a brook
it should be fed by mountain streams and hidden springs, until it broadened out into a deep river,
capable of reflecting in its **placid** surface, **billowy** hills, the **luminous** shadows of trees and the blue
heavens, as well as the sweet face of a little flower.

Any teacher can take a child to the classroom, but not every teacher can make him learn. He will not **P3**
15 work joyously unless he feels that liberty is his, whether he is busy or at rest; he must feel the flush of

yonder	fleecy	placid
a distant place that is usually within sight	covered or made of fleece, the wool usually from a sheep	peaceful; calm
billowy	**luminous**	
to swell out; puff up	radiating or reflecting light; shining; bright	

Developing Core Literacy Proficiencies

victory and the heart-sinking of disappointment before he takes with a will the tasks distasteful to him and resolves to dance his way bravely through a dull routine of textbooks.

My teacher is so near to me that I scarcely think of myself apart from her. How much of my delight   P4
in all beautiful things is **innate**, and how much is due to her influence, I can never tell. I feel that her
20 being is inseparable from my own, and that the footsteps of my life are in hers. All the best of me belongs to her—there is not a talent, or an aspiration or a joy in me that has not been awakened by her loving touch.

innate		
the essential character of something or someone		

TEXT 3

Changing Paradigms
Ken Robinson
TED Talk, 2010

TEXT 4

Only a Teacher
PBS

TEXT 5

"Kids Need Structure"
Colin Powell
TED Talk, 2012

I want to talk about young people and structure. This was last Wednesday afternoon at a school in **P1**
Brooklyn, New York, at Cristo Rey High School, run by the **Jesuits**. And I was talking to this group of
students, and take a look at them (shows a picture) . . . And there are about 300 kids in this school, and
the school's been going now for four years, and they're about to graduate their first class. Twenty-two
5 people are graduating, and all 22 are going to college. They all come from homes where there is, for
the most part, just one person in the home, usually the mother or the grandmother, and that's it, and
they come here for their education and for their structure . . .

Now I had this picture taken, and it was put up on my Facebook page last week, and somebody wrote **P2**
in, "Huh, why does he have him standing at attention like that?" And then they said, "But he looks
10 good." (Laughter)

He does look good, because kids need structure, and the trick I play in all of my school appearances **P3**
is that when I get through with my little **homily** to the kids, I then invite them to ask questions,
and when they raise their hands, I say, "Come up," and I make them come up and stand in front of
me. I make them stand at attention like a soldier. Put your arms straight down at your side, look up,
15 open your eyes, stare straight ahead, and speak out your question loudly so everybody can hear. No
slouching, no pants hanging down, none of that stuff. (Laughter) And this young man, his name is—
his last name Cruz—he loved it. That's all over his Facebook page and it's gone viral. (Laughter) So
people think I'm being unkind to this kid. No, we're having a little fun . . .

Jesuits	homily	
a member of a Roman Catholic religious order founded by Ignatius of Loyola in 1534	a sermon, usually religious and of a nondoctrine nature	

But anyway, it's a game I play, and it comes obviously from my military experience. Because for the   P4

20 majority of my adult life, I worked with young kids, teenagers with guns, I call them. And we would

bring them into the army, and the first thing we would do is to put them in an environment of

structure, put them in ranks, make them all wear the same clothes, cut all their hair off so they look

alike, make sure that they are standing in ranks. We teach them how to go right face, left face, so they

can obey instructions and know the consequences of not obeying instructions. It gives them structure.

25 And then we introduce them to somebody who they come to hate immediately, the drill sergeant.

And they hate him. And the drill sergeant starts screaming at them, and telling them to do all kinds of

awful things. But then the most amazing thing happens over time. Once that structure is developed,

once they understand the reason for something, once they understand, "Mama ain't here, son. I'm your

worst nightmare. I'm your daddy and your mommy. And that's just the way it is. You got that, son?

30 Yeah, and then when I ask you a question, there are only three possible answers: yes, sir; no, sir; and no

excuse, sir. Don't start telling me why you didn't do something. It's yes, sir; no, sir; no excuse, sir."

"You didn't shave." "But sir—"   P5

"No, don't tell me how often you scraped your face this morning. I'm telling you you didn't shave."   P6

"No excuse, sir." "Attaboy, you're learning fast."   P7

35 But you'd be amazed at what you can do with them once you put them in that structure. In 18 weeks,   P8

they have a skill. They are mature. And you know what, they come to admire the drill sergeant and

they never forget the drill sergeant. They come to respect him. And so we need more of this kind of

structure and respect in the lives of our children.

I spend a lot of time with youth groups, and I say to people, "When does the education process   P9

40 begin?" We're always talking about, "Let's fix the schools. Let's do more for our teachers. Let's put

more computers in our schools. Let's get it all online."

That isn't the whole answer. It's part of the answer. But the real answer begins with bringing a   P10

child to the school with structure in that child's heart and soul to begin with.

Developing Core Literacy Proficiencies

When does the learning process begin? Does it begin in first grade? No, no, it begins the first time a **P11**
45 child in a mother's arms looks up at the mother and says, "Oh, this must be my mother. She's the one
who feeds me. Oh yeah, when I don't feel so good down there, she takes care of me. It's her language
I will learn." And at that moment they shut out all the other languages that they could be learning
at that age, but by three months, that's her. And if the person doing it, whether it's the mother or
grandmother, whoever's doing it, that is when the education process begins. That's when language
50 begins. That's when love begins. That's when structure begins. That's when you start to imprint on
the child that "you are special, you are different from every other child in the world. And we're going
to read to you." A child who has not been read to is in danger when that child gets to school. A child
who doesn't know his or her colors or doesn't know how to tell time, doesn't know how to tie shoes,
doesn't know how to do those things, and doesn't know how to do something that goes by a word
55 that was drilled into me as a kid: mind. Mind your manners! Mind your adults! Mind what you're
saying! This is the way children are raised properly. And I watched my own young grandchildren now
come along and they're, much to the distress of my children, they are acting just like we did. You
know? You imprint them.

And that's what you have to do to prepare children for education and for school. And I'm working **P12**
60 at all the energy I have to sort of communicate this message that we need preschool, we need Head
Start, we need prenatal care. The education process begins even before the child is born, and if
you don't do that, you're going to have difficulty. And we are having difficulties in so many of our
communities and so many of our schools where kids are coming to first grade and their eyes are
blazing, they've got their little **knapsack** on and they're ready to go, and then they realize they're
65 not like the other first graders who know books, have been read to, can do their alphabet. And by
the third grade, the kids who didn't have that structure and minding in the beginning start to realize
they're behind, and what do they do? They act it out. They act it out, and they're on their way to jail
or they're on their way to being dropouts. It's predictable. If you're not at the right reading level at
third grade, you are a candidate for jail at age 18, and we have the highest **incarceration** rate because
70 we're not getting our kids the proper start in life.

knapsack	incarceration	
a bag made of nylon or leather and carried on the back of hikers or soldiers, etc.	imprisonment or confining to an enclosure	

TEXT 6

Dr. Montessori's Own Handbook
Maria Montessori
Frederick A. Stokes Co., 1914

Freedom

The success of these results is closely connected with the delicate intervention of the one who guides **P1**
the children in their development. It is necessary for the teacher to *guide* the child without letting
him feel her presence too much, so that she may be always ready to supply the desired help, but may
never be the obstacle between the child and his experience.

5 A lesson in the ordinary use of the word cools the child's enthusiasm for the knowledge of things, just **P2**
as it would cool the enthusiasm of adults. To keep alive that enthusiasm is the secret of real guidance,
and it will not prove a difficult task, provided that the attitude towards the child's acts be that of
respect, calm and waiting, and provided that he be left free in his movements and in his experiences.

Then we shall notice that the child has a personality which he is seeking to expand; he has initiative, **P3**
10 he chooses his own work, persists in it, changes it according to his inner needs; he does not shirk
effort, he rather goes in search of it, and with great joy overcomes obstacles within his capacity. He is
sociable to the extent of wanting to share with every one his successes, his discoveries, and his little
triumphs. There is therefore no need of intervention. "Wait while observing." That is the motto for the
educator.

15 Let us wait, and be always ready to share in both the joys and the difficulties which the child **P4**
experiences. He himself invites our sympathy, and we should respond fully and gladly. Let us have
endless patience with his slow progress, and show enthusiasm and gladness at his successes. If we
could say: "We are respectful and courteous in our dealings with children, we treat them as we should
like to be treated ourselves," we should certainly have mastered a great educational principle and
20 undoubtedly be setting an *example of good education*.

What we all desire for ourselves, namely, not to be disturbed in our work, not to find hindrances to   P5
our efforts, to have good friends ready to help us in times of need, to see them rejoice with us, to be
on terms of equality with them, to be able to confide and trust in them––this is what we need for
happy companionship. In the same way children are human beings to whom respect is due, superior
25 to us by reason of their "innocence" and of the greater possibilities of their future. What we desire
they desire also.

As a rule, however, we do not respect our children. We try to force them to follow us without regard to   P6
their special needs. We are overbearing with them, and above all, rude; and then we expect them to be
submissive and well-behaved, knowing all the time how strong is their instinct of imitation and how
30 touching their faith in and admiration of us. They will imitate us in any case. Let us treat them, therefore,
with all the kindness which we would wish to help to develop in them. And by kindness is not meant
caresses. Should we not call anyone who embraced us at the first time of meeting rude, vulgar and
ill-bred? Kindness consists in interpreting the wishes of others, in conforming one's self to them, and
sacrificing, if need be, one's own desire. This is the kindness which we must show towards children.

35 To find the interpretation of children's desires we must study them scientifically, for their desires are   P7
often unconscious. They are the inner cry of life, which wishes to unfold according to mysterious laws.
We know very little of the way in which it unfolds. Certainly the child is growing into a man by force
of a divine action similar to that by which from nothing he became a child. Our intervention in this
marvelous process is *indirect*; we are here to offer to this life, which came into the world by itself, the
40 *means* necessary for its development, and having done that we must await this development with
respect.

Let us leave the life *free* to develop within the limits of the good, and let us observe this inner life   P8
developing. This is the whole of our mission. Perhaps as we watch we shall be reminded of the words
of Him who was absolutely good, "Suffer the little children to come unto Me." That is to say, "Do not
45 hinder them from coming, since, if they are left free and unhampered, they will come."

submissive	caresses
passive, obedient	a light touch or embrace

TEXT 7

Good Citizenship: The Purpose of Education
Eleanor Roosevelt
Pictorial Review, 1930

What is the purpose of education? This question agitates scholars, teachers, statesmen, every group **P1**
of thoughtful men and women. The conventional answer is the acquisition of knowledge, the reading
of books, and the learning of facts. Perhaps because there are so many books and the branches of
knowledge in which we can learn facts are so multitudinous today, we begin to hear more frequently
5 that the function of education is to give children a desire to learn. Also to teach them how to use their
minds and where to go to acquire facts when their curiosity is aroused. Even more all-embracing than
this is the statement made not long ago, before a group of English headmasters, by the Archbishop of
York, that "the true purpose of education is to produce citizens." . . .

Theodore Roosevelt was teaching by precept and example. He believed that men owed something **P2**
10 at all times, whether in peace or in war, for the privilege of citizenship. He was saying that, no matter
what conditions existed, the blame lay no more heavily on the politician than on the shoulders of the
average citizen. For it was he who concerned himself so little with his government that he allowed
men to stay in power in spite of his dissatisfaction because he was too indifferent to exert himself to
get better men in office…

15 Gradually a change has come about. More young men and more young women (since the latter **P3**
have had the vote) are doing political work. And even if they do not hold political office they have
felt the need to understand their own government. In our schools are now given courses in civics,
government, economics, and current events. Very few children are as ignorant as I was. But there still
remains a vast amount to be done before we accomplish our first objective—informed and intelligent
20 citizens. Secondly, to bring about the realization that we are all responsible for the trend of thought
and the action of our times.

How shall we arrive at these objectives? We think of course of history as a first means of information. **P4**
Not the history which is a mere **recital** of facts, dates, wars, and kings, but a study of the life and
growth of other nations. These nations are ones in which we follow the general moral, intellectual,
25 and economic development through the ages. We note what brought about the rise and fall of
nations and what were the lasting contributions of peoples now passed away to the development of
the human family and the world as a whole.

Gradually from this study certain facts emerge. A nation must have leaders, men who have the power **P5**
to see a little farther, to imagine a little better life than the present. But if this vision is to be fulfilled, it
30 must also have a vast army of men and women capable of understanding and following these leaders
intelligently. These citizens must understand their government from the smallest election district to
the highest administrative office. It must be no closed book to them, and each one must carry his own
particular responsibility or the whole army will lag.

I would have our children visit national shrines, know why we love and respect certain men of the **P6**
35 past. I would have them see how government departments are run and what are their duties. I
would have them see how courts function, what juries are, what a legislative body is and what it
does. I would have them learn how we conduct our relationships with the rest of the world and what
are our contacts with other nations. The child seeing and understanding these things will begin to
envisage the varied pattern of the life of a great nation such as ours. He will see how his own life and
40 environment fit into the pattern and where his own usefulness may lie . . .

Learning to be a good citizen is learning to live to the maximum of one's abilities and opportunities, **P7**
and every subject should be taught every child with this in view. The teacher's personality and
character are of the greatest importance. I have known many erudite and scholarly men and women
who were dismal failures as teachers. I have known some less learned teachers who had the gift of
45 inspiring youth and sending them on to heights where perhaps they themselves were unable to
follow . . .

recital		
a formal or public delivery of a memorized nature		

You will be thinking that few teachers of this type exist and you will be right. The blame lies with the **P8**
attitude toward teachers and the teaching of our present generation. We have set up a money value, a
material gauge by which we measure success. We have frequently given more time and more material
50 compensation to our cooks and chauffeurs and day-laborers, bricklayers, carpenters, and painters
than we have to our nurses, governesses, and tutors and teachers in schools and colleges.

We entrust the building of our children's characters and the development of their minds to people **P9**
whom we, as a rule, compensate less **liberally** than we do the men and women who build our
houses and make our day-by-day existence more comfortable and luxurious. These men and women
55 teachers, paid from $1,200 to $5,000, and in extraordinary cases $10,000 a year, mold the future
citizens of our country. We do not treat them with the respect or consideration which their high
calling deserves. Nor do we reward them with the only reward which spells success according to our
present standards.

One of our hard-worked businessmen said to me not long ago, "Why, these teacher fellows have a **P10**
60 snap. Look at their long summer holidays, and you can't tell me it's as hard to tell a lot of youngsters
about logarithms or Scott's novels as it is to handle my board of directors at one end and my shop
committee at the other." My thought was that if he and his fellow members on the board of directors
and the men on the shop committee had had the right kind of teaching his job would be easier
because at both ends he would have men better able to understand the whole problem of **industry**
65 and realize the necessity of cooperation . . .

I believe that each one of us, if we delve in our memories, can find some similar experience which **P11**
will uphold my contention that a great teacher is more important than the most gorgeous building.
Where no such contacts have been experienced, the most ideal surroundings will not make our
school-days anything but a succession of dull and meaningless tasks.

liberally	industry	
allowing freedom of action, particularly with regards to personal belief	the management or ownership of businesses, etc.	

70 There are many inadequate teachers today. Perhaps our standards should be higher, but they cannot   **P12**
be until we learn to value and understand the function of the teacher in our midst. While we have
put much money in buildings and laboratories and gymnasiums, we have forgotten that they are
but the shell, and will never live and create a vital spark in the minds and hearts of our youth unless
some teacher furnishes the inspiration. A child responds naturally to high ideals, and we are all of us
creatures of habit.

75 Begin young to teach the standards that should prevail in public servants, in governmental   **P13**
administration, in national and international business and politics, and show by relating to daily life
and known experience the advantages derived from a well-run government. It will then be a logical
conclusion that the ends cannot be achieved without the cooperation of every citizen. This will be
readily grasped by the child because his daily experience in school illustrates the point.

TEXT 8

Notes on the State of Virginia
Thomas Jefferson
University of Chicago Press, 1784

Another object of the revisal is, to **diffuse** knowledge more generally through the mass of the people. **P1**
This bill proposes to lay off every county into small districts of five or six miles square, called hundreds,
and in each of them to establish a school for teaching reading, writing, and arithmetic. The tutor
to be supported by the hundred, and every person in it entitled to send their children three years

5   **gratis**, and as much longer as they please, paying for it. These schools to be under a **visitor**, who is
annually to chuse the boy, of best genius in the school, of those whose parents are too poor to give
them further education, and to send him forward to one of the grammar schools, of which twenty are
proposed to be erected in different parts of the country, for teaching Greek, Latin, geography, and
the higher branches of numerical arithmetic. Of the boys thus sent in any one year, trial is to be made

10   at the grammar schools one or two years, and the best genius of the whole selected, and continued
six years, and the residue dismissed. By this means twenty of the best geniusses will be raked from
the **rubbish** annually, and be instructed, at the public expense, so far as the grammar schools go. At
the end of six years instruction, one half are to be discontinued (from among whom the grammar
schools will probably be supplied with future masters); and the other half, who are to be chosen for

15   the superiority of their parts and disposition, are to be sent and continued three years in the study
of such sciences as they shall chuse, at William and Mary college, the plan of which is proposed to be
enlarged, as will be hereafter explained, and extended to all the useful sciences. The ultimate result
of the whole scheme of education would be the teaching all children of the state reading, writing,
and common arithmetic: turning out ten annually of superior genius, well taught in Greek, Latin,

diffuse	gratis	visitor
to spread or scatter widely or thinly	without charge or payment; free	acting as a superintendent of schools
rubbish		
worthless, unwanted material that is rejected or thrown out; trash		

                                                           Developing Core Literacy Proficiencies

20 geography, and the higher branches of arithmetic: turning out ten others annually, of still superior

parts, who, to those branches of learning, shall have added such of the sciences as their genius shall

have led them to: the furnishing to the wealthier part of the people convenient schools, at which

their children may be educated, at their own expense. —. But of all the views of this law none is more

important, none more legitimate, than that of rendering the people the safe, as they are the ultimate,

25 guardians of their own liberty. For this purpose the reading in the first stage, where *they* will receive

their whole education, is proposed, as has been said, to be chiefly historical.

History by **apprising** them of the past will enable them to judge of the future; it will avail them of the P2

experience of other times and other nations; it will qualify them as judges of the actions and designs

of men; it will enable them to know ambition under every disguise it may assume; and knowing it,

30 to defeat its views. In every government on earth is some trace of human weakness, some germ of

corruption and **degeneracy**, which cunning will discover, and wickedness insensibly open, cultivate,

and improve. Every government **degenerates** when trusted to the rulers of the people alone. The

people themselves therefore are its only safe **depositories**. And to render even them safe their minds

must be improved to a certain degree. This indeed is not all that is necessary, though it be essentially

35 necessary. An amendment of our constitution must here come in aid of the public education. The

influence over government must be shared among all the people. If every individual which composes

their mass participates of the ultimate authority, the government will be safe; because the corrupting

the whole mass will exceed any private resources of wealth: and public ones cannot be provided but

by levies on the people. In this case every man would have to pay his own price. The government

40 of Great-Britain has been corrupted, because but one man in ten has a right to vote for members of

parliament. The sellers of the government therefore get nine-tenths of their price clear. It has been

thought that corruption is restrained by confining the right of suffrage to a few of the wealthier of the

people: but it would be more effectually restrained by an extension of that right to such numbers as

would bid defiance to the means of corruption.

apprising	degeneracy	degenerates
to give notice to; inform; advise	to fall below a normal or desirable level in physical, mental, or moral qualities	to decline in standard
depositories		
a place where something valuable is kept		

TEXT 9

"The Vision of Education Reform in the United States"
Secretary Arne Duncan
United States Department of Education

Remarks to UNESCO in Paris, France, November 4, 2010

The promise of universal education was then a lonely beacon—a light to guide the way to peace and **P1**
the rebuilding of nations across the globe. Today, the world is no longer recovering from a tragic
global war. Yet the international community faces a crisis of a different sort, the global economic
crisis. And education is still the beacon lighting the path forward—perhaps more so today than ever
5 before.

Education is still the key to eliminating gender inequities, to reducing poverty, to creating a **P2**
sustainable planet, and to fostering peace. And in a knowledge economy, education is the new
currency by which nations maintain economic competitiveness and global prosperity. . . .

I want to make the case to you today that enhancing educational attainment and economic viability, **P3**
10 both at home and abroad, is really more of a win-win game; it is an opportunity to grow the economic
pie, instead of carve it up. As President Obama said in his speech to the Muslim world in Cairo last
year, "Any world order that elevates one nation or group of people over another will inevitably fail."

There is so much that the United States has to learn from nations with high- performing education **P4**
systems. And there is so much that America can share from its experience to the mutual benefit of
15 nations confronting similar educational challenges.

I am convinced that the U.S. education system now has an unprecedented opportunity to get dramatically better. Nothing—nothing—is more important in the long-run to American prosperity than boosting the skills and attainment of the nation's students.

P5

In the United States, we feel an economic and moral imperative to challenge the status quo. Closing

20 the achievement gap and closing the opportunity gap is the civil rights issue of our generation. One quarter of U.S. high school students drop out or fail to graduate on time. Almost one million students leave our schools for the streets each year. That is economically unsustainable and morally unacceptable.

P6

One of the more unusual and sobering press conferences I participated in last year was the release

25 of a report by a group of top retired generals and admirals. Here was the stunning conclusion of their report: 75 percent of young Americans, between the ages of 17 to 24, are unable to enlist in the military today because they have failed to graduate from high school, have a criminal record, or are physically unfit.

P7

Now, everyone here today knows that education is taking on more and more importance around the

30 globe. In the last decade, international competition in higher education and the job market has grown dramatically. As the *New York Times* columnist Thomas Friedman famously pointed out, the world economy has indeed "flattened." Companies now digitize, automate, and outsource work to the most competitive individuals, companies, and countries.

P8

In the knowledge economy, opportunities to land a good job are vanishing fast for young workers

35 who drop out of school or fail to get college experience. That is why President Obama often says that the nation that "out-educates us today is going to out-compete us tomorrow."

P9

Yet there is also a paradox at the heart of America's efforts to bolster international competitiveness.

P10

To succeed in the global economy, the United States, just like other nations, will have to become both more economically competitive and more collaborative.

P11

40 In the information age, more international competition has spawned more international P12
collaboration. Today, education is a global public good **unconstrained** by national boundaries.

In the United States, for example, concerns are sometimes raised about the large number of foreign- P13
born students earning masters and doctorates in science and engineering fields. Immigrants now
constitute nearly half of America's PhD scientists and engineers, even though they constitute only
45 12 percent of the workforce overall.

These foreign-born students more often return to the country of origin than in the past. But their P14
scientific skills and entrepreneurship strengthen not only their native economy but also stimulate
innovation and new markets that can help boost the U.S. economy.

The same borderless nature of innovation and ideas is evident when foreign-born students remain P15
50 in America. Immigrants to the U.S. started a quarter of all engineering and technology companies
from 1995 and 2005, including half of the start-ups in Silicon Valley, our high-tech capital. Sergey Brin,
Google's co-founder, was born in Moscow but educated in the United States. Google is now used
throughout the globe to gather information and advance knowledge. The brain drain, in short, has
become the brain gain.

55 It is no surprise that economic interdependence brings new global challenges and educational P16
demands.

The United States cannot, acting by itself, dramatically reduce poverty and disease or develop P17
sustainable sources of energy. America alone cannot combat terrorism or curb climate change. To
succeed, we must collaborate with other countries.

60 Those new partnerships require American students to develop better critical thinking abilities, cross- P18
cultural understanding, and facility in multiple languages. They also will require U.S. students to

unconstrained	
able to act freely	

strengthen their skills in science, technology, engineering, and math—the STEM fields that anchor much of our innovation in the global economy.

These new partnerships must also inspire students to take a bigger and deeper view of their civic **P19**
65 obligations—not only to their countries of origin but to the betterment of the global community. A just and socially responsible society must also be anchored in civic engagement for the public good.

In our view, the United States will be better off, in comparative terms, if we lead the world in **P20** educational attainment, rather than lagging behind. A generation ago, America did in fact lead the world in college attainment. But today among young adults, the U.S. is tied for ninth. That is why
70 President Obama has set a goal that America will once again have the highest proportion of college graduates in the world by 2020, a decade from now.

Yet even as the United States works to strengthen its educational system, it is important to remember **P21** that advancing educational attainment and achievement everywhere brings benefits not just to the U.S. but around the globe. In the knowledge economy, education is the new game-changer driving
75 economic growth. Education, as Nelson Mandela says, "is the most powerful weapon which you can use to change the world."

EXTENDED READING

Lectures and Biographical Sketches
Ralph Waldo Emerson
Houghton Mifflin and Co, 1863–1864

I believe that our own experience instructs us that the secret of Education lies in respecting the pupil. **P1**
It is not for you to choose what he shall know, what he shall do. It is chosen and **foreordained**, and
he only holds the key to his own secret. By your **tampering** and **thwarting** and too much governing
he may be **hindered** from his end and kept out of his own. Respect the child. Wait and see the new
5 product of Nature. Nature loves analogies, but not repetitions. Respect the child. Be not too much his
parent. Trespass not on his **solitude**.

But I hear the outcry which replies to this suggestion:—Would you verily throw up the reins of **P2**
public and private discipline; would you leave the young child to the mad career of his own
passions and **whimsies**, and call this anarchy a respect for the child's nature? I answer,—Respect
10 the child, respect him to the end, but also respect yourself. Be the companion of his thought, the
friend of his friendship, the lover of his virtue,—but no kinsman of his sin. Let him find you so true
to yourself that you are the **irreconcilable** hater of his **vice** and **imperturbable** slighter of
his trifling.

foreordained	tampering	thwarting
to predestine; predetermine	to make changes to something, especially in order to falsify or damage	to prevent from accomplishing a goal or purpose
hindered	**solitude**	**whimsies**
to have caused delay or interruption	the state of being or living alone	excessively playful; fanciful
irreconcilable	**vice**	**imperturbable**
a person who will not agree or compromise	a habit or practice that is immoral; a weakness	incapable of being upset or agitated; not easily excited

I confess myself utterly at a loss in suggesting particular reforms in our ways of teaching. No

15 **discretion** that can be lodged with a school-committee, with the overseers or visitors of an academy, of a college, can at all avail to reach these difficulties and perplexities, but they solve themselves when we leave institutions and address individuals. The will, the male power, organizes, imposes its own thought and wish on others, and makes that military eye which controls boys as it controls men; admirable in its results, a fortune to him who has it, and only dangerous when it leads the workman

20 to overvalue and overuse it and precludes him from finer means. Sympathy, the female force— which they must use who have not the first—deficient in instant control and the breaking down of resistance, is more subtle and lasting and creative. I advise teachers to cherish mother-wit. I assume that you will keep the grammar, reading, writing and arithmetic in order; 't is easy and of course you will. But smuggle in a little contraband wit, fancy, imagination, thought. If you have a taste which you

25 have suppressed because it is not shared by those about you, tell them that. Set this law up, whatever becomes of the rules of the school: they must not whisper, much less talk; but if one of the young people says a wise thing, greet it, and let all the children clap their hands. They shall have no book but school-books in the room; but if one has brought in a Plutarch or Shakespeare or Don Quixote or Goldsmith or any other good book, and understands what he reads, put him at once at the head of

30 the class. Nobody shall he disorderly, or leave his desk without permission, but if a boy runs from his bench, or a girl, because the fire falls, or to check some injury that a little **dastard** is inflicting behind his desk on some helpless sufferer, take away the medal from the head of the class and give it on the instant to the brave rescuer. If a child happens to show that he knows any fact about astronomy, or plants, or birds, or rocks, or history, that interests him and you, hush all the classes and encourage

35 him to tell it so that all may hear. Then you have made your school-room like the world. Of course you will insist on modesty in the children, and respect to their teachers, but if the boy stops you in your speech, cries out that you are wrong and sets you right, hug him!

discretion	dastard	
the power or right to decide or act according to one's own judgment; freedom of judgment or choice	a wrong-doing coward	

EXTENDED READING

Education and National Welfare
Horace Mann
Tennessee Criminal Law Resources, 1848

**EXCERPT OF THE TWELFTH ANNUAL REPORT OF HORACE MANN AS SECRETARY
OF MASSACHUSETTS STATE BOARD OF EDUCATION**

Now two or three things will doubtless be admitted to be true, beyond all controversy, in regard **P1**

to Massachusetts. By its industrial condition, and its business operations, it is exposed, far beyond

any other State in the Union, to the fatal extremes of overgrown wealth and desperate poverty. Its

population is far more dense than that of any other State. It is four or five times more dense than the

5 average of all the-other States taken together; and density of population has always been one of the

proximate causes of social inequality. According to population and territorial extent there is far more

capital in Massachusetts—capital which is movable, and instantaneously available—than in any other

State in the Union; and probably both these qualifications respecting population and territory could

be omitted without endangering the truth of the **assertion**. . . .

10 Now surely nothing but universal education can counterwork this tendency to the domination of **P2**

capital and the **servility** of labor. If one class possesses all the wealth and the education, while the

residue of society is ignorant and poor, it matters not by what name the relation between them may

be called: the latter, in fact and in truth, will be the servile dependents and subjects of the former.

But, if education be equally diffused, it will draw property after it by the strongest of all attractions;

15 for such a thing never did happen, and never can happen, as that an intelligent and practical body of

proximate	assertion	servility
approximate; fairly accurate	a positive statement or declaration, often without support or reason	oppressed as being in slavery
residue		
a remnant that remains after a part is discarded or removed		

men should be permanently poor. Property and labor in different classes are essentially **antagonistic**; but property and labor in the same class are essentially **fraternal**. The people of Massachusetts have, in some degree, appreciated the truth that the unexampled prosperity of the State—its comfort, its competence, its general intelligence and **virtue**—is attributable to the education, more or less

20 perfect, which all its people have received; but are they sensible of a fact equally important—namely, that it is to this same education that two-thirds of the people are indebted for not being to-day the **vassals** of as severe a **tyranny**, in the form of capital, as the lower classes of Europe are bound to in any form of brute force?

Education then, beyond all other devices of human origin, is a great equalizer of the conditions of   P3
25 men,—the balance wheel of the social machinery. I do not here mean that it so elevates the moral nature as to make men disdain and abhor the oppression of their fellow men. This idea pertains to another of its attributes. But I mean that it gives each man the independence and the means by which he can resist the selfishness of other men. It does better than to disarm the poor of their hostility toward the rich: it prevents being poor. **Agrarianism** is the revenge of poverty against wealth. The

30 wanton destruction of the property of others—the burning of hay-ricks, and corn-ricks, the demolition of machinery because it supersedes hand-labor, the sprinkling of vitriol on rich dresses—is only agrarianism run mad. Education prevents both the revenge and the madness. On the other hand, a fellow-feeling for one's class or caste is the common instinct of hearts not wholly sunk in selfish regard for a person or for a family. The spread of education, by enlarging the cultivated class or caste, will

35 open a wider area over which the social feelings will expand; and, if this education should be universal and complete, it would do more than all things else to obliterate factitious distinctions in society. . . .

For the creation of wealth, then,—for the existence of a wealthy people and a wealthy nation,—   P4
intelligence is the grand condition. The number of improvers will increase as the intellectual

antagonistic	fraternal	virtue
hostile; opposing	a society of men associated with brotherly union	moral excellence; goodness; righteousness
vassals	**tyranny**	**Agrarianism**
servants or slaves	oppressive or severe government	a social movement of the equal division of rural land

constituency, if I may so call it, increases. In former times, and in most parts of the world even at

40 the present day, not one man in a million has ever had such a development of mind as made it

possible for him to become a contributor to art or science. . . . Let this development proceed, and

contributions . . . of inestimable value, will be sure to follow. That political economy, therefore,

which busies itself about capital and labor, supply and demand, interests and rents, favorable and

unfavorable balances of trade, but leaves out of account the elements of a wide-spread mental

45 development, is naught but **stupendous folly**. The greatest of all the arts in political economy is to

change a consumer into a producer; and the next greatest is to increase the producing power,—and

this to be directly obtained by increasing his intelligence. For mere delving, an ignorant man is but

little better than a swine, whom he so much resembles in his appetites, and surpasses in his power of

mischief. . . .

stupendous	folly	
very large or great	an action or idea that is foolish	

READING CLOSELY
FOR TEXTUAL DETAILS

DEVELOPING CORE LITERACY PROFICIENCIES

GRADE 9

Literacy Toolbox

READING CLOSELY GRAPHIC

1.
APPROACHING
Where do I START?

- I determine my reading purposes and take note of important information about the text.

- Why am I reading this text, and how might that influence how I approach and read it?
- What do I know (or might find out) about the text's title, author, type, publisher, publication date, and history?
- **What sequence of questions might I use to focus my reading and increase my understanding of the text?**

2.
QUESTIONING
What details do I NOTICE?
- I use questions to help me investigate important aspects of the text.

3.
ANALYZING
What do I THINK about the details?
- I question further to analyze the details I notice and determine their meaning or importance.

4.
DEEPENING
How do I deepen my UNDERSTANDING?

- I consider others' questions and develop initial observations or claims.
- I explain why and cite my evidence.

5.
EXTENDING
Where does this LEAD me?

- I pose new questions to extend my investigation of the text and topic.
- I communicate my thinking to others.

READING CLOSELY: GUIDING QUESTIONS HANDOUT

- Why am I reading this text, and how might that influence how I approach and read it?
- What do I know (or might find out) about the text's title, author, type, publisher, publication date, and history?
- **What sequence of questions might I use to focus my reading and increase my understanding of the text?**

1. APPROACHING
Where do I START?
- I determine my reading purposes and take note of important information about the text.

LANGUAGE (CCSS R.4, L.3, L.4, L.5)	IDEAS (CCSS R.2, W.3, R.8, R.9)	PERSPECTIVE (CCSS R.6)	STRUCTURE (CCSS R.5)
2. QUESTIONING — *What details do I NOTICE?* — I use questions to help me investigate important aspects of the text.			
• What words or phrases stand out to me as powerful and important? • What do the author's words and phrases cause me to see, feel, or think? • How are key ideas, events, places, or characters described? • What unfamiliar words do I need to study or define to better understand the text?	• What do I think the text is mainly about—what is discussed in detail? • What new ideas or information do I find in the text? • Who are the main people, voices, or characters presented in the text? • What claims do I find in the text? • What ideas stand out to me as significant or interesting?	• What do I learn about the author and the purpose for writing the text? • What details or words suggest the author's perspective? • What seems to be the author's (narrator's) attitude or point of view?	• What do I notice about how the text is organized or sequenced? • What do I notice about the structure of specific elements (paragraphs, sentences, stanzas, lines, or scenes)? • In what ways does the text begin, end, and develop?
3. ANALYZING — *What do I THINK about the details?* — I question further to analyze the details I notice and determine their meaning or importance.			
• How do specific words or phrases influence the meaning or tone of the text? • How does the author's choice of words reveal his/her purposes and perspective? • How does context define or change the meaning of key words in the text? • How does the text's language influence my understanding of important ideas or themes?	• How might I summarize the main ideas of the text and the key supporting details? • How do the text's main ideas relate to what I already know, think, or have read? • How do the main ideas, events, or people change as the text progresses? • What evidence supports the claims in the text, and what is left uncertain or unsupported?	• How does the author's perspective influence his or her presentation of ideas, themes, or arguments? • How does the author's perspective and presentation of the text compare to others? • How does the author's perspective influence my reading of the text?	• In what ways are ideas, events, and claims linked together in the text? • How do specific sections or elements of the text develop its central ideas or themes? • How does the organization of the text influence my understanding of its information, themes, or arguments?

- **What relationships do I discover among the ideas and details presented, the author's perspective, and the language or structure of the text?**

4. DEEPENING
How do I deepen my UNDERSTANDING?
- I consider others' questions and develop initial observations or claims.
- I explain why and cite my evidence.

5. EXTENDING
Where does this LEAD me?
- I pose new questions to extend my investigation of the text and topic.
- I communicate my thinking to others.

ODELL EDUCATION

ATTENTING TO DETAILS HANDOUT

SEARCHING FOR DETAILS

I read the text closely and mark words and phrases that help me answer my question.

As I read, I notice authors use a lot of details and strategies to develop their ideas, arguments, and narratives. Following are examples of types of details authors often use in important ways.

SELECTING DETAILS

I select words or phrases from my search that I think are important for answering my questions.

Author's Facts and Ideas

- Statistics
- Examples
- Vivid description
- Characters and actors
- Events

Author's Language and Structure

- Repeated words
- Strong language
- Figurative language
- Tone
- Organizational structure and phrases

Opinions and Perspective

- Interpretations
- Explanation of ideas or events
- Narration
- Personal reflection
- Beliefs

ANALYZING DETAILS

I reread parts of the text and think about the meaning of the details and what they tell me about my questions.

By reading closely and thinking about the details, I can make connections among them. Following are some ways details can be connected.

Facts and Ideas

- Authors use hard facts to illustrate or define an idea.
- Authors use examples to express a belief or point of view.
- Authors use vivid description to compare or oppose different ideas.
- Authors describe different actors or characters to illustrate a comparison or contrast.
- Authors use a sequence of events to arrive at a conclusion.

Language and Structure

- Authors repeat specific words or structures to emphasize meaning or tone.
- Authors use language or tone to establish a mood.
- Authors use figurative language to infer emotion or embellish meaning.
- Authors use a specific organization to enhance a point or add meaning.

Opinions and Perspective

- Authors compare or contrast evidence to help define their point of view.
- Authors offer their explanation of ideas or events to support their beliefs.
- Authors tell their own story to develop their point of view.
- Authors use language to reveal an opinion or feeling about a topic.

READING CLOSELY FINAL WRITING AND DISCUSSION TASK HANDOUT

In this unit, you have been developing your skills as an investigator of texts. You have learned to do the following things:

- Ask and think about good questions to help you examine what you read closely
- Uncover key clues in the details, words, and information found in the texts
- Make connections among details and texts
- Discuss what you have discovered with your classmates and teacher
- Cite specific evidence from the texts to explain and support your thinking
- Record and communicate your thinking on graphic tools and in sentences and paragraphs

Your final assignments will provide you with opportunities to use all of these related skills and to demonstrate your proficiency and growth in Reading Closely.

FINAL ASSIGNMENTS

1. **Becoming a Text Expert:** You will first become an expert about one of the three final texts in the unit. To accomplish this, you will do the following:

   a. Read and annotate the text on your own and use Guiding Questions and an ***Analyzing Details Tool*** to make some initial connections about the text.

   b. Compare the notes and connections you make with those made by other students who are also becoming experts about the same text.

   c. In your expert group, come up with a new text-specific question to think about when rereading the text more closely. Complete a second ***Analyzing Details Tool*** for this question.

   d. Study your text notes and ***Analyzing Details Tools*** to come up with your own central idea about the text and topic—something new you have come to understand.

   e. Think about how your text and the central idea you have discovered relates and compares to other texts in the unit.

2. **Writing a Text-Based Explanation:** On your own, you will plan and draft a multiparagraph explanation of something you have come to understand by reading and examining your text. To accomplish this, you will do the following:

   a. Present and explain the central idea you have found in the text—what you think the text is about.

   b. Use quotations and paraphrased references from the text to explain and support the central idea you are discussing.

   c. Explain how the central idea is related to what you have found out about the author's purpose in writing the text and the author's perspective on (view of) the topic.

   d. Present and explain a new understanding about the unit's topic that your text has led you to.

   e. Work with other students to review and improve your draft—and to be sure it is the best possible representation of your ideas and your skills as a reader and writer.

   f. Reflect on how well you have used Literacy Skills in developing this final explanation.

READING CLOSELY FINAL TASK HANDOUT (Continued)

FINAL ASSIGNMENTS (Continued)

3. **Leading and Participating in a Text-Centered Discussion:** After you have become an expert about your text and written an explanation of what you understand, you will prepare for and participate in a final discussion. In this discussion, you and other students will compare your close readings of the final three texts in the unit. To accomplish this, you will do the following:

   a. Prepare a summary of what you have come to understand and written in your explanation to share with the other students in your discussion group.

   b. Reread the other two final texts so that you are prepared to discuss and compare them.

   c. Meet with your expert group to talk about your text and how to lead a discussion of it.

   d. Come up with a new question about your text that will get others to think about the connections between it and the other texts in the unit.

   e. Join a new discussion group, and share your summary about your text and the evidence you have found:

      ⇒ Point out key details to the other students in your group.

      ⇒ Explain your observations about your author's purpose and perspective.

      ⇒ Point out key words, phrases, or sentences that indicate your author's perspective.

      ⇒ Explain what you have come to understand about the topic from your text.

   f. Listen to other students' summaries and think about the connections to your text.

   g. Pose your question to the group, and lead a discussion about the three texts, asking students to present evidence from the texts that supports their thinking.

   h. Reflect on how well you have used Discussion Habits in this final discussion.

SKILLS AND HABITS TO BE DEMONSTRATED

As you become a text expert, write your text-based explanation, and participate in a text-centered discussion, think about demonstrating the Literacy Skills and Discussion Habits you have been working on to the best of your ability. Your teacher will evaluate your work and determine your grade based on how well you do the following things:

- **Attend to Details:** Identify words, details, or quotations that you think are important to understanding the text.

- **Interpret Language:** Understand how words are used to express ideas and perspectives.

- **Summarize:** Correctly explain what the text says about the topic.

- **Identify Relationships:** Notice important connections among details, ideas, or texts.

- **Recognize Perspective:** Identify and explain the author's view of the text's topic.

- **Use Evidence:** Use well-chosen details from the text to support your explanation. Accurately paraphrase or quote what the author says in the text.

- **Prepare:** Read the text(s) closely and think about the questions to prepare for a text-centered discussion.

READING CLOSELY FINAL TASK HANDOUT (Continued)

SKILLS AND HABITS TO BE DEMONSTRATED (Continued)

- **Question:** Ask and respond to questions that help the discussion group understand and compare the texts.
- **Collaborate:** Pay attention to other participants while you participate in and lead a text-centered discussion.
- **Communicate Clearly:** Present your ideas and supporting evidence so others can understand them.

NOTE

These skills and habits are also listed on the **Student Literacy Skills and Discussion Habits Checklist**, which you can use to assess your work and the work of other students.

PART 1

UNDERSTANDING CLOSE READING

Overview and Tools

"At the beginning I was only a little mass of possibilities."

OBJECTIVE:	You will learn what it means to read a text closely by paying attention to and analyzing details from the text.

MATERIALS:
- *Guiding Questions Handout*
- *Reading Closely Graphic*
- *Questioning Path Tools*

TEXTS:
- *1-Classroom Images*
- *2-The Story of My Life, Helen Keller, 1905*
- *3-"Changing Education Paradigms," Ken Robinson, 2010*
- *4-Only a Teacher, PBS*

ACTIVITIES

1. INTRODUCTION TO THE UNIT
Your teacher presents an overview of the unit, and discusses the purposes and parts of close reading.

2. ATTENDING TO DETAILS
You explore the idea of paying attention to details through examining images.

3. READING CLOSELY FOR DETAILS
You use Guiding Questions to look closely for details in a text.

4. ATTENDING TO DETAILS IN MULTIMEDIA
You use Guiding Questions to look closely for details in a multimedia text and write a few sentences explaining something you have learned.

5. INDEPENDENT READING AND RESEARCHING ACTIVITY
You use Guiding Questions to explore a multimedia website.

ODELL
EDUCATION

QUESTIONING PATH TOOL
Text 1—Classroom Photos

APPROACHING:
I determine my reading purposes and take note of key information about the text. I identify the LIPS domain(s) that will guide my initial reading.

I will initially focus on *ideas* and supporting details.

QUESTIONING: *I use Guiding Questions to help me investigate the text (from the **Guiding Questions Handout**).*

1. What details stand out to me as I examine this image? [I]

2. What do I think this image is mainly about? [I]

ANALYZING: *I question further to connect and analyze the details I find (from the **Guiding Questions Handout**).*

3. How do specific details help me understand what is being depicted in the image? [I]

DEEPENING: *I consider the questions of others.*

4. What do I notice about the arrangement of each classroom? How are the chairs and desks set up?

5. What do the details of the photos suggest about what the students are doing?

6. What connections or comparisons do I notice between the photos?

   What might these connections and comparisons suggest about the nature of education in the classrooms and historical eras they depict?

EXTENDING: *I pose my own questions.*

Examples:

7. Why is there such a big difference between the classrooms?

8. What do I think might influence the way they are set up?

QUESTIONING PATH TOOL
Text 2—*The Story of My Life*, Helen Keller (Model 1)

APPROACHING:
I determine my reading purposes and take note of key information about the text. I identify the LIPS domain(s) that will guide my initial reading.

I will initially note that this is an autobiography written in 1905. I will focus on the author's use of *language* to describe the teacher and student.

QUESTIONING: *I use Guiding Questions to help me investigate the text (from the **Guiding Questions Handout**).*

1. What words or phrases stand out to me as powerful and important? [L]
2. How are key ideas or characters described? [L]

ANALYZING: *I question further to connect and analyze the details I find (from the **Guiding Questions Handout**).*

3. What details or words suggest the author's perspective? [L/P]

DEEPENING: *I consider the questions of others.*

4. What words does Keller use to describe her teacher?

   What do these words suggest about how she feels about Anne Sullivan?
5. What does the figurative language phrase "a little mass of possibilities" in the first paragraph suggest about how Keller at first saw herself as a student?

   How does her use of the word *only* with this phrase further develop her view of herself?

   Based on details in this first paragraph, what does she think the role of a teacher is?
6. In paragraph 3, Keller claims that a student "will not work joyously unless he feels that liberty is his."

   What does this statement suggest about Keller's view of students, teachers, and education?

   What must the student experience in order to "dance bravely through a dull routine of textbooks"?
7. In paragraph 4, Keller writes, "How much of my delight in all beautiful things is innate, and how much is due to her influence, I can never tell."

   How does the word *innate* help me understand what Keller means?

   What does this statement suggest Keller thinks the relationship between a teacher and a student should be?

EXTENDING: *I pose my own questions.*

Example:
8. According to Keller, who has more responsibility when it comes to a student's education—the teacher or the student?

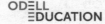
ODELL EDUCATION

QUESTIONING PATH TOOL

Text 3—"Changing Education Paradigms," Ken Robinson, 2010

APPROACHING: *I determine my reading purposes and take note of key information about the text. I identify the LIPS domain(s) that will guide my initial reading.*

I will initially focus on *ideas* and supporting details. I will think about the animation helps me to understand the author's words and ideas.

QUESTIONING: *I use Guiding Questions to help me investigate the text (from the Guiding Questions Handout).*

1. What new ideas or information do I find in the text (video)? [I]

2. What do I notice about how the text (video) is organized or sequenced? [S]

ANALYZING: *I question further to connect and analyze the details I find (from the Guiding Questions Handout).*

3. How might I summarize the main ideas of the text and the key supporting details? [I]

DEEPENING: *I consider the questions of others.*

4. Ken Robinson's TED Talk is brought to life through illustration and animation. What is one set of visual images from the video that stands out to me? What do these images suggest about Robinson's view of education?

5. What reasons does Robinson present for why "every country on earth is reforming public education"?

   What does he say is the "problem" with current approaches to improving education?

6. What does Robinson say is the old view of the value of education that "our kids don't believe"?

   Why don't students see the value in education that people once did?

   How has the world changed since the development of public education in the age of enlightenment and the industrial revolution?

7. Robinson says that the current model of education is "essentially about conformity." What details does he give to support this claim?

   How does he explain the modern "epidemic" of ADHD?

   Why might students see schoolwork as being about "boring stuff"?

8. Robinson contrasts the two words "aesthetic" and "anaesthetic." How does he define these two words?

   How does he use these words to talk about the differences between education that "puts students to sleep" and education that "wakes them up to what is inside of themselves"?

9. What does Robinson suggest about how and why schools are like factories? Why does he think this is not a good "model of learning"?

10. How does Robinson define the idea of "divergent thinking"?

    Robinson describes a longitudinal study on divergent thinking in young children. How does he use this information to support his claims about what is wrong or missing in current education?

11. The speech is titled, "Changing Education Paradigms." According to Robinson, why do education paradigms (or models) need to change? What evidence does he give to support his claim that a change must occur?

EXTENDING: *I pose my own questions.*

Students might explore a question they generate through Internet research.

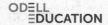

QUESTIONING PATH TOOL
Only a Teacher, PBS

APPROACHING: *I determine my reading purposes and take note of key information about the text. I identify the LIPS domain(s) that will guide my initial reading.*

I will focus on new *ideas* and information I can bring back to the class. I will note key information about the website I visit and its author or source.

QUESTIONING: *I use Guiding Questions to help me investigate the text (from the **Guiding Questions Handout**).*

1. What do I notice about how the website is organized? [S]

2. What new ideas or information do I find on the website? [I]

ANALYZING: *I question further to connect and analyze the details I find (from the **Guiding Questions Handout**).*

3. How might I summarize the main ideas of the website and the key supporting details? [I]

DEEPENING: *I consider the questions of others.*

4. What interesting details, examples, or ideas can I find that relate to the other texts we are studying?

5. From the Teaching Timeline, what details do I learn about Normal Schools? What was their primary purpose? How were they related to Common Schools?

6. For one of the Schoolhouse Pioneers or Teachers Today, what do I learn about his or her view of education?

EXTENDING: *I pose my own questions.*

Students might be asked to pose a question and bring back information related to their question.

ODELL EDUCATION

PART 2

QUESTIONING TEXTS

Overview and Tools

"The education process begins before the child is born."

OBJECTIVE:	You will learn how to use questioning paths to help you read and analyze texts.

MATERIALS:
- *Approaching Texts Tool*
- *Analyzing Details Tool*
- *Questioning Path Tools*

- *Reading Closely Graphic*
- *Guiding Questions Handout*
- *Attending to Details Handout*

TEXTS:
- *2-The Story of My Life, Helen Keller, 1905*
- *5-"Kids Need Structure" (speech), Colin Powell, 2012*

ACTIVITIES

1. HOW SKILLFUL READERS APPROACH TEXTS
Your teacher shows the class how to use the *Approaching Texts Tool* and then you practice using it in pairs.

2. APPROACHING A NEW TEXT
You read a new text and use the *Approaching Texts Tool* to guide your reading.

3. ANALYZING TEXT WITH TEXT-SPECIFIC QUESTIONS
Your teacher shows the class how to use the *Analyzing Details Tool*.

4. POSING TEXT-SPECIFIC QUESTIONS
You think of your own Text-Specific Questions you can use to analyze the text.

5. INDEPENDENT WRITING ACTIVITY
You write a short paragraph explaining your analysis of the text and list supporting textual details.

APPROACHING TEXTS TOOL

Name _____   Text _____

APPROACHING THE TEXT	
Before reading, I consider what my specific purposes for reading are.	**What are my reading purposes?**
	Title:
	Author: **Source/Publisher:**
	Text type: **Publication date:**
I also take note of key information about the text.	**What do I already think or understand about the text based on this information?**

QUESTIONING THE TEXT	
As I read the text for the first time, I use Guiding Questions that relate to my reading purpose and focus. (*Can be taken from the Guiding Questions Handout.*)	**Guiding Questions for *my first reading* of the text:**
	As I read I mark details on the text that relate to my Guiding Questions.
As I reread, I use questions I have about specific details that have emerged in my reading to focus my analysis and deepen my understanding.	**Text-specific questions to help focus *my rereading* of the text:**

ODELL EDUCATION

APPROACHING TEXTS TOOL

Name _____ Text _____

APPROACHING THE TEXT	
Before reading, I consider what my specific purposes for reading are.	**What are my reading purposes?**
I also take note of key information about the text.	Title:	Author:	Source/Publisher:
		Text type:	Publication date:
	What do I already think or understand about the text based on this information?	

➡

QUESTIONING THE TEXT	
As I read the text for the first time, I use Guiding Questions that relate to my reading purpose and focus. (*Can be taken from the Guiding Questions Handout.*)	**Guiding Questions for *my first reading* of the text:**
	As I read I mark details on the text that relate to my Guiding Questions.
As I reread, I use questions I have about specific details that have emerged in my reading to focus my analysis and deepen my understanding.	**Text-specific questions to help focus *my rereading* of the text:**

QUESTIONING PATH TOOL

Text 2—*The Story of My Life*, Helen Keller (Model 2)

APPROACHING: *I determine my reading purposes and take note of key information about the text. I identify the LIPS domain(s) that will guide my initial reading.*

I will focus on the author's use of *language* to describe her affection of her teacher and convey her *perspective*.

QUESTIONING: *I use Guiding Questions to help me investigate the text (from the **Guiding Questions Handout**).*

1. How do specific words or phrases influence the meaning or tone of the text? [L]

ANALYZING: *I question further to connect and analyze the details I find (from the **Guiding Questions Handout**).*

2. How does the author's choice of words reveal her purposes and perspective? [P]

DEEPENING: *I consider the questions of others.*

3. In the third sentence of paragraph 2, Keller sets up a comparison between a "shallow brook" and a "deep river."

   What language does she use to describe the brook and the river and how do the words help me think about the differences between the two?

   How does this comparison further develop Keller's perspective on what a teacher's role is?

EXTENDING: *I pose my own questions.*

Examples:

4. What does Keller think the role of a student is?

5. What about a teacher—what does she think the teacher's responsibility is?

ODELL
EDUCATION

APPROACHING TEXTS TOOL

Name _____   **Text** _____

APPROACHING THE TEXT

Before reading, I consider what my specific purposes for reading are.

What are my reading purposes?

I also take note of key information about the text.

Title:

Author:

Source/Publisher:

Text type:

Publication date:

What do I already think or understand about the text based on this information?

QUESTIONING THE TEXT

As I read the text for the first time, I use Guiding Questions that relate to my reading purpose and focus. (Can be taken from the Guiding Questions Handout.)

Guiding Questions for *my first reading* of the text:

As I read I mark details on the text that relate to my Guiding Questions.

As I reread, I use questions I have about specific details that have emerged in my reading to focus my analysis and deepen my understanding.

Text-specific questions to help focus *my rereading* of the text:

QUESTIONING PATH TOOL
Text 5, "Kids Need Structure," Colin Powell

APPROACHING:
I determine my reading purposes and take note of key information about the text. I identify the LIPS domain(s) that will guide my initial reading.

I will initially focus on the text's *ideas* and supporting details but will also pay attention to its *perspective* and *language.* I will think about how knowing the text comes from a US General of the Army might influence my reading.

QUESTIONING: *I use Guiding Questions to help me investigate the text (from the **Guiding Questions Handout**).*

1. What new ideas or information do I find in the text? [I]

2. What claims do I find in the text? [I]

ANALYZING: *I question further to connect and analyze the details I find (from the **Guiding Questions Handout**).*

3. What do I learn about the author and the purpose for writing the text? [P]

4. What details or words suggest the author's perspective? [P, L]

DEEPENING: *I consider the questions of others.*

5. Starting in paragraph 4, what does Powell describe?

   How does this description tell me something about his perspective on education?

   What experiences from Powell's life influence what he says in his speech?

6. What does Powell mean when he talks about *structure*? What examples does he give?

7. What does Powell mean when he makes a claim in paragraph 10 that "the real answer begins with bringing a child to the school with structure in that child's heart and soul to begin with"?

   How does the explanation he gives in the following paragraph help me understand what he means by structure in a child's soul?

8. What details in the final paragraph again point to Powell's perspective?

   How does he use the details he presents to support his view about why American education is not working?

EXTENDING: *I pose my own questions.*

Students will pose a new question in Activity 4.

ODELL
EDUCATION

APPROACHING TEXTS TOOL

Name _____   Text _____

APPROACHING THE TEXT

Before reading, I consider what my specific purposes for reading are.

What are my reading purposes?

I also take note of key information about the text.

Title:

Author:

Text type:

Source/Publisher:

Publication date:

What do I already think or understand about the text based on this information?

QUESTIONING THE TEXT

As I read the text for the first time, I use Guiding Questions that relate to my reading purpose and focus. (Can be taken from the Guiding Questions Handout.)

Guiding Questions for *my first reading* of the text:

As I read I mark details on the text that relate to my Guiding Questions.

As I reread, I use questions I have about specific details that have emerged in my reading to focus my analysis and deepen my understanding.

Text-specific questions to help focus *my rereading* of the text:

ODELL EDUCATION

ANALYZING DETAILS TOOL

Name _ _ _ _ _ _ _ _ _ Text _ _ _ _ _ _ _ _ _

Reading purpose:

A question I have about the text:

SEARCHING FOR DETAILS

I read the text closely and mark words and phrases that help me think about my question.

SELECTING DETAILS

I select words or phrases from my search that I think are the most important in thinking about my question.

Detail 1 (Ref.:)	Detail 2 (Ref.:)	Detail 3 (Ref.:)

ANALYZING DETAILS

I reread parts of the text and think about the meaning of the details and what they tell me about my question.

What I think about detail 1:	What I think about detail 2:	What I think about detail 3:

CONNECTING DETAILS

I compare the details and explain the connections I see among them.

How I connect the details:

ODELL EDUCATION

ANALYZING DETAILS TOOL

Name _____

Text _____

Reading purpose:
_____

A question I have about the text:
_____

SEARCHING FOR DETAILS

I read the text closely and mark words and phrases that help me think about my question.

SELECTING DETAILS

I select words or phrases from my search that I think are the most important in thinking about my question.

Detail 1 (Ref.:)

Detail 2 (Ref.:)

Detail 3 (Ref.:)

ANALYZING DETAILS

I reread parts of the text and think about the meaning of the details and what they tell me about my question.

What I think about detail 1:

What I think about detail 2:

What I think about detail 3:

CONNECTING DETAILS

I compare the details and explain the connections I see among them.

How I connect the details:

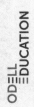

ODELL
EDUCATION

ANALYZING DETAILS TOOL

Name _____ Text _ _ _ _ _ _ _ _ _ _ _ _ _ _ _

Reading purpose:

A question I have about the text:

SEARCHING FOR DETAILS

I read the text closely and mark words and phrases that help me think about my question.

SELECTING DETAILS

I select words or phrases from my search that I think are the most important in thinking about my question.

Detail 1 (Ref.:)	Detail 2 (Ref.:)	Detail 3 (Ref.:)

ANALYZING DETAILS

I reread parts of the text and think about the meaning of the details and what they tell me about my question.

What I think about detail 1:	What I think about detail 2:	What I think about detail 3:

CONNECTING DETAILS

I compare the details and explain the connections I see among them.

How I connect the details:

ODELL EDUCATION

ANALYZING DETAILS

Overview and Tools

"Never be the obstacle between the child and his experience."

OBJECTIVE:	You will learn to analyze textual details as a key to discovering an author's perspective. You will read, analyze, and compare texts.

MATERIALS:
- *Approaching Texts Tool*
- *Analyzing Details Tool*
- *Questioning Path Tools*

- *Guiding Questions Handout*
- *Reading Closely Graphic*

TEXTS:
- 5-*"Kids Need Structure,"* Colin Powell, 2012
- 6-Dr. Montessori's Own Handbook, *Maria Montessori, 1914*

- 7-*"Good Citizenship: The Purpose of Education,"* Eleanor Roosevelt, 1930

ACTIVITIES

1. ANALYZING TEXTUAL DETAILS
You closely read and analyze a new text.

2. ANALYZING DETAILS ACROSS TEXTS
Your teacher guides and supports you as you compare two texts in a discussion.

3. EXPLAINING AND COMPARING TEXTS
In groups, you think about a comparative question and use the question to individually write a paragraph that compares two texts.

4. INDEPENDENT READING ACTIVITY
You independently read texts using Guiding Questions to guide you

QUESTIONING PATH TOOL
Text 6—*Dr. Montessori's Own Handbook*, Maria Montessori, 1914

APPROACHING:
I determine my reading purposes and take note of key information about the text. I identify the LIPS domain(s) that will guide my initial reading.

I will focus on the author's *ideas* and how it reveals her *perspective*. I will think about how the title of this section of text—"Freedom"—is reflected in what I read.

QUESTIONING: *I use Guiding Questions to help me investigate the text (from the **Guiding Questions Handout**).*

1. What words or phrases stand out to me as powerful and important? [L]

2. What ideas stand out to me as significant or interesting? [I]

ANALYZING: *I question further to connect and analyze the details I find (from the **Guiding Questions Handout**).*

3. What seems to be the author's attitude or point of view? [P]

DEEPENING: *I consider the questions of others.*

4. In the first paragraph, what does the word *delicate* suggest about how Montessori thinks a teacher should guide a student?

   What other words in the first two paragraphs convey similar ideas about how adults should provide "real guidance" to children?

   How is the subtitle of this section of Montessori's *Handbook*—"Freedom"—reflected in the ideas, details, and words of paragraphs 1 and 2?

5. In paragraphs 3–4, what words are used to describe the child and his or her actions?

   What words are used to explain what Montessori means with her "motto for the educator": "Wait while observing"?

   How might I sum up Montessori's perspective about how a teacher should teach?

6. At the end of paragraph 4, Montessori presents a "great educational principle" and an "example of good education." What is that principle?

   In the following paragraph, what phrases does Montessori use to explain this principle and communicate her view of children?

   Likewise in paragraph 6, what do the details and words communicate about Montessori's view of how adults treat children?

7. How does Montessori explain what "kindness" is (and is not) in paragraph 6?

   What does she say about what "kindness consists in" and why it is important to treat children with kindness?

8. Montessori italicizes two key words in paragraphs 7 and 8: *indirect* and *free*.

   How do these two words communicate Montessori's perspective on child development and teaching children?

9. How does her final paraphrasing of the Biblical quotation about "little children" represent her view of education?

EXTENDING: *I pose my own questions.*

Example:

10. How does Montessori's description of how a teacher should teach a child make me think differently about education?

54

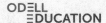

APPROACHING TEXTS TOOL

Name _____   Text _____

APPROACHING THE TEXT	What are my reading purposes?
Before reading, I consider what my specific purposes for reading are.	
I also take note of key information about the text.	Title:
	Author:
	Source/Publisher:
	Text type:
	Publication date:
	What do I already think or understand about the text based on this information?

QUESTIONING THE TEXT	Guiding Questions for *my first reading* of the text:
As I read the text for the first time, I use Guiding Questions that relate to my reading purpose and focus. (*Can be taken from the Guiding Questions Handout.*)	
	As I read I mark details on the text that relate to my Guiding Questions.
As I reread, I use questions I have about specific details that have emerged in my reading to focus my analysis and deepen my understanding.	Text-specific questions to help focus *my rereading* of the text:

ODELL EDUCATION

ANALYZING DETAILS TOOL

Name _ _ _ _ _ _ _ _ _ _ _ _ _ _ _ Text _ _ _ _ _ _ _ _ _ _ _ _ _ _ _ _ _ _

Reading purpose:

A question I have about the text:

SEARCHING FOR DETAILS

I read the text closely and mark words and phrases that help me think about my question.

SELECTING DETAILS

I select words or phrases from my search that I think are the most important in thinking about my question.

Detail 1 (Ref.:	)	Detail 2 (Ref.:	)	Detail 3 (Ref.:	)

ANALYZING DETAILS

I reread parts of the text and think about the meaning of the details and what they tell me about my question.

What I think about detail 1:	What I think about detail 2:	What I think about detail 3:

CONNECTING DETAILS

I compare the details and explain the connections I see among them.

How I connect the details:

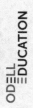

ODELL EDUCATION

ANALYZING DETAILS TOOL

Name _____ **Text** _____

Reading purpose:

A question I have about the text:

SEARCHING FOR DETAILS

I read the text closely and mark words and phrases that help me think about my question.

SELECTING DETAILS

I select words or phrases from my search that I think are the most important in thinking about my question.

Detail 1 (Ref.:)	Detail 2 (Ref.:)	Detail 3 (Ref.:)

ANALYZING DETAILS

I reread parts of the text and think about the meaning of the details and what they tell me about my question.

What I think about detail 1:	What I think about detail 2:	What I think about detail 3:

CONNECTING DETAILS

I compare the details and explain the connections I see among them.

How I connect the details:

ODELL EDUCATION

QUESTIONING PATH TOOL
Comparison of Text 5 and Text 6

APPROACHING:
I determine my reading purposes and take note of key information about the text. I identify the LIPS domain(s) that will guide my initial reading.

I will compare the two text's use of *language* and details to describe what student's need in education and also how they reflect the author's *perspective(s)*. I will think about the differences between the two authors concerning their backgrounds and views about how children should be educated.

QUESTIONING: *I use Guiding Questions to help me investigate the text (from the **Guiding Questions Handout**).*

1. What details or words suggest the author's perspective? [P-L]

ANALYZING: *I question further to connect and analyze the details I find (from the **Guiding Questions Handout**).*

2. How does the author's perspective influence the text's presentation of ideas, themes, or claims? [P]

3. How does the author's perspective and presentation of the text compare to others? [P]

DEEPENING: *I consider the questions of others.*

4. In his fourth and following paragraphs, Powell describes the relationships between the drill sergeant and young soldiers. What words are used to describe this relationship?

   In paragraph 6, Montessori describes how we ought to and ought not to treat children. What language does she use to describe the relationship between adult and child?

   Considering each author's choice of language, how do their perspectives about the relationship between teacher and student compare?

5. In his final paragraph, what warning does Powell give the audience about what happens when children have no structure in their lives?

   What is the measurable consequence according to him?

   Montessori also gives a warning, though it is not as obvious. In paragraph 6, what does she mean when she says, "we expect them to be submissive and well-behaved" and "they will imitate us in any case"?

   What is she warning the reader about?

   Each author gives a warning about what happens to children when something specific does not occur. According to each author, what needs to happen so that children are properly taught?

6. Colin Powell is a retired four-star general of the US Army. How might his position influence the ideas and language he uses in his talk?

   Given his perspective, how might he react to the educational philosophy of Montessori?

EXTENDING: *I pose my own questions.*

As an alternative to questions 4–6, students may develop their own comparative questions.

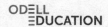
ODELL EDUCATION

ANALYZING DETAILS TOOL

Name _ _ _ _ _ _ _ _ _ _ _ _ _ _ _ _ Text _ _ _ _ _ _ _ _ _ _ _ _ _ _ _ _ _ _ _

Reading purpose:

A question I have about the text:

| SEARCHING FOR DETAILS | I read the text closely and mark words and phrases that help me think about my question. |

SELECTING DETAILS	Detail 1 (Ref.:)	Detail 2 (Ref.:)	Detail 3 (Ref.:)
I select words or phrases from my search that I think are the most important in thinking about my question.			

ANALYZING DETAILS	What I think about detail 1:	What I think about detail 2:	What I think about detail 3:
I reread parts of the text and think about the meaning of the details and what they tell me about my question.			

CONNECTING DETAILS	How I connect the details:
I compare the details and explain the connections I see among them.	

ANALYZING DETAILS TOOL

Name _ _ _ _ _ _ _ _ _ _ _ _ Text _ _ _ _ _ _ _ _ _ _ _ _ _ _ _ _ _ _

Reading purpose:

A question I have about the text:

SEARCHING FOR DETAILS

I read the text closely and mark words and phrases that help me think about my question.

SELECTING DETAILS

I select words or phrases from my search that I think are the most important in thinking about my question.

Detail 1 (Ref.:)	Detail 2 (Ref.:)	Detail 3 (Ref.:)

ANALYZING DETAILS

I reread parts of the text and think about the meaning of the details and what they tell me about my question.

What I think about detail 1:	What I think about detail 2:	What I think about detail 3:

CONNECTING DETAILS

I compare the details and explain the connections I see among them.

How I connect the details:

QUESTIONING PATH TOOL
Texts 7, 8, and 9

APPROACHING: *I determine my reading purposes and take note of key information about the text. I identify the LIPS domain(s) that will guide my initial reading.*

I will do a first reading of the text, thinking about the sequence of the text and events it presents, the author's use of *language* to describe key events, and the author's *perspective* on those events.

QUESTIONING: *I use Guiding Questions to help me investigate the text (from the **Guiding Questions Handout**).*

1. What words or phrases stand out to me as powerful and important? [L]

2. What do I think the text is mainly about—what is discussed in detail? [I]

3. What seems to be the author's attitude or point of view? [P]

4. In what ways are ideas and claims linked together in the text? [S]

ANALYZING: *I question further to connect and analyze the details I find (from the **Guiding Questions Handout**).*

DEEPENING: *I consider the questions of others.*

EXTENDING: *I pose my own questions.*

APPROACHING TEXTS TOOL

Name _____ **Text** _____

APPROACHING THE TEXT

Before reading, I consider what my specific purposes for reading are.

What are my reading purposes?

_____
_____
_____

I also take note of key information about the text.

Title:	Source/Publisher:
Author:	
Text type:	Publication date:

What do I already think or understand about the text based on this information?

_____
_____

QUESTIONING THE TEXT

As I read the text for the first time, I use Guiding Questions that relate to my reading purpose and focus. (Can be taken from the Guiding Questions Handout.)

Guiding Questions for _my first reading_ of the text:

_____
_____
_____

As I read I mark details on the text that relate to my Guiding Questions.

As I reread, I use questions I have about specific details that have emerged in my reading to focus my analysis and deepen my understanding.

Text-specific questions to help focus _my rereading_ of the text:

_____
_____

ODELL
EDUCATION

PART 4

EXPLAINING UNDERSTANDING

Overview and Tools

"The true purpose of education is to produce citizens."

OBJECTIVE: You will learn how to summarize and explain what you have learned from reading, questioning, and analyzing texts. You will read and analyze three related texts.

MATERIALS:
- *Approaching Texts Tool*
- *Analyzing Details Tool*
- *Questioning Path Tools*
- *Guiding Questions Handout*

TEXTS:
- *1-Classroom Images*
- *2-The Story of My Life,* Hellen Keller, 1905
- *3-"Changing Education Paradigms,"* Ken Robinson, 2010
- *4-Only a Teacher,* PBS
- *5-"Kids Need Structure,"* Colin Powell, 2012
- *6-Dr. Montessori's Own Handbook,* Maria Montessori, 1914
- *7-"Good Citizenship: The Purpose of Education,"* Eleanor Roosevelt, 1930
- *8-Notes on the State of Virginia,* Thomas Jefferson, 1784
- *9-"The Vision of Education Reform in the United States,"* Arne Duncan, 2010

≡ ACTIVITIES

1. INTRODUCTION TO CULMINATING ACTIVITY
Your teacher introduces the final text-centered writing assignment and comparative discussion.

2. READING AND DISCUSSING RELATED TEXTS
You read three related texts and discuss them as a class.

3. QUESTIONING AND ANALYZING TEXTS INDEPENDENTLY
You select (or are assigned) one of the texts to discuss with a small group and then analyze it independently.

4. INDEPENDENT WRITING ACTIVITY
You use your analysis to independently write a text-based explanation of one of the texts.

QUESTIONING PATH TOOL

Text 7—"Good Citizenship: The Purpose of Education," Eleanor Roosevelt, 1930

APPROACHING:
I determine my reading purposes and take note of key information about the text. I identify the LIPS domain(s) that will guide my initial reading.

I will do a close reading of my text, looking for key details related to its *structure, language, ideas,* or *perspective* in preparation for writing a text-based explanation and leading a comparative discussion. I will think about how the text discusses the role and purpose of education.

QUESTIONING: *I use Guiding Questions to help me investigate the text (from the **Guiding Questions Handout**).*

1. What words or phrases stand out to me as powerful and important? [L]

2. What do I think the text is mainly about—what is discussed in detail? [I]

ANALYZING: *I question further to connect and analyze the details I find (from the **Guiding Questions Handout**).*

3. What seems to be the author's attitude or point of view? [P]

4. In what ways are ideas and claims linked together in the text? [S]

DEEPENING: *I consider the questions of others.*

5. According to paragraph 1, what are the prevailing purposes for education?

   How does Roosevelt structure this paragraph so the reader knows what she believes the purpose of education really should be?

6. Based on paragraphs 3 and 4, how does Roosevelt believe education needs to change in order to meet "these objectives"?

7. What details in paragraphs 5 and 6 point to Roosevelt's perspective on the primary purpose of education?

   What will a child who is educated through the experiences Roosevelt describes be able to "envisage"? What does she suggest will be the result for the child and for society?

8. What shift in focus occurs between paragraphs 7 and 8, and why might Roosevelt have made this shift?

   What claims, and what evidence, does she present about how teachers are treated in the United States?

9. In the final paragraph, Roosevelt presents a comment made to her recently by a "hard-worked businessman."

   What is the implied societal attitude suggested by that comment?

   How does Roosevelt respond, and what does this indicate about her perspective on what needs to happen in United States education?

EXTENDING: *I pose my own questions.*

Students will develop an original question for their text in Part 4 and a comparative question in Part 5.

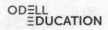
ODELL EDUCATION

QUESTIONING PATH TOOL

Text 8—*Notes on the State of Virginia*, Thomas Jefferson, 1784

APPROACHING:
I determine my reading purposes and take note of key information about the text. I identify the LIPS domain(s) that will guide my initial reading.

I will do a close reading of my text, looking for key details related to its *structure, language, ideas,* or *perspective* in preparation for writing a text-based explanation and leading a comparative discussion. I will think about how the text discusses the role and purpose of education.

QUESTIONING: *I use Guiding Questions to help me investigate the text (from the Guiding Questions Handout).*

1. What words or phrases stand out to me as powerful and important? [L]

2. What do I think the text is mainly about—what is discussed in detail? [I]

ANALYZING: *I question further to connect and analyze the details I find (from the Guiding Questions Handout).*

3. What seems to be the author's attitude or point of view? [P]

4. In what ways are ideas and claims linked together in the text? [S]

DEEPENING: *I consider the questions of others.*

5. What is the first thing Jefferson discusses in his "note"?

   What details does he present about the process by which "the best geniuses will be raked from the rubbish"?

   Why is this process important in his view of the purpose of education?

6. Jefferson's "note" is presented as a single paragraph, but is actually divided into several sections with different areas of focus.

   How does the focus of his discussion shift with the transitional phrase "But of all the views of this law none is more important…"?

   What do details and words in this section of the text communicate about Jefferson's perspective on the purpose of education?

7. According to Jefferson, why should education focus on the study of history?

8. What does Jefferson mean when he talks about the "degeneracy" of government and says "the people themselves . . . are the only safe depositories"?

   How is this claim related to his call for "an amendment of our constitution" to "come in aid of the public education" and to the Virginia bill and plan he outlines at the start of the text?

   Ultimately, according to Jefferson, what is the purpose of education?

EXTENDING: *I pose my own questions.*

Students will develop an original question for their text in Part 4 and a comparative question in Part 5.

QUESTIONING PATH TOOL

Text 9—"The Vision of Education Reform in the United States," Secretary Arne Duncan, 2010

APPROACHING:
I determine my reading purposes and take note of key information about the text. I identify the LIPS domain(s) that will guide my initial reading.

I will do a close reading of my text, looking for key details related to its *structure*, *language*, *ideas*, or *perspective*, in preparation for writing a text-based explanation and leading a comparative discussion. I will think about how the text discusses the role and purpose of education.

QUESTIONING: *I use Guiding Questions to help me investigate the text (from the **Guiding Questions Handout**).*

1. What words or phrases stand out to me as powerful and important? [L]

2. What do I think the text is mainly about—what is discussed in detail? [I]

ANALYZING: *I question further to connect and analyze the details I find (from the **Guiding Questions Handout**).*

3. What seems to be the author's attitude or point of view? [P]

4. In what ways are ideas and claims linked together in the text? [S]

DEEPENING: *I consider the questions of others.*

5. According to what Duncan details in the opening paragraphs of his speech, what purposes does education serve?

6. What details from paragraph 6 explain what the "achievement gap" and "opportunity gap" are?

   In this and the following paragraphs, what details does Duncan provide to support his assertion that "closing the achievement gap and closing the opportunity gap is the civil rights issue of our generation"?

7. Duncan describes "a paradox at the heart of America's efforts to bolster international competitiveness."

   What words and information does he use to explain this paradox?

   What are the implications for education in the United States, and what do "new partnerships" in the world "require" of American students?

8. At the end of the passage, Duncan quotes Nelson Mandela. What does this quotation say about the value of education?

   How are Mandela's words related to the perspective and claims about education that Duncan has presented throughout his speech?

EXTENDING: *I pose my own questions.*

Students will develop an original question for their text in Part 4 and a comparative question in Part 5.

ODELL EDUCATION

APPROACHING TEXTS TOOL

Name _____ **Text** _____

APPROACHING THE TEXT

Before reading, I consider what my specific purposes for reading are.

What are my reading purposes?

I also take note of key information about the text.

Title:	Author:	Source/Publisher:
	Text type:	Publication date:

What do I already think or understand about the text based on this information?

QUESTIONING THE TEXT

As I read the text for the first time, I use Guiding Questions that relate to my reading purpose and focus. (*Can be taken from the Guiding Questions Handout*.)

Guiding Questions for *my first reading* of the text:

As I read I mark details on the text that relate to my Guiding Questions.

As I reread, I use questions I have about specific details that have emerged in my reading to focus my analysis and deepen my understanding.

Text-specific questions to help focus *my rereading* of the text:

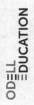

ANALYZING DETAILS TOOL

Name _ _ _ _ _ _ _ _ _ _ _ _ _ Text _ _ _ _ _ _ _ _ _ _ _ _ _

Reading purpose:

A question I have about the text:

SEARCHING FOR DETAILS

I read the text closely and mark words and phrases that help me think about my question.

SELECTING DETAILS

I select words or phrases from my search that I think are the most important in thinking about my question.

Detail 1 (Ref.:)	Detail 2 (Ref.:)	Detail 3 (Ref.:)

ANALYZING DETAILS

I reread parts of the text and think about the meaning of the details and what they tell me about my question.

What I think about detail 1:	What I think about detail 2:	What I think about detail 3:

CONNECTING DETAILS

I compare the details and explain the connections I see among them.

How I connect the details:

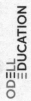

ODELL EDUCATION

ANALYZING DETAILS TOOL

Name _ _ _ _ _ _ _ _ _ _ _   Text _ _ _ _ _ _ _ _ _ _ _ _

Reading purpose:

A question I have about the text:

SEARCHING FOR DETAILS — I read the text closely and mark words and phrases that help me think about my question.

SELECTING DETAILS

I select words or phrases from my search that I think are the most important in thinking about my question.

Detail 1 (Ref.:)	Detail 2 (Ref.:)	Detail 3 (Ref.:)

ANALYZING DETAILS

I reread parts of the text and think about the meaning of the details and what they tell me about my question.

What I think about detail 1:	What I think about detail 2:	What I think about detail 3:

CONNECTING DETAILS

I compare the details and explain the connections I see among them.

How I connect the details:

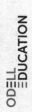

ODELL EDUCATION

PART 5

DISCUSSING IDEAS

Overview and Tools

"A great equalizer of the conditions of men"

OBJECTIVE:	You will learn how to successfully participate in a text-based discussion.

MATERIALS:
- *Approaching Texts Tool*
- *Analyzing Details Tool*

- *Student Reading Closely Literacy Skills and Discussion Habits Checklist*

TEXTS:
- *1-Classroom Images*
- *2-The Story of My Life,* Hellen Keller, 1905
- *3-"Changing Education Paradigms,"* Ken Robinson, 2010
- *4-Only a Teacher,* PBS
- *5-"Kids Need Structure,"* Colin Powell, 2012
- *6-Dr. Montessori's Own Handbook,* Maria Montessori, 1914

- *7-"Good Citizenship: The Purpose of Education,"* Eleanor Roosevelt, 1930
- *8-Notes on the State of Virginia,* Thomas Jefferson, 1784
- *9-"The Vision of Education Reform in the United States,"* Arne Duncan, 2010

ACTIVITIES

1. UNDERSTANDING TEXT-CENTERED DISCUSSIONS
Your teacher introduces you to productive, text-centered discussions.

2. PREPARING FOR A TEXT-CENTERED DISCUSSION
You discuss your analysis in groups and independently prepare to lead a text-centered discussion by writing down a comparative text-specific question.

3. LEADING A TEXT-CENTERED DISCUSSION
You lead and participate in text-centered discussions with other students who have analyzed different texts.

ANALYZING DETAILS TOOL

Name _ _ _ _ _ _ _ _ _ _ _ _ _ _ _ _ Text _

Reading purpose:

A question I have about the text:

SEARCHING FOR DETAILS

I read the text closely and mark words and phrases that help me think about my question.

SELECTING DETAILS

I select words or phrases from my search that I think are the most important in thinking about my question.

Detail 1 (Ref.:)	Detail 2 (Ref.:)	Detail 3 (Ref.:)

ANALYZING DETAILS

I reread parts of the text and think about the meaning of the details and what they tell me about my question.

What I think about detail 1:	What I think about detail 2:	What I think about detail 3:

CONNECTING DETAILS

I compare the details and explain the connections I see among them.

How I connect the details:

STUDENT READING CLOSELY LITERACY SKILLS AND DISCUSSION HABITS CHECKLIST

READING CLOSELY LITERACY SKILLS AND DISCUSSION HABITS	✔	EVIDENCE Demonstrating the SKILLS AND HABITS
READING AND THINKING		
1. **Attending to Details:** Identifies words, details, or quotations that are important to understanding the text		
2. **Interpreting Language:** Understands how words are used to express ideas and perspectives		
3. **Summarizing:** Correctly explains what the text says about the topic		
4. **Identifying Relationships:** Notices important connections among details, ideas, or texts		
5. **Recognizing Perspective:** Identifies and explains the author's view of the text's topic		
6. **Using Evidence:** Uses well-chosen details from the text to support explanations; accurately paraphrases or quotes		
DISCUSSION		
7. **Preparing:** Reads the text(s) closely and thinks about the questions to prepare for a text-centered discussion		
8. **Questioning:** Asks and responds to questions that help the discussion group understand and compare the texts		
9. **Collaborating:** Pays attention to other participants while participating in and leading a text-centered discussion		
10. **Communicating Clearly:** Presents ideas and supporting evidence so others can understand them		
General comments:		

UNIT 2

MAKING EVIDENCE-BASED CLAIMS

DEVELOPING CORE LITERACY PROFICIENCIES

GRADE 9

"The unexamined life is not worth living"

Apology, Plato

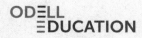

GOAL

In this unit you will develop your proficiency as a maker and defender of claims. You will learn how to do the following:

1. Use the details, connections, and evidence you find in a text to form a claim—a stated conclusion—about something you have discovered.
2. Organize evidence from the text to support your claim and make your case.
3. Express and explain your claim in writing.
4. Improve your writing so that others will clearly understand and appreciate your evidence-based claim—and think about the case you have made for it.

TOPIC

In this unit you will be reading and listening to the ancient Greek text, the *Apology*, written by Plato, an ancient Greek philosopher. The *Apology* is Plato's account of the speech delivered by his teacher, Socrates, as he stood trial in Athens. The title for the text, *Apology,* comes from the Greek word *apologia*, which is better translated into English as "defense." In essence then, Plato's *Apology* is not at all an account of an apology given by Socrates, but of Socrates's defense at his trial. As you study the speech, you will be learning about what a *claim* is, noting how Socrates makes claims that are based on the details of his own experiences and convictions. As you apply the skills from *Reading Closely for Details* of finding key details and making connections, you will take the next step as a reader and thinker: forming your own claims that come from your reading of the texts and supporting them with evidence that comes from what Socrates says.

ACTIVITIES

As you move through this unit from initial reading, to thinking, and to writing, the activities will help you do a close reading of an excerpt from the speech. You will first think about what Socrates tells his audience and then to what he seems to mean when you "read between the lines." As you learn about forming claims you will practice finding evidence from Socrates's defense to support a claim made by your teacher, then move on to forming your own first claims from details you notice in the text. As you read and listen to the text, you will continue to search for evidence that leads to and supports new claims. You will then learn how to organize that evidence. From this base, you will write and revise several claims, the final one a global claim about the overall meaning you have found in the speech. You will learn to work with other students in the class to review and improve your writing so that your final claim can be as clear, strong, and evidence-based as possible.

MAKING EVIDENCE-BASED CLAIMS
LITERACY TOOLBOX

In *Making Evidence-Based Claims*, you will continue to build your "literacy toolbox" by learning how to use the following handouts, tools and checklists organized in your Student Edition.

HANDOUTS

To support your work with the texts and the tools, you will be able to use the following informational handouts. You will also use handouts from *Reading Closely*:

Attending to Details Handout

from the *Reading Closely* unit

Guiding Questions Handout

from the *Reading Closely* unit

Writing Evidence-Based Claims Handout

This handout explains five key things you will need to think about as you write an evidence-based claim. These characteristics are also things your teacher will be looking for in the final claim you write and turn in. The handout includes examples related to one of the speeches in the unit so you can see what each of the key characteristics might look like.

Making Evidence-Based Claims - Final Writing Tasks

This handout will explain to you what you will be doing in the final assignments for this unit: writing a multiparagraph essay that presents, explains, and uses evidence to support a claim you have formed about the meaning of one or more of the texts you have read. The handout will also help you know what your teacher will be looking for so you can be successful on the essay assignment.

TOOLS

In *Making Evidence-Based Claims,* you will continue to build your **Literacy Toolbox** by learning how to use the following tools organized in your Student Edition. You will also apply tools from *Reading Closely*:

Approaching the Text Tool

from the *Reading Closely* unit

Analyzing Details Tool

from the *Reading Closely* unit

Questioning Path Tool

from the *Reading Closely* unit

Model Questioning Path Tools

For each section of the text you will read, there is a **Questioning Path Tool** that has been filled out for you to frame and guide your reading. These model Questioning Paths are just starting points, and your teacher or you may prefer to develop your own paths. The model paths are organized by the steps from the **Reading Closely Graphic** (approaching, questioning, analyzing, deepening, and extending). They include general Guiding Questions from the **Guiding Questions Handout** and some questions that are specific to each text and its content. You will use these model paths to guide your reading, frame your discussions with your teacher and other students, and help you when you are doing the final activities in the unit.

Forming Evidence-Based Claims Tool

This three-part tool will help you move in your thinking from *finding* important details, to *connecting* those details and explaining your connections, to *making a claim* based on the details and connections you have found. You can also use the tool to record evidence to support your claim and indicate where in the text you found the evidence.

Supporting Evidence-Based Claims Tool

This tool provides spaces in which you can record one or more claims about the text (either your teacher's or your own) and then quote or paraphrase supporting evidence for the claim(s)—which you will later use in organizing and writing your claim.

Organizing Evidence-Based Claims Tool

This tool provides support as you move from forming a claim and finding supporting evidence to writing the claim. The tool provides space for writing down two or three supporting points you will want to make to explain and prove your claim. Under each of these points, you can then organize the evidence you have found that relates to the point and supports your overall claim.

 **CHECKLISTS**

You will also use these checklists throughout the unit to support peer- and self-review:

Making Evidence-Based Claims Skills and Habits Checklists

These two checklists present and briefly describe the Literacy Skills and Habits you will be working on during the unit. You can use the checklists to remind you of what you are trying to learn; to reflect on what you have done when reading, discussing, or writing; or to give feedback to other students. Your teacher may use them to let you know about your areas of strength and areas in which you can improve.

MAKING EVIDENCE-BASED CLAIMS
UNIT TEXT

Apology
Plato
cir. 360 BCE
Excerpted and translated by Peter Heinegg, 2013

Lexile Measure 980L

In 399 BC, Socrates (an ancient Greek philosopher) was put on trial by his fellow Athenian citizens. The Apology is Plato's account of the speech that Socrates gave in defense of his actions at the trial.

Let me begin by asking what's the charge that has gotten me **slandered** and that gave **Meletus** the   P1

confidence to **indict** me as he has. What did the people who slandered me say? I'll have to read their

sworn statement, as if they were prosecuting me. It runs something like this: "Socrates is a criminal

and meddles in matters where he has no business. He's always poking under the earth and up in the

5 sky. He makes the worse case look better; and he teaches this sort of stuff to others." You yourselves

have seen **Aristophanes** make this claim in his comedy (*The Clouds*), which had a character called

Socrates strolling around sand saying, "I walk on air," and spouting all sorts of other nonsense about

which I know absolutely nothing. And I'm not saying that because I look down on that sort of science,

if someone actually knows it. I just hope Meletus never brings charges against me for that! But,

10 Athenians, I've never gotten mixed up with that sort of thing; and I can call most of you here today as

slandered	Meletus	indict
falsely accused	Ancient Greek Athenian who was the prosecutor in the trial of Socrates	charge with an offense; bring someone to trial
Aristophanes		
Ancient Greek dramatist and comedy playwright		

my witnesses to this. I ask as many of you who've ever heard me speaking in public—and lots of you have—whether anyone ever heard me discussing such things, either briefly or at length.—(*Voices of agreement in the audience.*) You see, and so you'll know what to think of the other accusations most people make against me. None of it's true. And if you've heard anyone say that I set up to be an

15 educator and charge money for it, that's false too.

Perhaps somebody here might reply: "But, Socrates, what's wrong with you? Where do these charges **P2** come from? Surely, none of this talk and publicity about you would have arisen if you behaved like everyone else. So, tell us what your problem is, because we don't want to treat you unfairly." That sounds fair enough to me, and I'll try to show you what has led people to talk about and accuse me.

20 Listen, please. Some of you may think I'm joking, but you can be sure I'll tell you the whole truth.

Athenians, I got this reputation thanks to a certain kind of wisdom I have. What kind of wisdom, you **P3** ask. Just a human sort of wisdom, I'd say; and I may really be wise in this respect. Perhaps the people I just mentioned have some type of superhuman wisdom, or something I can't put into words. That's because I just don't understand it; and anyone who says I do is lying and slandering me.

25 And now please quiet down, Athenians, even if I say something that strikes you as over the top; **P4** because the statement I'm about to make isn't mine. The person I'm referring to deserves to be trusted. The witness I call on with respect to my wisdom—if it be wisdom—is the god of Delphi (Apollo). You know what sort of man **Chaerephon** was, my companion from early on and a friend to your democracy. He took part in the recent **exile** and returned from exile with you. You certainly know

30 what Chaerephon was like, how **impetuous** he was in everything he set his mind to. Well, he went to Delphi and asked the oracle—please don't interrupt—asked the **oracle** if there was anyone wiser than

Chaerephon	exile	impetuous
Ancient Greek Athenian who was the follower and friend of Socrates	banished from your country or place of residence	acting hastily with little thought
oracle		
priest or priestess who could deliver the prophesies of God		

myself. And the priestess of Apollo replied that there was nobody wiser. Chaerephon has since died; but his brother can testify to all of it.

Why do I bring this up? Because I'm going to show you where the accusations against me came from. **P5**

35 When I heard from Chaerephon, I thought, "What ever does the god mean? What is this riddle all about? I'm not aware of being wise, not a lot and not a little. So what does he mean by calling me the wisest? He can't be telling a lie. That just wouldn't be right." So, with great **toil** and trouble I began to look into what he said.

I paid a visit to one of those people with a reputation for being wise. I thought that there, if anywhere, **P6**

40 I could prove the oracle wrong: "Look, this man is wiser than I am; but you said I was the wisest. I checked this man out—there's no need to give his name; he happened to be one of the politicians. And, after conversing with him, I felt that, although many people and especially this gentleman himself took him to be wise, he wasn't. And then I tried to show him that while he thought he was wise, he was no such thing. But that just turned the man and many of those with him against me. As I

45 walked away, I thought to myself, "At least I'm wiser than *this* fellow. Neither of us actually knows what Beauty and Goodness are, but he *thinks* he knows, even though he doesn't; whereas I neither know nor think I know." Then I went to see someone else reputed to be wiser than the first man; but I came away with the same impression, which made me an object of hatred both to him and many others.

Afterwards I went to talk to one person after another, sensing how **odious** I had become to them. I **P7**

50 was sad and fearful; but I felt it was necessary to make the god's work my highest priority. So I had to go consult all those with a reputation for knowing anything, and find out what the oracle's answer meant. And **by the dog**, Athenians, I have to tell you the truth. When I went on my godly quest, I discovered that the people with the finest reputation struck me as just about the most lacking in wisdom, whereas others who were rated lower were actually more sensible.

toil	odious	by the dog
effort; difficulty	disliked; offensive	reference to Anubis, the Egyptian jackal-like god who represented reasoned judgment

55 Now this investigation has made me a lot of bitter enemies, which led in turn to a lot of slander being   P8

spread about me. I've come to be called "the wise man," because the people who listen to me always

assume that I know all about the subjects that I show others are ignorant of. But the truth is more

likely that the god is the only wise one; and the oracle's response means that human wisdom is worth

little or nothing. And it seems that the god isn't talking about Socrates in person; he's just using my

60 name and taking me as an example, as if to say, "O humans, the wisest one among you is somebody

like Socrates—he realizes that in fact he's worthless when it comes to wisdom."

That's why I still go around seeking and searching at the god's command for anyone, whether citizen   P9

or foreigner, who I think is wise. And in my task of helping the god, if I find anybody who fails this test,

I point out that he's not wise. As a result of this assignment I have no leisure time to devote to any of

65 the city's business worth mentioning or to my own private affairs; and I'm completely poverty-stricken

because of my service to the god.

In addition, the young men with the most time on their hands—the ones from the upper classes—like P10

to come along with me and listen to people being questioned. These fellows often imitate me and try

questioning others. I suspect they find a large supply of folks who think they know something when

70 they actually know little or nothing. And then the people who have been grilled by those youngsters

get angry, not at themselves, but at me. "This Socrates," they say, "is the most **abominable** man; and

he corrupts the youth." When someone asks how I do that, with what sort of actions or teaching,

they don't have any answer. They don't know; but rather than appear to be stumped, they repeat

the handy old **clichés** about philosophers: "things up in the air" and "things beneath the earth,"

75 "not believing in the gods" and "making the worse case look better." I imagine, they'd rather not tell

the truth, that they've been caught pretending to know something when they know nothing. And

because there are a lot of them; and they're extremely concerned about their **prestige**, and they line

up and speak **plausibly** about me, they've long since filled your ears with violent slander. Meletus

abominable	clichés	prestige
unpleasant; awful	common expression or thought	reputation
plausibly		
speaking with reason		

Developing Core Literacy Proficiencies

and **Anytus** and **Lycon** have angrily attacked me: Meletus on behalf of the poets, Anytus on behalf of
80 the craftsmen and the politicians, and Lycon on behalf of the orators. What I've told you, Athenians, is
the truth. I've concealed nothing; I've **evaded** nothing, big or little. And yet I'm pretty sure that what
I've done has made them hate me. That hatred shows that I'm speaking the truth. It's the reason why
they've slandered me, as you'll find out whenever you investigate this, now or later….

Now then, Athenians, I'm going to present my defense, not for my own sake, as one might suppose, P11
85 but for your sake. I mean, so that you don't condemn me and thereby sin against the gift the god gave
you. For if you kill me, you'll find it hard to find someone like me, someone who—if I find someone
like me, someone who—if I can use a **crude** and ridiculous expression— goes after the city the way a
gadfly goes after a big thoroughbred horse that's sluggish because of his great size and that needs to
be **roused** by stinging. It seems to me that the god has inflicted me on the city in some such fashion:
90 I never stop rousing and persuading and **chiding** every one of you, landing on you everywhere all
day long. You're not likely to get another gadfly like me; so take my advice and spare me. You might
get vexed, the way sleepy people do when they're waked up, and you might swat me, if you listen
to Anytus, and easily kill me. Then you'd spend the rest of your lives sleeping, unless the god in his
kindness were to send you someone else like me. I happen to be a gift of the god to the city; and this
95 is how you can tell: Unlike most people, I have neglected all my own interests, and I've put up with
this private neglect for so many years now, while always attending to your business. I've taken each
one of you aside, like a father or elder brother, and encouraged you to have a care for virtue. Now if
I had gotten any profit out of this or been paid for my advice, that would have made sense. But now
you yourselves can see that my accusers, who shamelessly throw every other charge at me, haven't
100 taken their shamelessness so far as to get somebody to testify that I ever charged anyone a fee or
asked for pay. And I think I myself have a witness to the fact that I'm speaking the truth here: my
poverty.

(The jury returns a guilty verdict. Meletus asks for the death penalty.)

Anytus and Lycon	**evaded**	**crude**
Athenian prosecutors of Socrates	avoided	unrefined
gadfly	**roused**	**chiding**
a small insect that bites horses	excited, became active	talking with disapproval

105 There are many reasons, Athenians, why I'm not disturbed by your vote condemning me. It's what **P12**
I expected. But I was much more surprised by the number of votes for and against. I didn't think I'd
lose by a narrow margin, but by a much wider one. Look, if only thirty votes had gone the other way, I
would have been **acquitted.**

You may think that by arguing this way, as in my remarks about wailing and pleading, I'm just putting **P13**
up a bold front. That's not true. No, I'm convinced that I never deliberately harmed anyone; but I
110 can't convince you about this, because we've only had a short time for our discussion. I think that you
would be convinced if you had a law, as other places have, requiring death-penalty cases to be judged
not in a single day but over several days. But, as things stand, it's hard to **quash** these slanders in a
short time. Anyhow, convinced as I am that I never harmed anyone, I'm not about to harm myself by
saying that I deserve anything bad or propose a penalty like that for myself. What do I have to fear?
115 Am I worried about the penalty Meletus proposes, when I've said that I don't know whether death is a
good thing or a bad thing? Should I choose instead something that I'm sure is bad? Should I propose
to be sent to prison? But why should I offer to live in a prison, slaving away for whichever magistrates
have been elected? Should I propose a fine—and be kept in chains until I pay it? But then my old
problem comes up: I don't have any money to pay a fine. Should I propose being sent off into exile?

120 That punishment might suit you. But I would have to be madly in love with life if I failed to realize that **P14**
if you, my fellow citizens, can't endure my arguments and discussions—so bothersome and irritating
do you find them that you want to get rid of them for good—then other people wouldn't endure
them either. Not a chance. And what a wonderful life I'd lead if I went off, a man of my age, moving
from one city to another, only to be driven out. Because I'm well aware that wherever I go, the young
125 people will listen to what I say, as they do here. And if I antagonize them, they'll drive me out by
persuading their elders to do so. Or if I don't antagonize them, their fathers and family members will
drive me out on their own.

acquitted	quash	
found not guilty	suppress	

Developing Core Literacy Proficiencies

Some might say, "Socrates, why can't you just go away from here, keep quiet and not say anything?"   P15
This is the hardest thing to get some of you to understand. Because if I tell you that doing that would
130 mean disobeying the god, and so I can't keep quiet, you'll think I'm putting you on, and you won't
believe me. And if I say that the best thing for everyone is to spend some time every day talking about
virtue and the other things you hear me discussing and examining myself and others about; if I say
that the unexamined life is not worth living, you'll believe me even less. That's how it is, and that's
why it's hard to persuade you.

135 Athenians, you won't save a lot of time by condemning me now. And the people who want to pour   P16
abuse on the city will give you a bad name for killing Socrates, "the wise man." That's because the
ones who want to blame you will say that I'm wise, even though I'm not. If you had waited a little
while, you would have gotten your wish without lifting a finger. You see how old I am, how far gone in
life and how close to death. I'm not saying this to all of you, but to those who voted for my death. And
140 I have another thing to tell them. Perhaps you think I've been convicted for lack of arguments that
would have persuaded you—if only I had thought it right to say and do everything possible to win an
acquittal. Far from it. I was convicted not by a lack of arguments, but by my lack of ruthlessness and
shamelessness and willingness to tell you what you most wanted to hear. You would have found it
sweet to hear me groaning and grieving and doing all sorts of things that are beneath me—you know,
145 the kind of things you're used to hearing from others.

But I didn't think then that because I was in danger I ought to do anything unworthy of a free person; P17
nor do I now regret defending myself the way I did. I would much rather die for that sort of defense
than to live after giving the other sort. For neither in the courtroom nor on the battlefield should I or
anyone else **scheme** to escape death any which way. It's often clear in battle that you can avoid death
150 by throwing down your weapons and pleading for mercy from those pursuing you. And there are
many other schemes for dodging death amid all sorts of dangers—if you have it in you to do or say
anything at all. It's not hard to escape death; but it's much harder to escape wickedness, because it
runs faster than death. Old and slow as I am, I have been caught by the slower runner, death; while my

scheme		
an underhand plan		

accusers, who are clever and swift, have been caught by the faster runner, wickedness. Now I'm going

155 away, found guilty by you and condemned to death, while they go away—but it's the truth that has

found them guilty of evil and injustice. I'll stand by my sentence; and they'll stand by theirs. Perhaps

this is how it has to be. I think it's all right.

And now, for those of you who voted to condemn me, I'd like to make a **prophecy**. I am, in fact, at   **P18**

the place where most people do prophesy: the point when they're about to die. You have killed me;

160 but I have to tell you that you'll be punished immediately after my death. And the punishment will be

a lot harsher than the one you gave by putting me to death. You did that, thinking you'd get off the

hook, that you wouldn't have to **render** an account of the lives you've led. But I'd say that things will

work out very differently for you. There will be *more* people demanding an account of you. You didn't

notice it, but I held them back. And they'll be all the harder on you insofar as they'll be younger—

165 which will only make you angrier. Because if you think that by killing people you can avoid being

taken to task for not living as you should, then you're wrong. That kind of escape is neither available

nor honorable. The easiest and finest escape is not by doing people in, but by making yourself the

best person possible. That's my prophecy to those of you who have condemned me. And now I bid

you farewell.

170 But for those of you who voted to acquit me, I'd like to say a few words about this event—while the   **P19**

magistrates are still busy and before I head for where I must die. Stay a bit longer with me. Nothing

prevents us from conversing while we can. You're my friends, and I want to show you the meaning of

what's just happened to me . . .

Let's think this over in another way. Consider how there's every reason to hope that death is a good   **P20**

175 thing. To have died means one of two things: either to be in a state of nothingness and to have no

awareness of anything; or else, as they say, it's a kind of change and migration of the soul from where

it is to somewhere else. If there's no consciousness, as in a sleep where you sleep the whole night

through without dreaming, then death would be a marvelous gain. I think that if someone had to

prophesy	render		
a prediction	perform		

Developing Core Literacy Proficiencies

pick a night when he or she slept soundest without even dreaming, and then compared it with all the
180 other days and nights of his life, that person would have to say: "How many days and nights of my

life have I lived through more sweetly and pleasantly than this one?" I think that not only an ordinary

individual, but the King of Persia himself could find precious few days or nights like that one. If that's

the nature of death, I'd call it a gain, for then all time turns out to be nothing more than a single night.

But if, on the other hand, death is a departure to another place, and what they say about it is true,   P21
185 and all the dead are there, then what greater good could there be than this? For if a person arrives in

the underworld, having gotten away from these so-called judges, and he or she finds there the real

judges who are said to preside there—**Minos** and **Rhadamanthus** and **Aeacus** and **Triptolemos**

and the demigods who lived righteous lives—that would be a splendid journey. And what would you

give to get together with **Orpheus** and **Musaeus** and **Hesiod** and **Homer**? I'd be willing to die many
190 times over if this is true. And I'd find it marvelous to live there and meet Palamedes or Ajax the son of

Telamon and any other of the ancients who died because of an unjust judgment—I could compare

my troubles with theirs. I think that would be quite pleasurable. Best of all would be to spend my time

examining and questioning the people there as I do here to discover who's wise and who thinks he is

but isn't. What price would you pay, judges, to question Agamemnon, who led the great army against
195 Troy, or Odysseus or Sisiphus and countless others, men and women? Talking to them, and being

with them, examining them—what indescribable happiness. I don't suppose they kill people there for

doing that, since everyone is immortal forever afterwards, as well as being happier in other ways than

people here, if what they say is true.

But now you, my judges, must take a hopeful view of death and reflect on this one truth: nothing evil   P22
200 can befall a good person either in life or in death; and the god will not neglect his or her fate. Thus,

Minos and Rhadamanthus	Aeacus and Triptolemos	Orpheus and Musaeus
in Greek mythology, the judges of the dead in the underworld	in Greek mythology, judges of the dead in the underworld	the earliest and most revered of the Ancient Greek poets and philosophers
Hesiod and Homer		
the earliest and most revered of the Ancient Greek poets and philosophers		

my case didn't play out by chance. It's clear to me that it's better for me to die now and be free from all my troubles. That's why the special sign that I get from heaven never warned me off in this matter. Now I don't hold it against my accusers and the ones who voted to condemn me. Yet in accusing and condemning me, they *did* mean to injure me; and they're to blame for that. But I beg this of them:

205   when my sons grow up, punish them by getting in their face as I've gotten in yours. If you think they care more about money or anything else than they do about virtue; and if they take themselves to be very important when they aren't, rebuke them for, the way I've **rebuked** you, for not paying attention to what they should and for thinking they're important when they're worthless. If you do that, the treatment you give me and my sons will have been fair.

210   But now it's time to leave, time for me to die and for you to live. But which of us is headed to a better P23 destiny, nobody knows but God.

rebuked		
expressed disapproval		

Developing Core Literacy Proficiencies

MAKING EVIDENCE-BASED CLAIMS

DEVELOPING CORE LITERACY PROFICIENCIES

GRADE 9

Literacy Toolbox

WRITING EVIDENCE-BASED CLAIMS: PLATO

Writing evidence-based claims is a little different from writing stories or just writing about something. You need to **follow a few steps** as you write.

1. ESTABLISH THE CONTEXT

Your readers must know **where your claim is coming from** and **why it's relevant**.

Depending on the scope of your piece and the claim, the context differs. If your whole piece is one claim or if you're introducing the first major claim of your piece, the entire context must be established:

> In Plato's *Apology*, Socrates believes . . .

Purposes of evidence-based writing vary. In some cases, naming the book and author might be enough to establish the relevance of your claim. In other cases, you might want to supply additional information:

> In Plato's *Apology*, Socrates is put on trial for meddling in "matters where he has no business." To begin his defense, Socrates argues that . . .

If your claim is part of a larger piece with multiple claims, then the context might be simpler:

> According to Socrates, . . .   *or*   In paragraph 3, Socrates argues . . .

2. STATE YOUR CLAIM CLEARLY

How you state your claim is important; it must **precisely and comprehensively express your analysis**. Figuring out how to state claims is a **process**; writers revise them continually as they write their supporting evidence. Here's a claim about Socrates's role in Athenian society from Plato's *Apology*:

> In Plato's *Apology*, Socrates believes that the annoyance he causes helps Athens and they will suffer if they put him to death.

When writing claims it is often useful to describe parts of the claim before providing the supporting evidence. In this case, the writer might want to connect the "annoyance" to Socrates's social role.

> In Plato's *Apology*, Socrates believes that the annoyance he causes helps Athens and they will suffer if they put him to death. Socrates thinks he plays a unique role in Athenian society.

The idea in the second sentence is relevant to the claim and begins connecting the claim to ideas that will be used as evidence.

Remember, you should continually return and rephrase your claim as you write the supporting evidence to make sure you are capturing exactly what you want to say. Writing out the evidence always helps you figure out what you really think.

ODELL EDUCATION

WRITING EVIDENCE-BASED CLAIMS: PLATO (Continued)

3. ORGANIZE YOUR SUPPORTING EVIDENCE

Many claims contain multiple parts that require different evidence and should be expressed in separate paragraphs. This claim can be **broken down into two parts:**

The **HELPFUL ANNOYANCE**

and

the **EFFECTS OF SOCRATES'S DEATH ON ATHENS**

Here are two paragraphs that support the claim with evidence organized into these two parts.

A description of the HELPFUL ANNOYANCE:

> Socrates explains that he will argue not for his own sake, but instead for the benefit of the Athenians. He explains that he "goes after the city the way a gadfly goes after a big thoroughbred horse" and that "god has inflicted me on the city" to "never stop rousing and persuading and chiding every one of you, landing on you everywhere all day long" (paragraph 11). Socrates likens himself to a fly that was sent by god to wake up the people from their state of sleep. This suggests that it is the god's will to wrest the Athenian citizens from their ignorance, and Socrates is merely doing what he has been called to do (paragraph 11). In fact, by remaining loyal to this godly calling, Socrates had to put aside his own personal interests and remained impoverished in order to help out the Athenians (paragraph 11). Socrates thus defends himself by proving to the Athenians how much of a help to society he is.

A description of the EFFECTS OF SOCRATES'S DEATH ON ATHENS:

> To strengthen his argument, Socrates tells the Athenians that even though they "might get vexed" and "swat" at him, it is for their own benefit, for without him they will "spend the rest of your lives sleeping" (paragraph 11). Further, he explains that putting him to death will give the Athenians a "bad name" (paragraph 16) and that once he is killed, his accusers' punishment will be much worse than what they gave to Socrates (paragraph 18). Socrates argues that though his condemners have successfully quieted him, they will still be held accountable for their dishonest lives (paragraph 18).

Notice the phrase "to strengthen his argument even further" starting the second paragraph. **Transitional phrases** like this aid the organization by showing how the ideas relate to each other.

4. PARAPHRASE AND QUOTE

Written evidence from texts can be paraphrased or quoted. It's up to the writer to decide which works better for each piece of evidence. Paraphrasing is **putting the author's words into your own.** This works well when the author originally expresses the idea you want to include across many sentences. You might write it more briefly. The fourth line from paragraph 11 paraphrases the evidence from Plato's text. The ideas are his, but the exact way of writing them is not.

> Socrates says that he is not going to make a defense for the benefit of himself, but for the benefit of the Athenians (paragraph 11).

Some evidence is better quoted than paraphrased. If an author has found the quickest way to phrase the idea or the words are especially strong, you might want to use the author's words. The second line from paragraph 11 quotes the text exactly, incorporating important phrases.

> He explains that he "goes after the city the way a gadfly goes after a big thoroughbred horse" and that "god has inflicted me on the city" to "never stop rousing and persuading and chiding every one of you, landing on you everywhere all day long" (paragraph 11).

WRITING EVIDENCE-BASED CLAIMS: PLATO (Continued)

5. REFERENCE YOUR EVIDENCE

Whether you paraphrase or quote the author's words, you must include **the exact location where the ideas come from**. Direct quotes are written in quotation marks. How writers include the reference can vary depending on the piece and the original text. Here the writer puts the paragraph numbers from the original text in parentheses at the end of the sentence.

ODELL
EDUCATION

MAKING EVIDENCE-BASED CLAIMS FINAL WRITING TASKS: PLATO

In this unit, you have been developing your skills as a reader who can make text-based claims and prove them with evidence from the text.

- Uncovering key clues in the details, words, and central ideas found in the text
- Making connections among details and central ideas in the text
- Using the details, connections, and evidence you find in the text to form a claim—a stated conclusion—about something you have discovered
- Organizing evidence from the text to support your claim and make your case
- Expressing and explaining your claim in writing
- Improving your writing so that others will clearly understand and appreciate your evidence-based claim—and think about the case you have made for it

Your final two writing assignments will provide you with opportunities to use all of these related skills and to demonstrate your proficiency and growth in making evidence-based claims.

FINAL ASSIGNMENTS

1. **Developing and Writing an Evidence-Based Claim:** On your own, you will read the final part of the text in the unit closely and develop an evidence-based claim. To accomplish this, you will do the following:

   a. Read and annotate a section of text on your own and use Guiding Questions and a ***Forming Evidence-Based Claims Tool*** to develop an initial claim about the text.

   b. Compare the notes and initial claim you make with those made by other students—reframe or revise your claim.

   c. Complete an ***Organizing Evidence-Based Claims Tool*** to plan subpoints and evidence you will use to explain and support your claim.

   d. Study the ***Writing Evidence-Based Claims Handout*** to know what a written EBC needs to do and what examples might look like.

   e. Draft a one- to two-paragraph written presentation and explanation of your claim, making sure that you do the things listed on the ***Writing Evidence-Based Claims Handout***:

   ⇒ Establish the context by connecting the claim to the text.

   ⇒ State the claim clearly to fully communicate your ideas about the text.

   ⇒ Organize supporting evidence found in the text.

   ⇒ Paraphrase and quote from the text.

   ⇒ Reference the evidence drawn from the text.

   f. Work with other students to review and improve your draft—and to be sure it is the best possible representation of your claim and your skills as a reader and writer. Work on improving at least one of these aspects of your claim:

   ⇒ How clear your presentation and explanation of your claim is

   ⇒ How defensible (based on the evidence you present) your claim is

FINAL WRITING TASKS: PLATO (Continued)

FINAL ASSIGNMENT (Continued)

⇒ How well you have <u>presented and referenced evidence</u> to support your claim

⇒ How well you have <u>organized</u> your subpoints and evidence into a unified claim

g. Reflect on how well you have used Literacy Skills in developing this written claim.

2. **Writing and Revising a Global Evidence-Based Claims Essay:** On your own, you will plan and draft a multiparagraph essay that presents a global claim—one based on connections you have found between details in the text you have read in the unit. To accomplish this, you will do the following:

a. Review the text you have read, the tools you have completed, and the claims you have formed throughout the unit, looking for connections or comparisons.

b. Use a **Forming Evidence-Based Claims Tool** to make a new claim that develops a global conclusion about the meaning of the text.

c. Use an **Organizing Evidence-Based Claims Tool** to plan the subpoints and evidence you will use to explain and support your claim.

d. Draft a multiparagraph essay that explains, develops, and supports your global claim—keeping in mind these three criteria for this final writing assignment. Your essay should do the following:

⇒ Demonstrate an accurate reading and insightful analysis of the text you have read in the unit.

⇒ Develop a supported claim that is clearly connected to the content of the text.

⇒ Successfully accomplish the five key elements of a written EBC (**Writing Evidence-Based Claims Handout**).

e. Use a collaborative process with other students to review and improve your draft in two key areas: (1) its content (quality of the claim and its evidence) and (2) its organization and expression (unity of the discussion and clarity of the writing).

f. Reflect on how well you have used Literacy Skills in developing this final explanation.

SKILLS TO BE DEMONSTRATED

As you become a text expert and write your evidence-based claims, think about demonstrating the Literacy Skills listed in the following to the best of your ability. Your teacher will evaluate your work and determine your grade based on how well you do.

Read

- **Attend to Details:** Identify words, details, or quotations that you think are important to understanding the text
- **Interpret Language:** Understand how words are used to express ideas and perspectives
- **Identify Relationships:** Notice important connections among details, ideas, or texts
- **Recognize Perspective:** Identify and explain the author's view of the unit's topic

Think

- **Make Inferences:** Draw sound conclusions from reading and examining the text closely
- **Form a Claim:** State a meaningful conclusion that is well supported by evidence from the text

FINAL WRITING TASKS: PLATO (Continued)

SKILLS TO BE DEMONSTRATED (Continued)

- **Use Evidence:** Use well-chosen details from the texts to support your explanation; accurately paraphrase or quote what the authors say in the text

Write

- **Present Details:** Insert details and quotations effectively into your essay
- **Organize Ideas:** Organize your claim, supporting ideas, and evidence in a logical order
- **Use Language:** Write clearly so others can understand your claim and supporting ideas
- **Use Conventions:** Correctly use sentence elements, punctuation, and spelling to produce clear writing
- **Publish:** Correctly use, format, and cite textual evidence to support your claim

HABITS TO BE DEVELOPED

Your teacher may also want you to reflect on how well you have used and developed the following habits of text-centered discussion when you worked with others to understand the text and improve your writing:

- **Engage Actively:** Focus your attention on the assigned tasks when working individually and with others
- **Collaborate:** Work respectfully and productively to help your discussion or review group be successful
- **Communicate Clearly:** Present your ideas and supporting evidence so others can understand them
- **Listen:** Pay attention to ideas from others and take time to think about them
- **Understand Purpose and Process:** Understand why and how a text-centered discussion or peer writing review should be accomplished
- **Revise:** Rethink your ideas and refine your writing based on feedback from others
- **Remain Open:** Modify and further justify ideas in response to thinking from others.

NOTE

These skills and habits are also listed on the **Student Making EBC Literacy Skills** and **Academic Habits Checklists**, which you can use to assess your work and the work of other students.

PART 1

UNDERSTANDING EVIDENCE-BASED CLAIMS

Overview and Tools

"Just a human sort of wisdom"

OBJECTIVE: You will learn about making evidence-based claims through reading a text.

MATERIALS:
- *Guiding Questions Handout*
- *Reading Closely Graphic*
- *Questioning Path Tool*
- *Attending to Details Handout*
- *Forming EBC Tool*
- *Supporting EBC Tool*

OPTIONAL:
- *Approaching Texts Tool*
- *Analyzing Details Tool*

TEXT:
- *Apology, Plato, paragraphs 1–3*

ACTIVITIES

1. INTRODUCTION TO UNIT
Your teacher presents the purpose of the unit and explains the idea of making evidence-based claims.

2. INDEPENDENT READING
You independently read part of the text with a Guiding Question to help focus your reading.

3. READ ALOUD AND CLASS DISCUSSION
You follow along as you listen to the text being read aloud, and your teacher leads a discussion about it.

4. MODEL THE FORMING OF EBCs
Your teacher shows you how to form evidence-based claims about texts.

ODELL
EDUCATION

QUESTIONING PATH TOOL

Plato's *Apology,* paragraphs 1–3

APPROACHING:
I determine my reading purposes and take note of key information about the text. I identify the LIPS domain(s) that will guide my initial reading.

I will initially focus on the author's *ideas* and *perspective,* then consider *language,* *structure,* and supporting details.

QUESTIONING: *I use Guiding Questions to help me investigate the text (from the Guiding Questions Handout).*

1. What do the author's words and phrases cause me to see, feel, or think? [L]

2. What details or words suggest the author's perspective? [I]

ANALYZING: *I question further to connect and analyze the details I find (from the Guiding Questions Handout).*

3. How might I summarize the main ideas of the text and the key supporting details? [I]

4. How are key ideas, events, places, or characters described? [L]

DEEPENING: *I consider the questions of others.*

5. What is Socrates being accused of?

6. What does Socrates's use of the word *slandered* reveal about his position? How does Socrates make it clear that he is innocent?

7. In paragraph 3, Socrates says he is on trial because of "a certain kind of wisdom." According to Socrates, what kind of wisdom does he not have? What does this suggest about the wisdom he does have?

8. In paragraph 2, why does Socrates ask a question to himself as if the audience asked him? How does this paragraph relate to the first and third paragraphs? Why would Socrates pretend the audience is asking him questions?

9. Why is this text titled the Apology? What does the word apology mean when translated from the Greek *apologia*? How does this definition help you understand what Socrates is doing?

EXTENDING: *I pose my own questions.*

APPROACHING TEXTS TOOL

Name _____   Text _____

APPROACHING THE TEXT	What are my reading purposes?
Before reading, I consider what my specific purposes for reading are.	

	Title:	Author:	Source/Publisher:
I also take note of key information about the text.		Text type:	Publication date:

What do I already think or understand about the text based on this information?

QUESTIONING THE TEXT	Guiding Questions for *my first reading* of the text:
As I read the text for the first time, I use Guiding Questions that relate to my reading purpose and focus. (*Can be taken from the Guiding Questions Handout.*)	

As I read I mark details on the text that relate to my Guiding Questions.

As I reread, I use questions I have about specific details that have emerged in my reading to focus my analysis and deepen my understanding.	Text-specific questions to help focus *my rereading* of the text:

ODELL
EDUCATION

ANALYZING DETAILS TOOL

Name _____

Text _____

Reading purpose:

A question I have about the text:

SEARCHING FOR DETAILS

I read the text closely and mark words and phrases that help me think about my question.

SELECTING DETAILS

I select words or phrases from my search that I think are the most important in thinking about my question.

Detail 1 (Ref.:)	Detail 2 (Ref.:)	Detail 3 (Ref.:)

ANALYZING DETAILS

I reread parts of the text and think about the meaning of the details and what they tell me about my question.

What I think about detail 1:	What I think about detail 2:	What I think about detail 3:

CONNECTING DETAILS

I compare the details and explain the connections I see among them.

How I connect the details:

FORMING EVIDENCE-BASED CLAIMS TOOL

Name _____   Text _____

A question I have about the text:

	Detail 1 (Ref:)	Detail 2 (Ref:)	Detail 3 (Ref.:)
FINDING DETAILS I find interesting details that are <u>related</u> and that stand out to me from reading the text closely.			

	What I think about detail 1:	What I think about detail 2:	What I think about detail 3:
CONNECTING THE DETAILS I reread and think about the details, and <u>explain</u> the connections I find among them.			

How I connect the details:

	My claim about the text:
MAKING A CLAIM I state a conclusion that I have come to and can support with <u>evidence</u> from the text after reading and thinking about it closely.	

SUPPORTING EVIDENCE-BASED CLAIMS TOOL

Name _____ **Text** _____

CLAIM:

Supporting Evidence	Supporting Evidence	Supporting Evidence
(Reference:)	(Reference:)	(Reference:)

CLAIM:

Supporting Evidence	Supporting Evidence	Supporting Evidence
(Reference:)	(Reference:)	(Reference:)

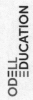

ODELL EDUCATION

PART 2

MAKING EVIDENCE-BASED CLAIMS

Overview and Tools

"I neither know nor think I know."

OBJECTIVE:	You will develop the ability to make evidence-based claims through a close reading of a second section of text

MATERIALS:
- *Supporting EBC Tool*
- *Attending to Details Handout*
- *Forming EBC Tool*
- *Questioning Path Tool*

TEXT:
- *Apology, Plato, paragraphs 4–10*

ACTIVITIES

1. INDEPENDENT READING TO FIND SUPPORTING EVIDENCE
You independently read a second section of text and use the **Supporting EBC Tool** to look for evidence to support a claim made by your teacher.

2. READ ALOUD AND CLASS DISCUSSION
You follow along as you listen to the same part of the text being read aloud and then discuss it.

3. FIND SUPPORTING EVIDENCE IN PAIRS
In pairs, you use the **Supporting EBC Tool** to look for evidence to support additional claims about the text made by your teacher.

4. CLASS DISCUSSION OF EBCs
The class discusses the evidence you have found in support the claims.

5. FORMING EBCs IN PAIRS
In pairs, you use the **Forming EBC Tool** to make an evidence-based claim of your own and present it to the class.

SUPPORTING EVIDENCE-BASED CLAIMS TOOL

Name _____

Text _____

CLAIM:

Supporting Evidence	Supporting Evidence	Supporting Evidence

(Reference:)   (Reference:)   (Reference:)

CLAIM:

Supporting Evidence	Supporting Evidence	Supporting Evidence

(Reference:)   (Reference:)   (Reference:)

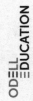
ODELL EDUCATION

QUESTIONING PATH TOOL

Plato's *Apology*, paragraphs 4–10

APPROACHING:
I determine my reading purposes and take note of key information about the text. I identify the LIPS domain(s) that will guide my initial reading.

I will initially focus on the narrator's *perspective*, then consider his *ideas* and supporting details.

QUESTIONING: *I use Guiding Questions to help me investigate the text (from the **Guiding Questions Handout**).*

1. What seems to be the author's point of view? [P]

2. What claims do I find in the text? [I]

ANALYZING: *I question further to connect and analyze the details I find (from the **Guiding Questions Handout**).*

3. How does the narrator's perspective influence his presentation of ideas or arguments? [P]

4. How do the main ideas, events, or people change as the text progresses? [I]

DEEPENING: *I consider the questions of others.*

5. How does Socrates view the oracle's message? In what way does Socrates use the oracle to for his defense?

6. What realization does Socrates come to while trying to prove the oracle wrong? How does Socrates interpret the oracle's words?

7. What does Socrates mean when he says that the god is using him "as an example"? How does his pursuit to understand the oracle come to affect his life?

EXTENDING: *I pose my own questions.*

ODELL
EDUCATION

SUPPORTING EVIDENCE-BASED CLAIMS TOOL

Name _ _ _ _ _ _ _ _ _ _ _ _ _ _ _ _ **Text** _ _ _ _ _ _ _ _ _ _ _ _ _ _ _

CLAIM:

Supporting Evidence	Supporting Evidence	Supporting Evidence

(Reference:)   (Reference:)   (Reference:)

CLAIM:

Supporting Evidence	Supporting Evidence	Supporting Evidence

(Reference:)   (Reference:)   (Reference:)

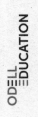
ODELL EDUCATION

SUPPORTING EVIDENCE-BASED CLAIMS TOOL

Name _____   Text _____

CLAIM:

Supporting Evidence	Supporting Evidence	Supporting Evidence
(Reference: _____)	(Reference: _____)	(Reference: _____)

CLAIM:

Supporting Evidence	Supporting Evidence	Supporting Evidence
(Reference: _____)	(Reference: _____)	(Reference: _____)

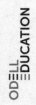

FORMING EVIDENCE-BASED CLAIMS TOOL

Name _____   **Text** _____

A question I have about the text:

FINDING DETAILS

I find interesting details that are related and that stand out to me from reading the text closely.

Detail 1 (Ref.:)	Detail 2 (Ref.:)	Detail 3 (Ref.:)

CONNECTING THE DETAILS

I reread and think about the details, and explain the connections I find among them.

What I think about detail 1:	What I think about detail 2:	What I think about detail 3:

How I connect the details:

MAKING A CLAIM

I state a conclusion that I have come to and can support with evidence from the text after reading and thinking about it closely.

My claim about the text:

ORGANIZING EVIDENCE-BASED CLAIMS

Overview and Tools

"You're not likely to get another gadfly like me."

OBJECTIVE:	You will learn to develop and explain evidence-based claims through the selection and organization of supporting evidence.

MATERIALS:
- *Organizing EBC Tool*
- *Forming EBC Tool*
- *Questioning Path Tool*

TEXT:
- *Aplogy, Plato,* paragraphs 11–18

≡ ACTIVITIES

1. INDEPENDENT READING AND FINDING EBCs
You independently read part of the text and use the *Forming EBC Tool* to make an evidence-based claim.

2. COMPARING EBCs
You compare your claims with your peers. Then you read or listen to the text begin read aloud to look for more evidence to support your claim.

3. MODEL THE ORGANIZING OF EBCs
Your teacher shows you how to organize evidence to develop and explain claims.

4. DEEPENING UNDERSTANDING
As a class, you use questions to deepen your understanding of the text and develop another evidence-based claim.

5. ORGANIZING EBCs IN PAIRS
In pairs, you develop and organize a new claim using the *Organizing EBC Tool*.

6. CLASS DISCUSSION OF STUDENT EVIDENCE-BASED CLAIMS
You discuss the evidence-based claims you have developed with the class.

ODELL EDUCATION

QUESTIONING PATH TOOL

Plato's _Apology_, paragraphs 11–18

APPROACHING:
I determine my reading purposes and take note of key information about the text. I identify the LIPS domain(s) that will guide my initial reading.

I will initially focus on the _ideas_ the narrator presents through details and how his perspective influences his ideas.

QUESTIONING: _I use Guiding Questions to help me investigate the text (from the **Guiding Questions Handout**)._

1. What do I think the text is mainly about—what is discussed in detail? [I]

2. What claims do I find in the text? [I]

ANALYZING: _I question further to connect and analyze the details I find (from the **Guiding Questions Handout**)._

3. In what ways are ideas, events, and claims linked together in the text? [I]

4. How does the author's perspective influence his presentation of ideas, themes, or claims? [P]

DEEPENING: _I consider the questions of others._

5. In paragraph 11, Socrates states that he will give his defense, "not for my own sake . . . but for your sake." What details does Socrates give to support this stance? How does Socrates arrive at such a conclusion?

6. The topic of money comes up throughout paragraphs 11–17. Why is it important for Socrates to bring up the issue of poverty? How does he use his economic status in his defense?

7. In paragraph 11, Socrates compares himself to a gadfly. According to him, why is it important for Athenians to have a gadfly? What is the consequence if Athens has no gadfly?

8. In paragraph 13, Socrates says he is "convinced that I never deliberately harmed anyone." Throughout paragraphs 13–17, he claims that it is difficult to persuade the Athenians. Finally, in paragraph 17, Socrates claims that his accusers have been found guilty by truth. What does this language reveal about Socrates's perspective of himself and his audience?

EXTENDING: _I pose my own questions._

FORMING EVIDENCE-BASED CLAIMS TOOL

Name _____

Text _

A question I have about the text:

FINDING DETAILS	**Detail 1 (Ref.:)**	**Detail 2 (Ref.:)**	**Detail 3 (Ref.:)**
I find interesting details that are <u>related</u> and that stand out to me from reading the text closely.			

CONNECTING THE DETAILS	**What I think about detail 1:**	**What I think about detail 2:**	**What I think about detail 3:**
I reread and think about the details, and <u>explain</u> the connections I find among them.			

How I connect the details:

MAKING A CLAIM	**My claim about the text:**
I state a conclusion that I have come to and can support with <u>evidence</u> from the text after reading and thinking about it closely.	

ODELL
EDUCATION

ORGANIZING EVIDENCE-BASED CLAIMS TOOL (2 POINTS)

Name _ _ _ _ _ _ _ _ _ _ _   **Text** _ _ _ _ _ _ _ _ _ _

CLAIM:

Point 1

A	Supporting Evidence	B	Supporting Evidence
(Reference:)		(Reference:)	

C	Supporting Evidence	D	Supporting Evidence
(Reference:)		(Reference:)	

Point 2

A	Supporting Evidence	B	Supporting Evidence
(Reference:)		(Reference:)	

C	Supporting Evidence	D	Supporting Evidence
(Reference:)		(Reference:)	

ODELL EDUCATION

ORGANIZING EVIDENCE-BASED CLAIMS TOOL (3 POINTS)

Name _ _ _ _ _ _ _ _ _ _ _ _ _ Text _ _ _ _ _ _ _ _ _ _ _ _ _ _ _ _ _

CLAIM:

Point 1	Point 2	Point 3
A Supporting Evidence	**A** Supporting Evidence	**A** Supporting Evidence
(Reference:)	(Reference:)	(Reference:)
B Supporting Evidence	**B** Supporting Evidence	**B** Supporting Evidence
(Reference:)	(Reference:)	(Reference:)
C Supporting Evidence	**C** Supporting Evidence	**C** Supporting Evidence
(Reference:)	(Reference:)	(Reference:)

ODELL
EDUCATION

FORMING EVIDENCE-BASED CLAIMS TOOL

Name _ _ _ _ _ _ _ _ _ _ _ _ _ _ _ _ _   Text _ _ _ _ _ _ _ _ _ _ _ _ _ _ _

A question I have about the text:

FINDING DETAILS I find interesting details that are <u>related</u> and that stand out to me from reading the text closely.	**Detail 1 (Ref.:**)	**Detail 2 (Ref.:**)	**Detail 3 (Ref.:**)
CONNECTING THE DETAILS I reread and think about the details, and <u>explain</u> the connections I find among them.	**What I think about detail 1:**	**What I think about detail 2:**	**What I think about detail 3:**
	How I connect the details:		
MAKING A CLAIM I state a conclusion that I have come to and can support with <u>evidence</u> from the text after reading and thinking about it closely.	**My claim about the text:**		

FORMING EVIDENCE-BASED CLAIMS TOOL

Name -

Text -

A question I have about the text:

FINDING DETAILS	**Detail 1 (Ref.:**)	**Detail 2 (Ref.:**)	**Detail 3 (Ref.:**)
I find interesting details that are related and that stand out to me from reading the text closely.			

CONNECTING THE DETAILS	**What I think about detail 1:**	**What I think about detail 2:**	**What I think about detail 3:**
I reread and think about the details, and explain the connections I find among them.			

How I connect the details:

MAKING A CLAIM	**My claim about the text:**
I state a conclusion that I have come to and can support with evidence from the text after reading and thinking about it closely.	

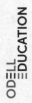

ODELL
EDUCATION

ORGANIZING EVIDENCE-BASED CLAIMS TOOL (2 POINTS)

Name _ _ _ _ _ _ _ _ _ _ _ _ Text _ _ _ _ _ _ _ _ _ _

CLAIM:

Point 1

A Supporting Evidence	B Supporting Evidence
(Reference:)	(Reference:)
C Supporting Evidence	D Supporting Evidence
(Reference:)	(Reference:)

Point 2

A Supporting Evidence	B Supporting Evidence
(Reference:)	(Reference:)
C Supporting Evidence	D Supporting Evidence
(Reference:)	(Reference:)

ODELL
EDUCATION

ORGANIZING EVIDENCE-BASED CLAIMS TOOL (3 POINTS)

Name _____   Text _____

CLAIM: _____

Point 1	Point 2	Point 3
A Supporting Evidence	**A** Supporting Evidence	**A** Supporting Evidence
(Reference:)	(Reference:)	(Reference:)
B Supporting Evidence	**B** Supporting Evidence	**B** Supporting Evidence
(Reference:)	(Reference:)	(Reference:)
C Supporting Evidence	**C** Supporting Evidence	**C** Supporting Evidence
(Reference:)	(Reference:)	(Reference:)

FORMING EVIDENCE-BASED CLAIMS TOOL

Name _ Text _ _ _ _ _ _ _ _

A question I have about the text:

FINDING DETAILS	Detail 1 (Ref.:)	Detail 2 (Ref.:)	Detail 3 (Ref.:)
I find interesting details that are _related_ and that stand out to me from reading the text closely.			

CONNECTING THE DETAILS	What I think about detail 1:	What I think about detail 2:	What I think about detail 3:
I reread and think about the details, and _explain_ the connections I find among them.			

How I connect the details:

MAKING A CLAIM	My claim about the text:
I state a conclusion that I have come to and can support with _evidence_ from the text after reading and thinking about it closely.	

ODELL EDUCATION

PART 4

WRITING EVIDENCE-BASED CLAIMS

Overview and tools

"The unexamined life is not worth living"

OBJECTIVE:	You will develop the ability to express text-based claims through writing.

MATERIALS:
- *Writing EBC Handout*
- *Questioning Path Tool*
- *Forming EBC Tool*
- *Organizing EBC Tool*

TEXT:
- *Apology, Plato, paragraphs 1–23*

ACTIVITIES

1. MODEL THE COMMUNICATION OF AN EBC THROUGH WRITING
Your teacher shows you how to write a paragraph that expresses an evidence-based claim.

2. MODEL AND PRACTICE THE USE OF QUESTIONS AND CRITERIA TO IMPROVE A WRITTEN EBC
Your teacher introduces a process for improving writing with your classmates.

3. WRITING EBCs IN PAIRS
You reread the section of the text and use a *Forming EBC Tool* to make a new claim and support it with evidence. In pairs, you develop a paragraph that expresses an evidence-based claim.

4. REVIEWING AND IMPROVING WRITTEN EBCs
You and your partner present your written evidence-based claims to your other classmates for feedback.

5. INDEPENDENT READING, DEVELOPING QUESTIONING PATHS, AND MAKING EBCs
You reread the text and develop your own *Questioning Path Tool*. You use the *Forming EBC Tool* to develop another evidence-based claim.

6. READ ALOUD AND CLASS DISCUSSION
You discuss your new evidence-based claim with the class.

7. INDEPENDENT WRITING OF EBCs

You organize your claim with an *Organizing EBC Tool* and draft a one- to two-paragraph evidence-based claim.

8. USING PEER FEEDBACK TO REVISE A WRITTEN EBC

You review and improve your claim with help from a partner.

QUESTIONING PATH TOOL

Name: _____   **Text:** _____

APPROACHING: *I determine my reading purposes and take note of key information about the text. I identify the LIPS domain(s) that will guide my initial reading.*

Purpose:

Key information:

LIPS domain(s):

QUESTIONING: *I use Guiding Questions to help me investigate the text (from the **Guiding Questions Handout**).*

1.

2.

ANALYZING: *I question further to connect and analyze the details I find (from the **Guiding Questions Handout**).*

1.

2.

DEEPENING: *I consider the questions of others.*

1.

2.

3.

EXTENDING: *I pose my own questions.*

1.

2.

ODELL EDUCATION

FORMING EVIDENCE-BASED CLAIMS TOOL

Name _ Text _ _ _ _ _ _ _ _ _ _ _ _ _ _ _ _ _

A question I have about the text:

FINDING DETAILS

I find interesting details that are related and that stand out to me from reading the text closely.

Detail 1 (Ref.:)	Detail 2 (Ref.:)	Detail 3 (Ref.:)

CONNECTING THE DETAILS

I reread and think about the details, and explain the connections I find among them.

What I think about detail 1:	What I think about detail 2:	What I think about detail 3:

How I connect the details:

MAKING A CLAIM

I state a conclusion that I have come to and can support with evidence from the text after reading and thinking about it closely.

My claim about the text:

ORGANIZING EVIDENCE-BASED CLAIMS TOOL (2 POINTS)

Name _____

Text _____

CLAIM:

Point 1

Point 2

A	Supporting Evidence	B	Supporting Evidence
(Reference:)		(Reference:)	
C	Supporting Evidence	D	Supporting Evidence
(Reference:)		(Reference:)	

A	Supporting Evidence	B	Supporting Evidence
(Reference:)		(Reference:)	
C	Supporting Evidence	D	Supporting Evidence
(Reference:)		(Reference:)	

ORGANIZING EVIDENCE-BASED CLAIMS TOOL (3 POINTS)

Name _____   Text _____

CLAIM:

Point 1	Point 2	Point 3
A Supporting Evidence	**A** Supporting Evidence	**A** Supporting Evidence
(Reference: _____)	(Reference: _____)	(Reference: _____)
B Supporting Evidence	**B** Supporting Evidence	**B** Supporting Evidence
(Reference: _____)	(Reference: _____)	(Reference: _____)
C Supporting Evidence	**C** Supporting Evidence	**C** Supporting Evidence
(Reference: _____)	(Reference: _____)	(Reference: _____)

PART 5

DEVELOPING EVIDENCE-BASED WRITING

Overview and Tools

"If you think that by killing people you can avoid being taken to task for not living as you should, then you're wrong."

OBJECTIVE: You will develop the ability to express global evidence-based claims in writing.

MATERIALS:
- *Forming EBC Tool*
- *Organizing EBC Tool*
- *Writing EBC Handout*
- *Student Making EBC Literacy Skills Checklist*
- *Student Making EBC Academic Habits Checklist*

TEXT:
- *Apology, Plato, paragraphs 1–23*

☰ ACTIVITIES

1. INDEPENDENT READING AND CLASS DISCUSSION OF GLOBAL EBCs
You review the text you have read in the unit, and the class discusses global evidence-based claims.

2. FORMING GLOBAL EBCs
You review previous claims and use a *Forming EBC Tool* to frame a new global evidence-based claim.

3. REVIEWING AND ORGANIZING EBCs
You discuss your new claim in pairs and then with the class, thinking about how you will organize it with an *Organizing EBC Tool*.

4. INDEPENDENT DRAFTING OF A FINAL WRITTEN EBC ESSAY
You draft a final evidence-based essay using your new claim.

5. USING THE COLLABORATIVE, CRITERIA-BASED PROCESS TO IMPROVE ESSAYS
You use a criteria-based checklist and feedback from peers to revise and improve your evidence-based claim essay.

6. CLASS DISCUSSION OF FINAL EBC ESSAYS
You discuss your final evidence-claims essays and reflect on the literacy skills and academic habits involved in making and communicating evidence.

ODELL
EDUCATION

FORMING EVIDENCE-BASED CLAIMS TOOL

Name _

Text _

A question I have about the text:

FINDING DETAILS I find interesting details that are related and that stand out to me from reading the text closely.	Detail 1 (Ref.:)	Detail 2 (Ref.:)	Detail 3 (Ref.:)

CONNECTING THE DETAILS I reread and think about the details, and <u>explain</u> the connections I find among them.	What I think about detail 1:	What I think about detail 2:	What I think about detail 3:
	How I connect the details:		

MAKING A CLAIM I state a conclusion that I have come to and can support with <u>evidence</u> from the text after reading and thinking about it closely.	My claim about the text:

SUPPORTING EVIDENCE-BASED CLAIMS TOOL

Name _ Text _

CLAIM:

Supporting Evidence	Supporting Evidence	Supporting Evidence

(Reference:)   (Reference:)   (Reference:)

CLAIM:

Supporting Evidence	Supporting Evidence	Supporting Evidence

(Reference:)   (Reference:)   (Reference:)

ORGANIZING EVIDENCE-BASED CLAIMS TOOL (2 POINTS)

Name _ _ _ _ _ _ _ _ _ _ _ _ _ _ _ _ Text _

CLAIM:

Point 1

A Supporting Evidence	B Supporting Evidence
(Reference:)	(Reference:)

C Supporting Evidence	D Supporting Evidence
(Reference:)	(Reference:)

Point 2

A Supporting Evidence	B Supporting Evidence
(Reference:)	(Reference:)

C Supporting Evidence	D Supporting Evidence
(Reference:)	(Reference:)

ODELL EDUCATION

ORGANIZING EVIDENCE-BASED CLAIMS TOOL (3 POINTS)

Name _____   Text _____

CLAIM:

Point 1	Point 2	Point 3
A Supporting Evidence	**A** Supporting Evidence	**A** Supporting Evidence
(Reference: _____)	(Reference: _____)	(Reference: _____)
B Supporting Evidence	**B** Supporting Evidence	**B** Supporting Evidence
(Reference: _____)	(Reference: _____)	(Reference: _____)
C Supporting Evidence	**C** Supporting Evidence	**C** Supporting Evidence
(Reference: _____)	(Reference: _____)	(Reference: _____)

ODELL EDUCATION

STUDENT MAKING EVIDENCE-BASED CLAIMS LITERACY SKILLS CHECKLIST

	LITERACY SKILLS USED IN THIS UNIT	✓	EVIDENCE Demonstrating the SKILLS
READING	1. **Attending to Details:** Identifies words, details, or quotations that are important to understanding the text		
	2. **Interpreting Language:** Understands how words are used to express ideas and perspectives		
	3. **Identifying Relationships:** Notices important connections among details, ideas, or texts		
	4. **Recognizing Perspective:** Identifies and explains the author's view of the text's topic		
THINKING	5. **Making Inferences:** Draws sound conclusions from reading and examining the text closely		
	6. **Forming Claims:** States a meaningful conclusion that is well-supported by evidence from the text		
	7. **Using Evidence:** Uses well-chosen details from the text to explain and support claims; accurately paraphrases or quotes		
WRITING	8. **Presenting Details:** Inserts details and quotations effectively into written or spoken explanations		
	9. **Organizing Ideas:** Organizes claims, supporting ideas, and evidence in a logical order		
	10. **Using Language:** Writes and speaks clearly so others can understand claims and ideas		
	11. **Using Conventions:** Correctly uses sentence elements, punctuation, and spelling to produce clear writing		
	12. **Publishing:** Correctly uses, formats, and cites textual evidence to support claims		
	General comments:		

STUDENT MAKING EVIDENCE-BASED CLAIMS ACADEMIC HABITS CHECKLIST

ACADEMIC HABITS USED IN THIS UNIT	✓	EVIDENCE demonstrating the HABITS
1. **Engaging Actively:** Focuses attention on the task when working individually and with others		
2. **Collaborating:** Works respectfully and productively to help a group be successful		
3. **Communicating Clearly:** Presents ideas and supporting evidence so others can understand them		
4. **Listening:** Pays attention to ideas from others and takes time to think about them		
5. **Understanding Purpose and Process:** Understands why and how a task should be accomplished		
6. **Revising:** Rethinks ideas and refines work based on feedback from others		
7. **Remaining Open:** Modifies and further justifies ideas in response to thinking from others		
General comments:		

UNIT 3

MAKING EVIDENCE-BASED CLAIMS ABOUT LITERARY TECHNIQUE

DEVELOPING CORE LITERACY PROFICIENCIES

GRADE 9

"Macomber laughed, a very natural hearty laugh."

GOAL

In this unit you will develop your proficiency as a maker and defender of claims. You will learn how to do the following:

1. Use the details, connections, and evidence you find in a text to form a claim—a stated conclusion—about something you have discovered.
2. Organize evidence from the text to support your claim and make your case.
3. Express and explain your claim in writing.
4. Improve your writing so that others will clearly understand and appreciate your evidence-based claim—and think about the case you have made for it.

You will also learn and make claims about these literary techniques:

- Character development
- Focus of narrative point of view
- Narrative structure

TOPIC

In this unit you will develop your abilities to make evidence-based claims about literary technique through activities based on a close reading of Ernest Hemingway's short story, "The Short Happy Life of Francis Macomber."

ACTIVITIES

As you move through this unit from initial reading, to thinking, and to writing, the activities will help you do a close reading of the text and to move from what Hemingway tells his audience to the various techniques he uses in creating his short story. As you learn about forming claims you will practice finding evidence from the text to support a claim, then move on to forming your own claims from details you notice in the text. You will continue to search for evidence that leads to and supports new claims. You will then learn how to organize that evidence. From this base, you will write and revise several claims, the final one a global claim about the effects of one of Hemingway's literary techniques. You will learn to work with other students in the class to review and improve your writing so that your final claim can be as clear, strong, and evidence-based as possible.

MAKING EVIDENCE-BASED CLAIMS LITERACY TOOLBOX

In *Making Evidence-Based Claims*, you will continue to build your "literacy toolbox" by learning how to use the following handouts, tools and checklists organized in your Student Edition.

HANDOUTS

To support your work with the texts and the tools, you will be able to use the following informational handouts. You will also use handouts from *Reading Closely*:

Attending to Details Handout

from the *Reading Closely* unit

Guiding Questions Handout

from the *Reading Closely* unit

Writing Evidence-Based Claims Handout

This handout explains five key things you will need to think about as you write an evidence-based claim. These characteristics are also things your teacher will be looking for in the final claim you write and turn in. The handout includes examples related to the text in the unit so you can see what each of the key characteristics might look like.

Making Evidence-Based Claims about Literary Technique—Final Writing Tasks

This handout will explain to you what you will be doing in the final assignments for this unit: writing an evidence-based claims paragraph and a multiparagraph essay that presents, explains, and uses evidence to support a claim you have formed about the meaning of the text you have read. The handout will also help you know what your teacher will be looking for so you can be successful on the essay assignment.

TOOLS

In *Making Evidence-Based Claims about Literary Technique*, you will continue to use your **Literacy Toolbox** and apply tools from *Reading Closely* and *Making Evidence-Based Claims*:

Approaching the Text Tool

from the *Reading Closely* unit

Analyzing Details Tool

from the *Reading Closely* unit

Questioning Path Tool

from the *Reading Closely* unit

Model Questioning Path Tools

For each section of the text you will read, there is a ***Questioning Path Tool*** that has been filled out for you to frame and guide your reading. These model Questioning Paths are just starting points, and your teacher or you may prefer to develop your own paths. The model paths are organized by the steps from the ***Reading Closely Graphic*** (approaching, questioning, analyzing, deepening, and extending). They include general Guiding Questions from the ***Guiding Questions Handout*** and some questions that are specific to each text and its content. You will use these model paths to guide your reading, frame your discussions with your teacher and other students, and help you when you are doing the final activities in the unit.

Forming Evidence-Based Claims Tool

This three-part tool will help you move in your thinking from *finding* important details, to *connecting* those details and explaining your connections, to *making a claim* based on the details and connections you have found. You can also use the tool to record evidence to support your claim and indicate where in the text you found the evidence.

Supporting Evidence-Based Claims Tool

This tool provides spaces in which you can record one or more claims about the text (either your teacher's or your own) and then quote or paraphrase supporting evidence for the claim(s)—which you will later use in organizing and writing your claim.

Organizing Evidence-Based Claims Tool

This tool provides support as you move from forming a claim and finding supporting evidence to writing the claim. The tool provides space for writing down two or three supporting points you will want to make to explain and prove your claim. Under each of these points, you can then organize the evidence you have found that relates to the point and supports your overall claim.

CHECKLISTS

You will also use these checklists throughout the unit to support peer- and self-review:

Making Evidence-Based Claims Skills and Habits Checklists

These two checklists present and briefly describe the Literacy Skills and Habits you will be working on during the unit. You can use the checklist to remind you of what you are trying to learn; to reflect on what you have done when reading, discussing, or writing; or to give feedback to other students. Your teacher may use them to let you know about your areas of strength and areas in which you can improve.

MAKING EVIDENCE-BASED CLAIMS ABOUT LITERARY TECHNIQUE

DEVELOPING CORE LITERACY PROFICIENCIES

GRADE 9

Literacy Toolbox

ODELL
EDUCATION

WRITING EVIDENCE-BASED CLAIMS

Writing evidence-based claims is a little different from writing stories or just writing about something. You need to **follow a few steps** as you write.

1. ESTABLISH THE CONTEXT

Your readers must know **where your claim is coming from** and why it's relevant.

Depending on the scope of your piece and claim, the context differs.

If your whole piece is one claim or if you're introducing the first major claim of your piece, the entire context must be established:

> In "The Short Happy Life of Francis Macomber," Ernest Hemingway develops…

Purposes of evidence-based writing vary. In some cases, naming the book and author might be enough to establish the relevance of your claim. In other cases, you might want to supply additional information:

> In literature, authors often use the technique *in media res* where they begin a story in the middle of the action rather than at the beginning. In his short story "The Short Happy Life of Francis Macomber," Ernest Hemingway develops…

If your claim is part of a larger piece with multiple claims, then the context might be simpler:

> To create this effect, Hemingway…   *or*   In paragraph 5, Hemingway…

2. STATE YOUR CLAIM CLEARLY

How you state your claim is important; it must **precisely and comprehensively express your analysis.** Figuring out how to state claims is a **process**; writers revise them continually as they write their supporting evidence. Here's a claim about how Hemingway uses various points of view to characterize the character of Francis Macomber:

> In "The Short Happy Life of Francis Macomber," Ernest Hemingway develops the characters of the short story by jumping from one character's point of view to another.

When writing claims, it is often useful to describe parts of the claim before providing the supporting evidence. In this case, the writer might want to briefly identify and describe the encounter between Macomber and the lion:

> In "The Short Happy Life of Francis Macomber," Ernest Hemingway develops the characters of the short story by jumping from one character's point of view to another. Although the hunting scene is largely told from Macomber's perspective, Hemingway alternates the perspective of both the lion and Macomber to highlight his fear and cowardice character.

The explanation in the second sentence about how Hemingway uses a shifting point of view is relevant to the claim. It also begins connecting the claim to ideas that will be used as evidence.

Remember, you should continually return to and re-phrase your claim as you write the supporting evidence to make sure you are capturing exactly what you want to say. Writing out the evidence always helps you figure out what you really think.

ODELL
EDUCATION

WRITING EVIDENCE-BASED CLAIMS (Continued)

3. ORGANIZE YOUR SUPPORTING EVIDENCE

Many claims contain multiple aspects that require different evidence that can be expressed in separate paragraphs. This claim can be organized sequentially, contrasting each perspective throughout the stages of the hunt: An account of **THE START OF THE ENOUNTER**, an account of **AFTER THE INITAL SHOTS**, and an account of **THE FINAL ENCOUNTER**.

Here are two paragraphs that support the claim with evidence for the first two stages.

An account of **THE START OF THE ENCOUNTER**:

> The comparison starts with the different ways the lion and Macomber begin their encounter. As Macomber got out of the car "the lion still stood looking majestically and coolly toward this object that his eyes only showed in silhouette, bulking like some super-rhino" (p168). This majestic coolness is contrasted with what the heavily armed Macomber was feeling at the time: "He only knew his hands were shaking and as he walked away from the car it was almost impossible for him to make his legs move. They were stiff in the thighs, but he could feel the muscles fluttering" (p169). Standing fearfully atop his "fluttering" thighs, Macomber manages to wound the lion with a few "gut-shot(s)" (p172).

An account of **AFTER THE INITAL SHOTS**:

> The next sequence of shifting perspective sets up another contrast of character. The lion, now facing an enemy who has just shot and wounded him unprovoked, prepares bravely and calmly for their next encounter: "He galloped toward the high grass where he could crouch and not be seen and make them bring the crashing thing close enough so he could make a rush and get the man that held it" (p168). In contrast, Macomber does everything he can to avoid going into the grass after the lion. "Can't we set the grass on fire?...Can't we send beaters?...What about the gun-bearers?...Why not just leave him?" (p195). He will put other men's lives in danger to avoid confronting the lion. At one point, he even blurts out uncontrollably, "I don't want to go in there" (p 197).

Notice the phrase, "The next sequence," starting the second paragraph. **Transitional phrases** like this one aid the organization by showing how the ideas relate to each other or are further developed.

4. PARAPHRASE AND QUOTE

Written evidence from texts can be paraphrased or quoted. It's up to the writer to decide which works better for each piece of evidence. **Paraphrasing is putting the author's words into your own**. This works well when the author originally expresses the idea you want to include across many sentences. You might write it more briefly.

The second sentence from paragraph 2 begins by paraphrasing Hemingway's description of the lion. The ideas are his, but the exact way of writing is not.

> The lion, now facing an enemy who has just shot and wounded him unprovoked, prepares bravely and calmly for their next encounter.

Some evidence is better quoted than paraphrased. If an author has found the quickest way to phrase the idea or the words are especially strong, you might want to **use the author's words**.

The second sentence in paragraph 1 quotes Hemingway exactly:

> As Macomber got out of the car "the lion still stood looking majestically and coolly toward this object that his eyes only showed in silhouette, bulking like some super-rhino" (p168).

WRITING EVIDENCE-BASED CLAIMS (Continued)

MAKING EVIDENCE-BASED CLAIMS ABOUT LITERARY TECHNIQUE FINAL WRITING TASKS

In this unit, you have been developing your skills as a reader who can make text-based claims about literary techniques and prove them with evidence from the text.

- Attending to various techniques authors use, such as characterization, narration, and chronology
- Uncovering key clues in the details, words, and central ideas found in the texts
- Making connections among details, central ideas, and texts
- Using the details, connections, and evidence you find in texts to form a claim—a stated conclusion—about something you have discovered
- Organizing evidence from the text to support your claim and make your case
- Expressing and explaining your claim in writing
- Improving your writing so that others will clearly understand and appreciate your evidence-based claim—and think about the case you have made for it

Your final two writing assignments will provide you with opportunities to use all of these related skills and to demonstrate your proficiency and growth in making evidence-based claims about literary technique.

FINAL ASSIGNMENTS

1. **Developing and Writing an Evidence-Based Claim:** On your own, you will read the final text in the unit closely and develop an evidence-based claim. To do this, you will do the following:

   a. Read and annotate the text (or section of text) on your own and use Guiding Questions and a **Forming EBC Tool** to develop an initial claim about the effects of a technique Hemingway uses.

   b. Compare the notes and initial claim you make with those made by other students—reframe or revise your claim.

   c. Complete an **Organizing EBC Tool** to plan subpoints and evidence you will use to explain and support your claim.

   d. Study the **Writing EBC Handout** to know what a written EBC needs to do and what examples might look like.

   e. Draft a one- to two-paragraph written presentation and explanation of your claim, making sure that you do the things listed on the **Writing EBC Handout**:

      ⇒ Establish the context by connecting the claim to the text.

      ⇒ State the claim clearly to fully communicate your ideas about the text.

      ⇒ Organize supporting evidence found in the text.

      ⇒ Paraphrase and quote from the text.

      ⇒ Reference the evidence drawn from the text.

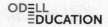

FINAL WRITING TASKS (Continued)

   f. Work with other students to review and improve your draft—and to be sure it is the best possible representation of your claim and your skills as a reader and writer. Work on improving at least one of these aspects of your claim:

      ⇒ How <u>clear</u> your presentation and explanation of your claim is

      ⇒ How <u>defensible</u> (based on the evidence you present) your claim is

      ⇒ How well you have <u>presented and referenced evidence</u> to support your claim

      ⇒ How well you have <u>organized</u> your subpoints and evidence into a unified claim

   g. Reflect on how well you have used Literacy Skills in developing this written claim.

2. **Writing and Revising a Global Evidence-Based Claim Essay:** On your own, you will plan and draft a multiparagraph essay that presents a global claim about the cumulative effects of a technique Hemingway uses. To accomplish this, you will do the following:

   a. Review the short story, the tools you have completed, and the claims you have formed throughout the unit, looking for connections or comparisons.

   b. Use a ***Forming EBC Tool*** to make a new claim that develops a global conclusion about the meaning of the text and Hemingway's use of a literary technique.

   c. Use an ***Organizing EBC Tool*** to plan the subpoints and evidence you will use to explain and support your claim.

   d. Draft a multiparagraph essay that explains, develops, and supports your global claim—keeping in mind these three criteria for this final writing assignment. Your essay should do the following:

      ⇒ Demonstrate an accurate reading and insightful analysis of the text.

      ⇒ Develop a supported claim that is clearly connected to the text.

      ⇒ Successfully accomplish the five key elements of a written EBC (***Writing EBC Handout***).

   e. Use a collaborative process with other students to review and improve your draft in two key areas: (1) its content (quality of the claim and its evidence) and (2) its organization and expression (unity of the discussion and clarity of the writing).

   f. Reflect on how well you have used Literacy Skills in developing this final explanation.

As you become a text expert and write your evidence-based claims, think about demonstrating the Literacy Skills listed in the following to the best of your ability. Your teacher will evaluate your work and determine your grade based on how well you do.

Read

- **Attend to Details:** Identify words, details, or quotations that you think are important to understanding the text

- **Interpret Language:** Understand how words are used to express ideas and perspectives

- **Identify Relationships:** Notice important connections among details, themes, or sections of the text

- **Recognize Perspective:** Identify and explain the author's or narrator's perspective and how it affects the story

ODELL
EDUCATION

FINAL WRITING TASKS (Continued)

SKILLS TO BE DEMONSTRATED (Continued)

Think

- **Make Inferences:** Draw sound conclusions from reading and examining the text closely
- **Form a Claim:** State a meaningful conclusion that is well supported by evidence from the texts
- **Use Evidence:** Use well-chosen details from the text to support your explanation; accurately paraphrase or quote the text

Write

- **Present Details:** Insert details and quotations effectively into your essay
- **Organize Ideas:** Organize your claim, supporting ideas, and evidence in a logical order
- **Use Language:** Write clearly so others can understand your claim and supporting ideas
- **Use Conventions:** Correctly use sentence elements, punctuation, and spelling to produce clear writing
- **Publish:** Correctly use, format, and cite textual evidence to support your claim

HABITS TO BE DEVELOPED

Your teacher may also want you to reflect on how well you have used and developed the following habits of text-centered discussion when you worked with others to understand the text and improve your writing:

- **Engage Actively:** Focus your attention on the assigned tasks when working individually and with others
- **Collaborate:** Work respectfully and productively to help your discussion or review group be successful
- **Communicate Clearly:** Present your ideas and supporting evidence so others can understand them
- **Listen:** Pay attention to ideas from others and take time to think about them
- **Understand Purpose and Process:** Understand why and how a text-centered discussion or peer writing review should be accomplished
- **Revise:** Rethink your ideas and refine your writing based on feedback from others
- **Remain Open:** Modify and further justify ideas in response to thinking from others.

NOTE

These skills and habits are also listed on the **Student Making EBC Literacy Skills** and **Academic Habits Checklists**, which you can use to assess your work and the work of other students.

PART 1

UNDERSTANDING EVIDENCE-BASED CLAIMS

Overview and Tools

"I'll have a gimlet too. I need something."

OBJECTIVE: You will learn about making evidence-based claims through reading a text.

MATERIALS:
- *Guiding Questions Handout*
- *Reading Closely Graphic*
- *Questioning Path Tool*

- *Attending to Details Handout*
- *Forming EBC Tool*
- *Supporting EBC Tool*

OPTIONAL:
- *Approaching Texts Tool*

- *Analyzing Details Tool*

TEXT:
- *"The Short Happy Life of Francis Macomber,"*
  Ernest Hemingway

☰ ACTIVITIES

1. INTRODUCTION TO UNIT
Your teacher presents the purpose of the unit and explains the idea of making evidence-based claims.

2. INDEPENDENT READING
You independently read the first sentence of the text with a Guiding Question to help focus your reading.

3. READ ALOUD AND CLASS DISCUSSION
You follow along as you listen to a section of the text being read aloud, and your teacher leads a discussion about it.

4. MODEL THE FORMING OF EBCs
Your teacher shows you how to form evidence-based claims about texts.

QUESTIONING PATH TOOL

Name: _____ **Text:** _____

APPROACHING: *I determine my reading purposes and take note of key information about the text. I identify the LIPS domain(s) that will guide my initial reading.*	Purpose: Key information: LIPS domain(s):
QUESTIONING: *I use Guiding Questions to help me investigate the text (from the **Guiding Questions Handout**).*	1. 2.
ANALYZING: *I question further to connect and analyze the details I find (from the **Guiding Questions Handout**).*	1. 2.
DEEPENING: *I consider the questions of others.*	1. 2. 3.
EXTENDING: *I pose my own questions.*	1. 2.

APPROACHING TEXTS TOOL

Name _____ Text _____

APPROACHING THE TEXT	
Before reading, I consider what my specific purposes for reading are.	**What are my reading purposes?**
I also take note of key information about the text.	**Title:**
	Author: **Source/Publisher:**
	Text type: **Publication date:**
	What do I already think or understand about the text based on this information?

QUESTIONING THE TEXT	
As I read the text for the first time, I use Guiding Questions that relate to my reading purpose and focus. (*Can be taken from the Guiding Questions Handout.*)	**Guiding Questions for *my first reading* of the text:**
	As I read I mark details on the text that relate to my Guiding Questions.
As I reread, I use questions I have about specific details that have emerged in my reading to focus my analysis and deepen my understanding.	**Text-specific questions to help focus *my rereading* of the text:**

ANALYZING DETAILS TOOL

Name _ _ _ _ _ _ _ _ _ _ _ _ _ _ _ _ _ _ _ Text _ _ _ _ _ _ _ _ _ _ _ _ _

Reading purpose:

A question I have about the text:

SEARCHING FOR DETAILS

I read the text closely and mark words and phrases that help me think about my question.

SELECTING DETAILS

I select words or phrases from my search that I think are the most important in thinking about my question.

Detail 1 (Ref.:)	Detail 2 (Ref.:)	Detail 3 (Ref.:)

ANALYZING DETAILS

I reread parts of the text and think about the meaning of the details and what they tell me about my question.

What I think about detail 1:	What I think about detail 2:	What I think about detail 3:

CONNECTING DETAILS

I compare the details and explain the connections I see among them.

How I connect the details:

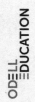

FORMING EVIDENCE-BASED CLAIMS TOOL

Name _ _ _ _ _ _ _ _ _ _ _ _ _ _ _ _ _ Text _

A question I have about the text:

	Detail 1 (Ref.:)	Detail 2 (Ref.:)	Detail 3 (Ref.:)
FINDING DETAILS I find interesting details that are related and that stand out to me from reading the text closely.			

	What I think about detail 1:	What I think about detail 2:	What I think about detail 3:
CONNECTING THE DETAILS I reread and think about the details, and explain the connections I find among them.			

How I connect the details:

	My claim about the text:
MAKING A CLAIM I state a conclusion that I have come to and can support with evidence from the text after reading and thinking about it closely.	

ODELL EDUCATION

SUPPORTING EVIDENCE-BASED CLAIMS TOOL

Name _ _ _ _ _ _ _ _ _ _ _ _ _ _ _

Text _ _ _ _ _ _ _ _ _ _ _ _ _ _ _

CLAIM:

Supporting Evidence	Supporting Evidence	Supporting Evidence
(Reference:)	(Reference:)	(Reference:)

CLAIM:

Supporting Evidence	Supporting Evidence	Supporting Evidence
(Reference:)	(Reference:)	(Reference:)

ODELL
EDUCATION

MAKING EVIDENCE-BASED CLAIMS ABOUT LITERARY TECHNIQUE

Overview and Tools

"Still drinking their whisky"

OBJECTIVE:	You will learn about making evidence-based claims through reading a text.

MATERIALS:
- *Supporting EBC Tool*
- *Attending to Details Handout*
- *Forming EBC Tool*
- *Questioning Path Tool*

TEXT:
- *"The Short Happy Life of Francis Macomber,"*
  Ernest Hemingway

ACTIVITIES

1. INDEPENDENT READING TO FIND SUPPORTING EVIDENCE
You independently read a section of the text and use the *Supporting EBC Tool* to look for evidence to support a claim made by your teacher.

2. READ ALOUD AND CLASS DISCUSSION
You follow along as you listen to the same part of the text being read aloud and then discuss it.

3. FINDING SUPPORTING EVIDENCE IN PAIRS
In pairs, you use the *Supporting EBC Tool* to look for evidence to support additional claims about the text made by your teacher.

4. CLASS DISCUSSION OF EBCs
The class discusses the evidence you have found to support the claims.

5. FORMING EBCs IN PAIRS
In pairs, you use the *Forming EBC Tool* to make an evidence-based claim of your own and present it to the class.

SUPPORTING EVIDENCE-BASED CLAIMS TOOL

Name _____

Text _____

CLAIM:

Supporting Evidence	Supporting Evidence	Supporting Evidence
(Reference:)	(Reference:)	(Reference:)

(Reference:)

CLAIM:

Supporting Evidence	Supporting Evidence	Supporting Evidence
(Reference:)	(Reference:)	(Reference:)

(Reference:)

QUESTIONING PATH TOOL

Ernest Hemingway's "The Short Happy Life of Francis Macomber" (P18–P106)

APPROACHING: *I determine my reading purposes and take note of key information about the text. I identify the LIPS domain(s) that will guide my initial reading.*

I will initially focus on the author's *language, ideas,* and *supporting details.*

QUESTIONING: *I use Guiding Questions to help me investigate the text (from the **Guiding Questions Handout**).*

1. How are key characters described? [L]

2. What seems to be the narrator's attitude or point of view?

ANALYZING: *I question further to connect and analyze the details I find (from the **Guiding Questions Handout**).*

3. How does the text's language influence my understanding of important characters or themes?

4. How does the narrator's perspective influence the presentation of themes or characterizations?

DEEPENING: *I consider the questions of others.*

5. Why does Margaret begin to cry in paragraph 36? What specific details provide clues? How do these details develop the characterization of Francis and Margaret Macomber?

6. In paragraph 55, why does Wilson think it is "bad form" for Macomber to ask if anyone will hear about "the lion business"? What specific details provide clues? How do these details develop the characterization of Macomber and Wilson? How does the use of point of view in this section affect the characterization of Wilson and Macomber?

7. Who does Wilson like more, Francis or Margaret? What details provide clues? How do these details develop the characterization of Wilson, Francis, and Margaret?

EXTENDING: *I pose my own questions.*

ODELL
EDUCATION

SUPPORTING EVIDENCE-BASED CLAIMS TOOL

Name _ _ _ _ _ _ _ _ _ _ _ _ _ _ _ Text _ _ _ _ _ _ _ _ _ _ _ _ _ _ _

CLAIM:

Supporting Evidence

Supporting Evidence

Supporting Evidence

(Reference:)   (Reference:)   (Reference:)

CLAIM:

Supporting Evidence

Supporting Evidence

Supporting Evidence

(Reference:)   (Reference:)   (Reference:)

ODELL EDUCATION

SUPPORTING EVIDENCE-BASED CLAIMS TOOL

Name _ _ _ _ _ _ _ _ _ _ _ _ _ _ _ Text _ _ _ _ _ _ _ _ _ _ _ _ _ _ _

CLAIM:

Supporting Evidence	Supporting Evidence	Supporting Evidence

(Reference:) | (Reference:) | (Reference:)

CLAIM:

Supporting Evidence	Supporting Evidence	Supporting Evidence

(Reference:) | (Reference:) | (Reference:)

FORMING EVIDENCE-BASED CLAIMS TOOL

Name _ **Text** _

A question I have about the text:

FINDING DETAILS	**Detail 1 (Ref.:)**	**Detail 2 (Ref.:)**	**Detail 3 (Ref.:)**
I find interesting details that are related and that stand out to me from reading the text closely.			

CONNECTING THE DETAILS	**What I think about detail 1:**	**What I think about detail 2:**	**What I think about detail 3:**
I reread and think about the details, and explain the connections I find among them.			

How I connect the details:

MAKING A CLAIM	**My claim about the text:**
I state a conclusion that I have come to and can support with evidence from the text after reading and thinking about it closely.	

ODELL EDUCATION

PART 3

ORGANIZING EVIDENCE-BASED CLAIMS ABOUT LITERARY TECHNIQUE

Overview and Tools

"Hell of a fine lion"

OBJECTIVE:	You will learn to develop and explain evidence-based claims through the selection and organization of supporting evidence.

MATERIALS:
- *Organizing EBC Tool*
- *Forming EBC Tool*

- *Questioning Path Tool*

TEXT:
- *"The Short Happy Life of Francis Macomber,"*
  Ernest Hemingway

ACTIVITIES

1. INDEPENDENT READING AND FINDING EBCs
You independently read a section of the text and use the *Forming EBC Tool* to make an evidence-based claim.

2. COMPARING EBCs
You compare claims with your peers. Then you read the text to look for more evidence to support your claim.

3. MODEL THE ORGANIZING OF EBCs
Your teacher shows you how to organize evidence to develop and explain claims.

4. DEEPENING UNDERSTANDING
As a class, you listen to the text being read aloud, use questions to deepen your understanding of the text, and develop another claim.

5. ORGANIZING EBCs IN PAIRS
In pairs, you develop and organize a new claim using the *Organizing EBC Tool*.

6. CLASS DISCUSSION OF STUDENT EBCs
You discuss the evidence-based claims you have developed with the class.

ODELL
EDUCATION

QUESTIONING PATH TOOL

Ernest Hemingway's "The Short Happy Life of Francis Macomber" (paragraphs 107–237)

APPROACHING:
I determine my reading purposes and take note of key information about the text. I identify the LIPS domain(s) that will guide my initial reading.

I will initially focus on how the author uses narrative *perspective* and *structure* to convey *ideas*.

QUESTIONING: *I use Guiding Questions to help me investigate the text (from the **Guiding Questions Handout**).*

1. What do I notice about how the text is organized or sequenced? [S]

2. What are the narrators' points of view? [P]

ANALYZING: *I question further to connect and analyze the details I find (from the **Guiding Questions Handout**).*

3. What details or words suggest the narrators' perspectives? [P, L]

4. How do the narrators' perspectives influence their presentation of ideas and themes? [P]

5. How does the organization of the text influence my understanding of its information and themes? [S]

DEEPENING: *I consider the questions of others.*

6. How does the shift in perspective of narration in this section relate to the sequence of action?

7. How does the shift to the lion's perspective during points in the hunt affect the characterization of Macomber?

8. How does Hemingway show Wilson's perspective in this section? Are there any moments when his thoughts are reported? How does Hemingway develop Wilson's character in this section?

EXTENDING: *I pose my own questions.*

FORMING EVIDENCE-BASED CLAIMS TOOL

Name _____

Text _____

A question I have about the text:

FINDING DETAILS

I find interesting details that are related and that stand out to me from reading the text closely.

Detail 1 (Ref.:)	Detail 2 (Ref.:)	Detail 3 (Ref.:)

CONNECTING THE DETAILS

I reread and think about the details, and explain the connections I find among them.

What I think about detail 1:	What I think about detail 2:	What I think about detail 3:

How I connect the details:

MAKING A CLAIM

I state a conclusion that I have come to and can support with evidence from the text after reading and thinking about it closely.

My claim about the text:

ODELL
EDUCATION

ORGANIZING EVIDENCE-BASED CLAIMS TOOL (2PT)

Name _ _ _ _ _ _ _ _ _ _ _ _ _ _ _   Text _ _ _ _ _ _ _ _ _ _ _ _ _ _ _

CLAIM:

Point 1

A Supporting Evidence	B Supporting Evidence
(Reference:)	(Reference:)
C Supporting Evidence	D Supporting Evidence
(Reference:)	(Reference:)

Point 2

A Supporting Evidence	B Supporting Evidence
(Reference:)	(Reference:)
C Supporting Evidence	D Supporting Evidence
(Reference:)	(Reference:)

ORGANIZING EVIDENCE-BASED CLAIMS TOOL (3PT)

Name _ _ _ _ _ _ _ _ _ _ _ _ _ _ _ Text _ _ _ _ _ _ _ _ _ _ _ _ _ _ _

CLAIM:

Point 1	Point 2	Point 3
A Supporting Evidence	**A** Supporting Evidence	**A** Supporting Evidence
(Reference:)	(Reference:)	(Reference:)
B Supporting Evidence	**B** Supporting Evidence	**B** Supporting Evidence
(Reference:)	(Reference:)	(Reference:)
C Supporting Evidence	**C** Supporting Evidence	**C** Supporting Evidence
(Reference:)	(Reference:)	(Reference:)

ODELL EDUCATION

FORMING EVIDENCE-BASED CLAIMS TOOL

Name

Text

A question I have about the text:

FINDING DETAILS

I find interesting details that are <u>related</u> and that stand out to me from reading the text closely.

Detail 1 (Ref.:)	Detail 2 (Ref.:)	Detail 3 (Ref.:)

CONNECTING THE DETAILS

I reread and think about the details, and <u>explain</u> the connections I find among them.

What I think about detail 1:	What I think about detail 2:	What I think about detail 3:

How I connect the details:

MAKING A CLAIM

I state a conclusion that I have come to and can support with <u>evidence</u> from the text after reading and thinking about it closely.

My claim about the text:

ODELL
EDUCATION

FORMING EVIDENCE-BASED CLAIMS TOOL

Name _____

Text _____

A question I have about the text:

	Detail 1 (Ref.:)	Detail 2 (Ref.:)	Detail 3 (Ref.:)
FINDING DETAILS I find interesting details that are <u>related</u> and that stand out to me from reading the text closely.			

	What I think about detail 1:	What I think about detail 2:	What I think about detail 3:
CONNECTING THE DETAILS I reread and think about the details, and <u>explain</u> the connections I find among them.			

How I connect the details:

	My claim about the text:
MAKING A CLAIM I state a conclusion that I have come to and can support with <u>evidence</u> from the text after reading and thinking about it closely.	

ODELL EDUCATION

ORGANIZING EVIDENCE-BASED CLAIMS TOOL (2PT)

Name _____   Text _____

CLAIM:

Point 1

A	Supporting Evidence	B	Supporting Evidence

(Reference:)   (Reference:)

C	Supporting Evidence	D	Supporting Evidence

(Reference:)   (Reference:)

Point 2

A	Supporting Evidence	B	Supporting Evidence

(Reference:)   (Reference:)

C	Supporting Evidence	D	Supporting Evidence

(Reference:)   (Reference:)

ORGANIZING EVIDENCE-BASED CLAIMS TOOL (3PT)

Name _ _ _ _ _ _ _ _ _ _ _ _ _ _   Text _

CLAIM:

Point 1	**Point 2**	**Point 3**
A Supporting Evidence	**A** Supporting Evidence	**A** Supporting Evidence
(Reference:)	(Reference:)	(Reference:)
B Supporting Evidence	**B** Supporting Evidence	**B** Supporting Evidence
(Reference:)	(Reference:)	(Reference:)
C Supporting Evidence	**C** Supporting Evidence	**C** Supporting Evidence
(Reference:)	(Reference:)	(Reference:)

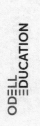
ODELL EDUCATION

FORMING EVIDENCE-BASED CLAIMS TOOL

Name _____

Text _____

A question I have about the text:

FINDING DETAILS

I find interesting details that are related and that stand out to me from reading the text closely.

Detail 1 (Ref.:)	Detail 2 (Ref.:)	Detail 3 (Ref.:)

CONNECTING THE DETAILS

I reread and think about the details, and explain the connections I find among them.

What I think about detail 1:	What I think about detail 2:	What I think about detail 3:

How I connect the details:

MAKING A CLAIM

I state a conclusion that I have come to and can support with evidence from the text after reading and thinking about it closely.

My claim about the text:

ODELL EDUCATION

PART 4

WRITING EVIDENCE-BASED CLAIMS ABOUT LITERARY TECHNIQUE

Overview and Tools

"Like a dam bursting"

OBJECTIVE:	You will develop the ability to express text-based claims through writing.

MATERIALS:
- *Writing EBC Handout*
- *Questioning Path Tool*
- *Forming EBC Tool*
- *Organizing EBC Tool*

TEXT:
- *"The Short Happy Life of Francis Macomber,"*
  Ernest Hemingway

 ACTIVITIES

1. **MODEL THE COMMUNICATION OF AN EBC THROUGH WRITING**
   Your teacher shows you how to write a paragraph that expresses an evidence-based claim.

2. **MODEL AND PRACTICE THE USE OF QUESTIONS AND CRITERIA TO IMPROVE A WRITTEN EBC**
   Your teacher introduces a process for improving writing with your classmates.

3. **WRITING EBCs IN PAIRS**
   In pairs, you develop a paragraph that expresses an evidence-based claim.

4. **REVIEWING AND IMPROVING WRITTEN EBCs**
   You and your partner present your written evidence-based claims to your other classmates for feedback.

5. **INDEPENDENT READING, DEVELOPING QUESTIONING PATHS, AND MAKING EBCs**
   You read the rest of the text and develop your own *Questioning Path Tool*. You use the *Forming EBC Tool* to develop another evidence-based claim.

ODELL
EDUCATION

6. READ ALOUD AND CLASS DISCUSSION

You discuss your new evidence-based claim with the class.

7. INDEPENDENT WRITING OF EBCs

You organize your claim with an *Organizing EBC Tool* and draft a one- to two-paragraph evidence-based claim.

8. USING PEER FEEDBACK TO REVISE A WRITTEN EBC

You review and improve your claim with help from a partner.

QUESTIONING PATH TOOL

Name: _____ **Text:** _____

APPROACHING: *I determine my reading purposes and take note of key information about the text. I identify the LIPS domain(s) that will guide my initial reading.*	Purpose: Key information: LIPS domain(s):

QUESTIONING: *I use Guiding Questions to help me investigate the text (from the **Guiding Questions Handout**).*

1.

2.

ANALYZING: *I question further to connect and analyze the details I find (from the **Guiding Questions Handout**).*

1.

2.

DEEPENING: *I consider the questions of others.*

1.

2.

3.

EXTENDING: *I pose my own questions.*

1.

2.

ODELL EDUCATION

FORMING EVIDENCE-BASED CLAIMS TOOL

Name _ **Text** _ _ _ _ _ _ _ _ _ _

A question I have about the text:

FINDING DETAILS	Detail 1 (Ref.:)	Detail 2 (Ref.:)	Detail 3 (Ref.:)
I find interesting details that are related and that stand out to me from reading the text closely.			

CONNECTING THE DETAILS	What I think about detail 1:	What I think about detail 2:	What I think about detail 3:
I reread and think about the details, and explain the connections I find among them.			

How I connect the details:

MAKING A CLAIM	My claim about the text:
I state a conclusion that I have come to and can support with evidence from the text after reading and thinking about it closely.	

ODELL EDUCATION

ORGANIZING EVIDENCE-BASED CLAIMS TOOL (2PT)

Name _____   Text _____

CLAIM:

Point 1

A Supporting Evidence

B Supporting Evidence

(Reference:)

C Supporting Evidence

D Supporting Evidence

(Reference:)

Point 2

A Supporting Evidence

B Supporting Evidence

(Reference:)

C Supporting Evidence

D Supporting Evidence

(Reference:)

ORGANIZING EVIDENCE-BASED CLAIMS TOOL (3PT)

Name _____

Text _____

CLAIM: _____

Point 1	Point 2	Point 3
A Supporting Evidence	**A** Supporting Evidence	**A** Supporting Evidence
(Reference:)	(Reference:)	(Reference:)
B Supporting Evidence	**B** Supporting Evidence	**B** Supporting Evidence
(Reference:)	(Reference:)	(Reference:)
C Supporting Evidence	**C** Supporting Evidence	**C** Supporting Evidence
(Reference:)	(Reference:)	(Reference:)

ODELL EDUCATION

PART 5

DEVELOPING EVIDENCE-BASED WRITING

Overview and Tools

"Mrs. Macomber, in the car, had shot at the buffalo"

OBJECTIVE: You will develop the ability to express global evidence-based claims in writing.

MATERIALS:
- *Forming EBC Tool*
- *Organizing EBC Tool*
- *Writing EBC Handout*
- *Student Making EBC Literacy Skills Checklist*
- *Student Making EBC Academic Habits Checklist*

TEXT:
- *"The Short Happy Life of Francis Macomber,"*
  Ernest Hemingway

ACTIVITIES

1. INDEPENDENT READING AND CLASS DISCUSSION OF GLOBAL EBCs ABOUT LITERARY TECHNIQUE
You independently reread the text, and the class discusses global evidence-based claims.

2. FORMING GLOBAL EBCs ABOUT LITERARY TECHNIQUE
You review previous claims and use a *Forming EBC Tool* to plan a new global evidence-based claim.

3. REVIEWING AND ORGANIZING EBCs
You discuss your new claim in pairs and then think with the class about how you will organize it with an *Organizing EBC Tool*.

4. INDEPENDENT DRAFTING OF A FINAL WRITTEN EBCs ESSAY
You draft a final evidence-based essay using your new claim.

5. USING THE COLLABORATIVE, CRITERIA-BASED PROCESS TO IMPROVE ESSAYS
You use a criteria-based checklist and feedback from peers to revise and improve your essay.

6. CLASS DISCUSSION OF FINAL EVIDENCE-BASED ESSAYS
You discuss your final essays and reflect on the literacy skills and academic habits involved in making and communicating evidence-based claims

ODELL EDUCATION

FORMING EVIDENCE-BASED CLAIMS TOOL

Name _____   Text _____

A question I have about the text:

	Detail 1 (Ref.:)	Detail 2 (Ref.:)	Detail 3 (Ref.:)
FINDING DETAILS I find interesting details that are related and that stand out to me from reading the text closely.			

	What I think about detail 1:	What I think about detail 2:	What I think about detail 3:
CONNECTING THE DETAILS I reread and think about the details, and <u>explain</u> the connections I find among them.			
	How I connect the details:		

	My claim about the text:
MAKING A CLAIM I state a conclusion that I have come to and can support with evidence from the text after reading and thinking about it closely.	

ODELL EDUCATION

SUPPORTING EVIDENCE-BASED CLAIMS TOOL

Name _ _ _ _ _ _ _ _ _ _ _ _ _ _ _ **Text** _ _ _ _ _ _ _ _ _ _ _ _ _ _ _

CLAIM:

Supporting Evidence	Supporting Evidence	Supporting Evidence

(Reference:) (Reference:) (Reference:)

CLAIM:

Supporting Evidence	Supporting Evidence	Supporting Evidence

(Reference:) (Reference:) (Reference:)

ODELL EDUCATION

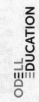

ORGANIZING EVIDENCE-BASED CLAIMS TOOL (2PT)

Name _ _ _ _ _ _ _ _ _ _ _ _ _ _ _ Text _

CLAIM: _____

Point 1

A	Supporting Evidence	B	Supporting Evidence
(Reference:)		(Reference:)	

C	Supporting Evidence	D	Supporting Evidence
(Reference:)		(Reference:)	

Point 2

A	Supporting Evidence	B	Supporting Evidence
(Reference:)		(Reference:)	

C	Supporting Evidence	D	Supporting Evidence
(Reference:)		(Reference:)	

ODELL
EDUCATION

ORGANIZING EVIDENCE-BASED CLAIMS TOOL (3PT)

Name

Text

CLAIM:

Point 1	Point 2	Point 3
A Supporting Evidence	**A** Supporting Evidence	**A** Supporting Evidence
(Reference:)	(Reference:)	(Reference:)
B Supporting Evidence	**B** Supporting Evidence	**B** Supporting Evidence
(Reference:)	(Reference:)	(Reference:)
C Supporting Evidence	**C** Supporting Evidence	**C** Supporting Evidence
(Reference:)	(Reference:)	(Reference:)

STUDENT MAKING EVIDENCE-BASED CLAIMS LITERACY SKILLS CHECKLIST

LITERACY SKILLS USED IN THIS UNIT	✔	EVIDENCE Demonstrating the SKILLS
READING		
1. **Attending to Details:** Identifies words, details, or quotations that are important to understanding the text		
2. **Interpreting Language:** Understands how words are used to express ideas and perspectives		
3. **Identifying Relationships:** Notices important connections among details, ideas, or texts		
4. **Recognizing Perspective:** Identifies and explains the author's or narrator's perspective		
THINKING		
5. **Making Inferences:** Draws sound conclusions from reading and examining the text closely		
6. **Forming Claims:** States a meaningful conclusion that is well supported by evidence from the text		
7. **Using Evidence:** Uses well-chosen details from the text to explain and support claims; accurately paraphrases or quotes		
WRITING		
8. **Presenting Details:** Inserts details and quotations effectively into written or spoken explanations		
9. **Organizing Ideas:** Organizes claims, supporting ideas, and evidence in a logical order		
10. **Using Language:** Writes and speaks clearly so others can understand claims and ideas		
11. **Using Conventions:** Correctly uses sentence elements, punctuation, and spelling to produce clear writing		
12. **Publishing:** Correctly uses, formats, and cites textual evidence to support claims		

General comments:

STUDENT MAKING EVIDENCE-BASED CLAIMS ACADEMIC HABITS CHECKLIST

Academic Habits Used in This Unit	✔	Evidence Demonstrating the Habits
1. Engaging Actively: Focuses attention on the task when working individually and with others		
2. Collaborating: Works respectfully and productively to help a group be successful		
3. Communicating Clearly: Presents ideas and supporting evidence so others can understand them		
4. Listening: Pays attention to ideas from others and takes time to think about them		
5. Understanding Purpose and Process: Understands why and how a task should be accomplished		
6. Revising: Rethinks ideas and refines work based on feedback from others		
7. Remaining Open: Modifies and further justifies ideas in response to thinking from others		
General comments:		

ODELL
EDUCATION

UNIT 4

RESEARCHING TO DEEPEN UNDERSTANDING

DEVELOPING CORE LITERACY PROFICIENCIES

GRADE 9

Music: What Role Does It Play in Our Lives?

GOAL

In this unit you will develop your proficiency as an investigator and user of information. You will learn how to do the following:

1. Have an inquiring mind and ask good questions.
2. Search for information—in texts, interviews, and on the Internet—that can help you answer your questions.
3. Record and organize the information you find.
4. Decide what is relevant and trustworthy in the sources of your information.
5. Come to a research-based perspective on a topic.
6. Clearly communicate what you have learned and "tell the story" of how you've come to learn it.

TOPIC

In this unit, you will explore the various ways that music affects our lives. You might investigate online pirating and the consequences of the digital world for musicians, discover how music affects our brains, or explore what life would be like without music.

ACTIVITIES

Throughout the unit, you will watch videos and read texts that foster classroom discussions about the role music plays in our lives. As you explore the topic, you will determine what you want to explore through research. As you read sources closely, you will keep an organized portfolio. Using your notes, you will express your new knowledge in a reflective research narrative or presentation.

TERMS AND DEFINITIONS USED IN THIS UNIT

Topic

The general topic chosen for class exploration

Area of Investigation

A particular theme, question, problem, or more focused subtopic within the general topic that warrants investigation

Inquiry Questions

Questions posed by researchers about their Areas of Investigation to be answered through inquiry

Developing Core Literacy Proficiencies

Inquiry Path

A realm of inquiry stemming from one or more related Inquiry Questions; a path can be framed by a general question that summarizes more specific questions or subtopics

Research Frame

An organized set of Inquiry Questions or Paths that guide the research process

Research Portfolio

The binder or electronic folder where students physically or electronically store and organize all the material related to their personal research

Research Plan

An organizer presenting the process students follow to guide them through the various stages of inquiry

RESEARCHING TO DEEPEN UNDERSTANDING LITERACY TOOLBOX

In *Researching to Deepen Understanding*, you will continue to build your "literacy toolbox" by learning how to use the following handouts, tools and checklists organized in your Student Edition.

 ## HANDOUTS

To support your work with the texts and the tools, you will be able to use the following informational handouts. You will also use handouts from previous Core Proficiencies units:

Research Plan

This handout presents the process you will follow during the various stages of inquiry.

Research Portfolio

This handout will help you to organize your tools and analysis throughout the research process.

Attending to Details Handout

from the *Reading Closely* unit

Guiding Questions Handout

from the *Reading Closely* unit

Posing Inquiry Questions Handout

This handout helps you come up with good questions to ask about a topic. These questions help you find important information throughout your research.

Assessing Sources Handout

This handout helps you evaluate how useful a potential source will be for your research.

Connecting Ideas Handout

This handout gives you examples of words to use in making connections among ideas in your writing.

Researching to Deepen Understanding—Final Writing Task Handout

This handout explains to you what you will be doing in the final assignment for this unit: writing a reflective research narrative that tells the story of how you arrived at your research-based perspective on the topic and communicates your experience with the inquiry process. The handout will also help you know what your teacher will be looking for so you can be successful writing your narrative.

TOOLS

In addition to using the handouts, you will learn how to use the following tools. You will also use tools from previous Developing Core Literacy Proficiencies units:

Forming Evidence-Based Claims Research Tool

from the *Making Evidence-Based Claims* unit (with Inquiry Question)

Organizing Evidence-Based Claims Research Tool

from the *Making Evidence-Based Claims* unit (with Inquiry Path)

Exploring a Topic Tool

This tool helps you think about and document potential areas of the topic you want to explore through research. You also have a space to write down notes from class discussion.

Potential Sources Tool

This tool helps you collect and organize information on sources you find that might be useful in your research. You can write down basic information about the source and later rate the source based on criteria such as Credibility, Relevance, and Interest.

Taking Notes Tool

This tool helps you make and organize notes from the various sources you find throughout your research.

Research Frame Tool

This tool helps you determine what you need to explore in order to develop a deep understanding of your Area of Investigation.

Research Evaluation Tool

This tool helps you work with your peers and teacher to determine if you have found enough information on your Area of Investigation.

 **CHECKLISTS**

You will also use these checklists throughout the unit to support peer- and self-review:

Research to Deepen Understanding Skills and Habits Checklist

This checklist presents and briefly describes the literacy skills and habits you will be working on during the unit. You can use it to remind you of what you are trying to learn. You can also use it to reflect on what you have done when reading, discussing, or writing. It can help you give feedback to other students about their research. Your teacher may use it to let you know about your areas of strength and areas in which you need to improve.

Area Evaluation Checklist

This checklist helps your class choose an area to investigate through research.

RESEARCHING TO DEEPEN UNDERSTANDING COMMON SOURCE SET

☰ MUSIC: WHAT ROLE DOES IT PLAY IN OUR LIVES?

Source 1: The first Common Source introduces a broad topic area in which to conduct research. It should be a high-interest source, preferably a video or multimedia resource. This source is used to stimulate curiosity and thinking about the topic and opens up many possibilities for research questions and learning within the topic area. This source is introduced and used in Part 1, Activity 2.

Common Source: "Imagine Life Without Music"—Leah Stevens. This video can be found on YouTube.com and was published on May 18, 2013.

Overview: This five-minute video introduces the topic of music by demonstrating the many ways that music influences our lives. Through a montage of pictures and video, enhanced by a classical music soundtrack, the videographer provides many ideas about how music plays an essential role in our lives including its impact on leisure, self-expression, and culture.

Discussion Questions: What does the video suggest about the topic area of music? What other questions about the topic of music does the video make you think about?

Source 2: The second Common Source provides background information and is used to extend discussion about the topic area. It also provides an opportunity to work on close-reading skills used during an independent research project. It is a print source that presents new information but is fairly easy to read and understand, and may be an Internet-based text. The source should expand thinking about the topic and open up additional paths for asking questions and learning within the topic area. All students read this source. This source is introduced and used in Part 1, Activity 2.

Common Source 2A: "A Brief History of the Music Industry" by Theo Smith, June 7, 2012. This Internet-based article can be found on the musicthinktank.com website.

Overview: In this article, the author provides an overview of the life and history of the music industry with insights into current and future states. Because it touches on so many facets of music, the article can provoke students to think more broadly about the topic and begin to explore people or things they did not know previously about music. Through nonfiction narrative and graphics, it describes the roles played by technological advancements, such as the printing press and the Internet, and the differences among live music, published music, and recorded music. The article also addresses how digital rights issues, such as copyright and piracy, shape the music industry as we know it today.

Discussion Questions: What does the text suggest about the topic area, "Music: What Role Does It Play in Our Lives?" What other connections to music does it make you think about?

Source 3: The third Common Source is a set of resources that introduce various subtopics within the general topic area. These sources provide additional background information and thinking to help make decisions about a more focused direction for research. The texts in this source set are also used to practice the skills of assessing sources for their relationship to research questions, their accessibility and interest, and their credibility and relevance within the topic area. Students read *one* of these sources, depending on their interests. This source is introduced and used in Part 1, Activity 3.

Common Sources:

Source 3A: Music on the Web: "What Is Online Piracy?" by the Recording Industry Association of America (RIAA), Date (NA). This source can be found on the RIAA website.—1210L

Source 3B: Relationship between Music and the Brain: "Why Your Brain Craves Music" by Michael D. Lemonick, April 15, 2013. This source can be found on the Time Magazine website.—1350L

Source 3C: Role of Music in History: "The 25 Most Important Civil Rights Moments in Music History" by Matthew Trammel, David Drake, Ernest Baker, Insanul Ahmed, and Rob Kenner, February 7, 2013. This source can be found on the complex.com website.

Overview: These three sources each focus on different aspects of the topic of "Music: What Role Does It Play in Our Lives?" and open up possible subtopic areas for research.

Source 3A: The Recording Industry Association of America (RIAA) is the trade organization that supports and promotes the creative and financial aspects of the major music companies. Its members are the music labels that comprise the most vibrant record industry in the world. This website, through its links, provides explanation about the topic of music piracy and why it is harmful to the music industry at large.

Source 3B: The article "Why Your Brain Craves Music" explores the physiological and neurological reasons for why we like music, but it also considers intellectual factors such as how paying for music stimulates our brains more than free music. The article considers how music affects our brains, thus our emotions, and how music might have even affected our evolutionary progress.

Source 3C: "25 Most Important Civil Rights Moments in Music History" shows the important role music and musicians can play during historical events and movements and presents several avenues for further research—either by artist or event. The article features images and commentary on key moments in history when civil rights and music collided, from the 1956 integration of southern dancehalls to Elton John and Eminem's duet at the 2001 Grammys.

Discussion Questions: What does the text suggest about the topic area "Music: What Role Does It Play in Our Lives?" What questions or directions for research does it suggest to you?

Text Assessment Questions: How accessible and interesting is the text for you? How credible and relevant is the source as a starting point for further research?

Source 4: The fourth Common Source Set provides information about websites (or other resources) that can be used to start a search for new sources and information in one of several possible subtopic areas. Students investigate *one* of these websites, depending on their interests. This source is introduced and used in Part 1, Activity 3.

Common Sources and Overviews

Source 4A: Music on the Web: "The True Cost of Sound Recording Piracy to the U.S. Economy" by Stephen E. Siwek, August 21, 2007. This article is available on The Institute for Policy Innovation website and provides a study by the conservative think tank discussing the adverse economic influence of music piracy.

Source 4B: Relationship between Music and the Brain: "Study Shows Some Are Unmoved by Music" by the *Los Angeles Times*, adapted by Newsela staff, March, 11, 2014. This article is available on the Newsela website. If the school or classroom does not already have an account, tell students they will have to create a username and password to log in to the Newsela website. This article explores how some people find it difficult to relate to music because of certain biological conditions.

Source 4C: Role of Music in History: "The Evolution of Music: How Genres Rise and Fall Over Time" by Kyle Kim, May 6, 2015. This article is available on the *Los Angeles Times* website. The article provides research on how scientists used Billboard music charts from the past to track how music genres evolved since 1960. The researchers were able to chart the popularity of thirteen different musical categories including hip-hop and country music.

Discussion Questions: What does the website suggest about the topic area "Music: What Role Does It Play in Our Lives?" What questions or directions for research does it suggest to you?

Text Assessment Questions: How accessible and interesting is the website's text for you? How credible and relevant is the source as a starting point for further research?

Source 5: The fifth Common Source is a set of texts that present a range of perspectives on a subtopic within the overall topic area. These texts are ones that have been written for various purposes by a range of organizations or authors who view the topic area in somewhat different ways. This Source Set is used to practice the skills of reading to understand a text's perspective on a topic and to compare perspectives and the ways they are presented by different authors. Students read *one* of these sources as a class and *another* individually. This source is introduced and used in Part 3, Activity 2.

Common Sources

Source 5A: "Why I Pirate" by Sebastian Anthony, January 18, 2012. This source is an article on the Extreme Tech website and is available through Extremetech.com.

Source 5B: "Why I No Longer Give Away My Music: How the digital music biz makes it difficult for musicians to offer free downloads" by Bob Ostertag, June 6, 2013. This source is an article on the *Commons Magazine* website and is available through Onthecommons.org.

Source 5C: "How the web changed music forever: it's both a boon and a bane to musicians" by Veronica Majerol, March 11, 2013. This source can be found using the Gale Virtual Reference Library.

Source 5D: "Are Musicians Going Up a Music Stream Without a Fair Payout?" by the *Philadelphia Inquirer,* adapted by Newsela staff, November 12, 2014. Available through the Newsela website.

Overview: These four sources all present specific and differing perspectives on the subtopic area of music piracy. They can be used to further understanding in the subtopic area and also to practice the skills of determining a source's perspective and therefore also its bias, credibility, and relevance to research in the topic area.

Source 5A: In his article, "Why I Pirate," Anthony Sebastian justifies his practice of music piracy. Citing profit sharing between labels and musicians, criticizing the value of a music product, and highlighting the access of music for the economically disadvantaged, this argumentative piece lays out a position defending the controversial, if not illegal, practice of pirating and sharing music content regardless of copyright laws. Reading and discussion could focus on his perspective and whether or not Sebastian's claims are credible.

Source 5B: In his article "Why I No Longer Give Away My Music: How the digital music biz makes it difficult for musicians to offer free downloads," sound artist Bob Ostertag recounts the unexpected issues concerned with giving away his music for free. Specifically, he talks about the idea that a large audience downloading more music than they will actually be able to listen to over a lifetime actually cheapens or degrades music. The author also describes how other laws negatively affect Creative Commons licenses.

Source 5C: "How the web changed music forever: it's both a boon and a bane to musicians" explores how smaller music groups are getting by in the new era of music streaming services such as Spotify and Pandora. The author explains that unknown musicians release their music on free, open, and public networks in order to become known, but then they might not make any money. This article considers the freedom of music access, exposing vulnerabilities in traditional music markets while admitting that open-source music platforms provide economic opportunities for lesser-known artists.

Source 5D: In the article "Are Musicians Going Up a Music Stream Without a Fair Payout?," the author explores several musicians' arguments that music should not be streamed and should, instead, be purchased. The author discusses why musicians such as Taylor Swift feel that the art form of making music should be valued and therefore purchased, not streamed for small payouts.

Evaluating Perspective Questions:
- What do I learn about the author and the purpose for writing the text? (GQH)
- What are the author's qualifications or credentials relative to the topic area? (ASH)
- What is the author's personal relationship to the topic area? (ASH)
- What details or words suggest the author's perspective? (GQH)
- How does the author's perspective influence the text's presentation of ideas or arguments? (GQH)
- How does the author's perspective and presentation of the text compare to others? (GQH)
- How does the author's perspective influence my reading of the text—and my use of the text in research? (GQH)

> **NOTE**
>
> Questions are referenced to handouts from the toolbox: GQH is the *Guiding Questions Handout* and ASH is the *Assessing Sources Handout*.

≡ ADDITIONAL RESOURCES IN THE TOPIC AREA

Music on the Web

- "Spotify's Daniel Ek: The Most Important Man In Music" by Steven Bertoni, January 4, 2012. Available through the Forbes.com website.

- "SoundScan Mid-Year: Albums Down, Stream Equivalents Nearly Double, Vinyl Continues Gain" by Ed Christman, July 3, 2014. Available through the Billboard.com website.

- "Are YOU Ruining the Music Industry?" by Suzanne Fitzpatrick, July 1, 2010. Available through the Siouxtrick.hubpages.com.

- "Digital Music Consumption on the Internet: Evidence from Clickstream Data" by Luis Aguiar and Bertin Martens, March 2013. Available through the Institute for Prospective Technological Studies as part of the Joint Research Centre.

- "The Music Video, Before Music Television" by History.Com staff, August 1, 2011. Available through the History.com website.

- "Are Musicians Going Up a Music Stream Without a Fair Payout?" by the Philadelphia Inquirer, adapted by Newsela staff, November 12, 2014. Available through the Newsela.com website.

Music and Therapy

- "What Is Music Therapy," American Music Therapy Association. Available through the Musictherapy.org website.

- "The transformative power of classical music," Benjamin Zander, TED Talk, February 2008. Available through the Ted.com website.

- "Music is medicine, music is sanity," Robert Gupta, TED Talk, February 2010. Available through the Ted.com website.

RESEARCHING TO DEEPEN UNDERSTANDING

DEVELOPING CORE LITERACY PROFICIENCIES

GRADE 9

Literacy Toolbox

STUDENT RESEARCH PLAN

STUDENT RESEARCH PLAN		TOOLS AND HANDOUTS
I. INITIATING INQUIRY *I determine what I want to know about a topic and develop Inquiry Questions that I will investigate.*	**1. Exploring a Topic** **2. Choosing an Area of Investigation** **3. Generating Inquiry Questions**	Exploring a Topic Potential Sources Area Evaluation Checklist Posing Inquiry Questions Handout
II. GATHERING INFORMATION *I find and take notes on sources that will help me answer my Inquiry Questions and define the scope of my investigation.*	**1. Finding and Assessing Sources** **2. Making and Recording Notes** **3. Framing Inquiry**	Potential Sources Assessing Sources Handout Taking Notes Research Frame Posing Inquiry Questions Handout
III. DEEPENING UNDERSTANDING *I analyze key sources to deepen my understanding and answer my Inquiry Questions.*	**1. Selecting Key Sources** **2. Analyzing Researched Information** **3. Writing Evidence-Based Claims**	Potential Sources Assessing Sources Handout Taking Notes Forming Evidence-Based Claims Student Research Literacy Skills and Discussion Habits Checklist Connecting Ideas Handout
IV. FINALIZING INQUIRY *I synthesize my information to determine what I have learned and what more I need to know about my Area of Investigation. I gather and analyze more information to complete my inquiry.*	**1. Organizing Evidence** **2. Evaluating Research** **3. Refining and Extending Inquiry**	Research Frame Forming Evidence-Based Claims Organizing Evidence-Based Claims Student Research Literacy Skills and Discussion Habits Checklist *Repeat parts II and III*
V. DEVELOPING AND COMMUNICATING AN EVIDENCE-BASED PERSPECTIVE *I review and synthesize my research to develop and communicate an evidence-based perspective on my area of investigation.*	**1. Reviewing Research** **2. Expressing an Evidence-Based Perspective** **3. Communicating an Evidence-Based Perspective**	Research Frame Organizing Evidence-Based Claims Student Research Literacy Skills and Discussion Habits Checklist Connecting Ideas Handout

STUDENT RESEARCH PORTFOLIO DESCRIPTION

The research portfolio helps you store and organize your findings and analysis throughout every step of the research process. Various tools help you develop a research strategy and record, analyze, and annotate your sources. Every time you complete a tool or annotate a source, file it in the corresponding section of your portfolio. Keeping an organized portfolio helps you make connections, see what you already have, and determine what you still have left to investigate. It will also provide everything you need to write your conclusions when you finish your research. The portfolio may be in either electronic or paper format.

PORTFOLIO SECTIONS	CONTENT
SECTION 1: DEFINING AN AREA OF INVESTIGATION *This section stores all the work you do exploring the topic and choosing an Area of Investigation.*	Exploring a Topic Area Evaluation Checklist Potential Sources (from pre-searches)
SECTION 2: GATHERING AND ANALYZING INFORMATION *This section stores all the information you gather throughout your investigation. It also stores your notes and analysis of sources.* *All the tools should be grouped by source.*	Potential Sources Annotated Sources Personal Drafts Taking Notes (about sources) Forming Evidence-Based Claims
SECTION 3: DRAWING CONCLUSIONS *This section stores your notes and Evidence-Based Claims about Inquiry Paths, your research evaluations, and the personal perspective that you come to at the end of your inquiry.* *Group the Taking Notes, Forming Evidence-Based Claim, or Organizing Evidence-Based Claim by Inquiry Path.*	Taking Notes (about Inquiry Paths) Forming Evidence-Based Claims Organizing Evidence-Based Claims Research Evaluation
SECTION 4: DISCARDED MATERIAL *This section stores all the sources and analysis that you have discarded throughout your investigation.* *The purpose of this section is to keep a record of discarded materials until the end of the research process in case you change your mind and want to use them.*	

ODELL EDUCATION

POSING INQUIRY QUESTIONS

Successful research results from posing good Inquiry Questions. When you have to solve a difficult problem or want to investigate a complex idea or issue, **developing questions about things you need to know helps guide your research and analysis**. But not all questions are created equal. Some lead to dead ends, and others open up vistas of knowledge and understanding . . . or best of all: *more questions!*

GENERATING QUESTIONS

Generating questions is most fun and effective with friends—the more minds the merrier. And **starting with lots of questions** helps you find the best ones. When brainstorming questions, consider many things about your Area of Investigation, for instance:

- **How is it defined?**
- **Where did it originate?**
- **What is its history?**
- **What are its important places, things, people, and experts?**
- **What are its major aspects?**
- **What are its causes and implications?**
- **What other things is it connected to or associated with?**

SELECTING AND REFINING QUESTIONS

Once you have a huge list of possible questions, select and refine them by asking yourself a few things about them:

Are you genuinely interested in answering your question?

Research requires hard work and endurance. If you don't care about your questions you won't do the work to answer them. The best questions are about things you actually want and need to know.

Can your question truly be answered through your research?

Some questions are unanswerable (How many walnuts are there in the world?) or take years to answer (What is the meaning of life?). Your Inquiry Questions must put you on a reachable path.

Is your question clear?

Can you pose your question in a way that you and others understand what you are asking? If it's confusing, then perhaps you are asking more than one thing. That's great: just break it into two questions. The more good Inquiry Questions you have the better.

What sort of answers does your question require?

Interesting, meaningful research comes from interesting questions. Good Inquiry Questions are rich enough to support lots of investigation that may even lead to multiple answers and more questions. Questions that can be answered with a simple Yes or No generally do not make good Inquiry Questions.

Do you already know what the answer is?

Good Inquiry Questions are actually questions. If you already have answered the questions for yourself, then you won't really be inquiring through your research. If you already know what you think, then you won't get the true reward of research: a deeper knowledge and understanding of things you want to know about.

ASSESSING SOURCES HANDOUT

ASSESSING A SOURCE'S ACCESSIBILITY AND INTEREST LEVEL

Consider your initial experience in reading the text, how well you understand it, and whether it seems interesting to you:

ACCESSIBILITY TO YOU AS A READER	INTEREST AND MEANING FOR YOU AS A READER
• Am I able to read and comprehend the text easily? • How do the text's structure and formatting either help or hinder me in reading it? • Do I have adequate background knowledge to understand the terminology, information, and ideas in the text?	• Does the text present ideas or information that I find interesting? • Which of my Inquiry Paths will the text provide information for? • Which Inquiry Questions does the text help me answer? How?

ASSESSING A SOURCE'S CREDIBILITY

Look at the information you can find about the text in the following areas, and consider the following questions to assess a source text's credibility:

PUBLISHER	DATE	AUTHOR	TYPE
• What is the publisher's relationship to the topic area? • What economic stake might the publisher have in the topic area? • What political stake might the publisher have in the topic area?	• When was the text first published? • How current is the information on the topic? • How does the publishing date relate to the history of the topic?	• What are the author's qualifications or credentials relative to the topic area? • What is the author's personal relationship to the topic area? • What economic or political stakes might the author have in the topic area?	• What type of text is it: explanation, informational article, feature, research study, op-ed, essay, argument, other? • What is the purpose of the text with respect to the topic area?

ASSESSING A SOURCE'S RELEVANCE AND RICHNESS

Using your Research Frame as a reference, consider the following questions:

RELEVANCE TO TOPIC AND PURPOSE	RELEVANCE TO AREA OF INVESTIGATION	SCOPE AND RICHNESS
• What information does the text provide on the topic? • How might the text help me accomplish the purpose for my research? • Does the text provide accurate information?	• How is the text related to the specific area I am investigating? • Which of my Paths of Inquiry might the text provide information for? • Which Inquiry Questions might the text help me address? How?	• How long is the text and what is the scope of the topic areas it addresses? • How extensive and supported is the information it provides? • How does the information in the text relate to other texts?

CONNECTING IDEAS HANDOUT

USING TRANSITIONAL WORDS AND PHRASES

Transitional words and phrases create links between your ideas when you are speaking and writing. They help your audience understand the logic of your thoughts. When using transitional words, make sure that they are the right match for what you want to express. And remember, transition words work best when they are connecting two or more strong ideas that are clearly stated. Here is a list of transitional words and phrases that you can use for different purposes.

ADD RELATED INFORMATION	GIVE AN EXAMPLE OR ILLUSTRATE AN IDEA	MAKE SURE YOUR THINKING IS CLEARLY UNDERSTOOD	COMPARE IDEAS OR SHOW HOW IDEAS ARE SIMILAR	CONTRAST IDEAS OR SHOW HOW THEY ARE DIFFERENT
• furthermore • moreover • too • also • again • in addition • next • further • finally • and, or, nor	• to illustrate • to demonstrate • specifically • for instance • as an illustration • for example	• that is to say • in other words • to explain • i.e., (that is) • to clarify • to rephrase it • to put it another way	• in the same way • by the same token • similarly • in like manner • likewise • in similar fashion	• nevertheless • but • however • otherwise • on the contrary • in contrast • on the other hand

EXPLAIN HOW ONE THING CAUSES ANOTHER	EXPLAIN THE EFFECT OR RESULT OF SOMETHING	EXPLAIN YOUR PURPOSE	LIST RELATED INFORMATION	QUALIFY SOMETHING
• because • since • on account of • for that reason	• therefore • consequently • accordingly • thus • hence • as a result	• in order that • so that • to that end, to this end • for this purpose • for this reason	• First, second, third . . . • First, then, also, finally	• almost • nearly • probably • never • always • frequently • perhaps • maybe • although

ODELL EDUCATION

RESEARCHING TO DEEPEN UNDERSTANDING—FINAL WRITING TASK

In this unit, you have been developing your skills as a researcher of a topic. You have learned to do the following things:

- Explore topics with your learning community
- Pose and refine inquiry questions
- Discover areas you wish to investigate
- Develop and refine a Research Frame (Area of Investigation with Inquiry Paths)
- Identify and assess pertinent sources
- Make claims about sources you find and connect them to your Research Frame
- Develop an evidence-based perspective on the topic

RESEARCH PORTFOLIO

- The Research Portfolio helps you store and organize your findings and analysis throughout every step of the research process. Various tools help you develop a research strategy and record, analyze, and annotate your sources. Every time you complete a tool or annotate a source, file it in the corresponding section of your portfolio.
- Keeping an organized portfolio helps you make connections, see what you already have, and determine what you still have left to investigate. It will also provide everything you need to write your reflective narrative when you finish your research. The portfolio may be in either electronic or paper format.

FINAL WRITING TASK: REFLECTIVE RESEARCH NARRATIVE

As you complete your research, you will have an opportunity to share what you've learned in a short reflective research narrative. Your narrative should clearly express your understanding of the topic and "tell the story" of how you have developed your new knowledge. *It does not need to fully summarize and include all of your research.*

In the reflective research narrative you will:

- Tell a story about what you've learned about the topic through your investigation
- Use notes and claims from your portfolio that you have already written
- Clearly connect your ideas to the sources where you have found them
- Reflect on what you have learned about the research process

To write this narrative, you will:

1. Review your Research Portfolio.
   a. Review the materials you have compiled and organized in your Research Portfolio:
      ⇒ *Taking Notes Tools*
      ⇒ *Forming EBC-Research Tools*

FINAL WRITING TASK (Continued)

⇒ *Organizing EBC-Research Tools*

⇒ *Written EBC(s)*

  b. Identify key materials that have helped you develop your thinking about the topic.

  c. Arrange key materials in a chronological order, to help you organize the narrative you will write.

2. Think of several different ways you and your classmates have come to understand the topic of "Music: What Role Does It Play in Our Lives?" based on the texts you have read.

  a. Select one or two of these ideas that match your own understanding, and return to the question:

   ⇒ *What do I think about this aspect of the topic of Music and Its Importance in Our Lives?*

  b. Your response to this question is the basis for your evidence-based perspective, which you will work into your narrative.

3. Think further about your perspective and your research by considering and discussing any of the following questions:

  ⇒ *Before starting my inquiry, what did I think about the topic? How did I view or understand it?*

  ⇒ *What specific steps did I take to research the topic? How did I address and answer my Inquiry Questions?*

  ⇒ *Which sources were the most interesting to me and why? What specifically did I find interesting about the sources?*

  ⇒ *What did I learn and discover about my Area of Investigation and Inquiry Question(s)?*

  ⇒ *What Inquiry Questions did I research but did not lead me anywhere?*

  ⇒ *What did I learn from my peers about the topic?*

  ⇒ *What moments were key in developing my understanding of the topic? When did I "get" something major about the topic?*

  ⇒ *What do I now think about the topic I have investigated, based on the research and reading I have done? What is my own perspective?*

  ⇒ *What did I learn about the research process? Where did I struggle and where did I triumph?*

4. Develop a plan or outline for your reflective research narrative.

  a. Think about telling the story of how you reached your perspective in a *chronological order*—from what you first thought or knew, through what you did to learn more about the topic, to how you arrived at your new understanding and perspective.

  b. Use your **Forming EBC Tools**, Written EBCs and **Organizing EBC Tools** to develop a detailed plan for your narrative.

5. Write a first draft of your reflective research narrative.

  a. Tell the story of how you researched the topic and arrived at your new perspective on it.

  b. Use your **Taking Notes Tools** to include evidence from relevant texts to support your story and your claims, accurately quoting and paraphrasing.

  c. Tell your story in the first person ("I"), present interesting details to help your reader understand it, and make good word choices to express and connect your ideas.

FINAL WRITING TASK (Continued)

FINAL WRITING TASK: REFLECTIVE RESEARCH NARRATIVE (Continued)

    d. Your reflective research narrative should do the following things, which will be evaluated in your final draft:

⇒ Express your original understanding of the research topic and tell the story of how you arrived at your new understanding.

⇒ Communicate a new perspective on the topic that is clearly connected to the area of investigation and supported by your research.

⇒ Explain and support the new perspective by discussing claims you have derived from inquiry questions.

⇒ Discuss evidence from relevant texts by accurately quoting and paraphrasing.

⇒ Use a clear narrative structure to sequence sentences and paragraphs and to present a coherent explanation of the perspective.

⇒ Use an informal narrative voice (first person) and effective words and phrases to communicate and connect ideas.

⇒ Present your reflections on what you have learned about the research process, using specific terminology from the unit.

6. Work with other students to review and improve your reflective research narrative.

    a. Use the following Guiding Review Questions to guide self and peer reviews of your narrative:

⇒ *Do I reflect on how I originally thought of the topic before I started to research it?*

⇒ *Do I recount the specific steps I took to think of Inquiry Questions around the Area of Investigation?*

⇒ *Do I tell how I found, read, and analyzed texts to help answer my Inquiry Questions?*

⇒ *Do I clearly communicate how I arrived at my research-based perspective?*

⇒ *What is the perspective and is it clearly stated?*

⇒ *Are the claims I present in my narrative "well supported," and is there enough evidence to explain or defend my perspective?*

⇒ *Are the sources cited accurately and consistently?*

⇒ *What can be added or revised to better express the perspective?*

7. Complete any additional drafts and peer reviews of your paper as instructed.

SKILLS AND HABITS TO BE DEMONSTRATED

As you develop and communicate a fine-tuned perspective on the topic, think about demonstrating the Literacy Skills and Academic Habits listed below to the best of your ability. Your teacher will evaluate your work and determine your grade based on how well you:

- **IDENTIFY RELATIONSHIPS:** Notice important connections among details, ideas, and texts
- **MAKE INFERENCES:** Draw sound conclusions from examining a text closely
- **SUMMARIZE:** Correctly explain what a text says about a topic
- **QUESTION:** Develop questions and lines of inquiry that lead to important ideas

ODELL
EDUCATION

FINAL WRITING TASK (Continued)

SKILLS AND HABITS TO BE DEMONSTRATED (Continued)

- **RECOGNIZE PERSPECTIVE:** Identify and explain the author's view of the text's topic
- **EVALUATE INFORMATION:** Assess the relevance and credibility of information in sources
- **FORM CLAIMS:** State a meaningful conclusion that is well supported by evidence from sources
- **USE EVIDENCE:** Use well-chosen details from sources to explain and support claims. Accurately paraphrase or quote.
- **ORGANIZE IDEAS:** Organize the narrative and its claims, supporting ideas, and evidence in a logical order
- **PRESENT DETAILS:** Describe and explain important details to tell the story
- **PUBLISH:** Use effective formatting and citations when paraphrasing, quoting, and listing sources
- **REFLECT CRITICALLY:** Use research concepts and terms to discuss and evaluate learning
- **GENERATE IDEAS:** Generate and develop ideas, perspectives, products, and solutions to problems
- **ORGANIZE WORK:** Maintain materials so that they can be used effectively and efficiently
- **COMPLETE TASKS:** Finish short and extended tasks by established deadlines
- **UNDERSTAND PURPOSE AND PROCESS:** Understand why and how a task should be accomplished

NOTE

These skills and habits are also listed on the *Student RDU Literacy Skills and Academic Habits Checklist* in your **Literacy Toolbox**, which you can use to assess your work and the work of other students.

PART 1

INITIATING INQUIRY

Overview and Tools

OBJECTIVE:	You will learn about inquiry and research. You will initially explore a topic and build background knowledge through reading and discussion. Then you will begin your inquiry by coming up with questions to direct your research. By the end of Part 1, you will have chosen an Area of Investigation and developed one or more Inquiry Questions.

MATERIALS:
- *Student Research Plan*
- *Questioning Path Tool*
- *Exploring a Topic Tool*

COMMON SOURCES:
- *Common Sources 1 through 4*

- *Guiding Questions Handout (Reading Closely Literacy Toolbox)*
- *Potential Sources Tool*
- *Area Evaluation Checklist*
- *Posing Inquiry Questions Handout*

ACTIVITIES

1. INTRODUCTION TO THE UNIT
Your teacher explains how critical readers use research to deepen their understanding and develop an evidence-based perspective on a topic. You are introduced to the purposes, the process, and the products of the unit.

2. EXPLORING A TOPIC
Your teacher leads a class exploration of a topic. You independently explore the research topic.

3. CONDUCTING PRE-SEARCHES
You conduct pre-searches for sources about one or two areas of investigation.

4. VETTING AREAS OF INVESTIGATION
You evaluate your potential areas of investigation and develop a research question or problem.

5. GENERATING INQUIRY QUESTIONS
You generate Inquiry Questions to guide your searches for information.

ODELL
EDUCATION

APPROACHING TEXTS TOOL

Name _____ **Text** _____

APPROACHING THE TEXT	What are my reading purposes?
Before reading, I consider what my specific purposes for reading are.	
I also take note of key information about the text.	Title: Author: Source/Publisher:
	Text type: Publication date:
	What do I already think or understand about the text based on this information?

QUESTIONING THE TEXT	Guiding Questions for *my first reading* of the text:
As I read the text for the first time, I use Guiding Questions that relate to my reading purpose and focus. (*Can be taken from the Guiding Questions Handout.*)	
	As I read I mark details on the text that relate to my Guiding Questions.
As I reread, I use questions I have about specific details that have emerged in my reading to focus my analysis and deepen my understanding.	Text-specific questions to help focus *my rereading of the text:*

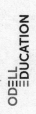
ODELL EDUCATION

QUESTIONING PATH TOOL

Name: _____   **Text:** _____

APPROACHING: *I determine my reading purposes and take note of key information about the text. I identify the LIPS domain(s) that will guide my initial reading.*

Purpose:

Key information:

LIPS domain(s):

QUESTIONING: *I use Guiding Questions to help me investigate the text (from the **Guiding Questions Handout**).*

1.

2.

ANALYZING: *I question further to connect and analyze the details I find (from the **Guiding Questions Handout**).*

1.

2.

DEEPENING: *I consider the questions of others.*

1.

2.

3.

EXTENDING: *I pose my own questions.*

1.

2.

ODELL EDUCATION

ANALYZING DETAILS TOOL

Name _____   Text _ _ _ _ _ _ _ _ _ _ _ _ _ _

Reading purpose:

....

A question I have about the text:

....

....

SEARCHING FOR DETAILS	I read the text closely and mark words and phrases that help me think about my question.

SELECTING DETAILS I select words or phrases from my search that I think are the most important in thinking about my question.	**Detail 1 (Ref.:**)	**Detail 2 (Ref.:**)	**Detail 3 (Ref.:**)

ANALYZING DETAILS I reread parts of the text and think about the meaning of the details and what they tell me about my question.	**What I think about detail 1:**	**What I think about detail 2:**	**What I think about detail 3:**

CONNECTING DETAILS I compare the details and explain the connections I see among them.	**How I connect the details:**

EXPLORING A TOPIC TOOL

Name _

Topic _

Write a brief account of the class conversation about the topic describing
what you know at this point about some of its aspects:

_____

_____

_____

_____

_____

_____

_____

_____

_____

_____

POTENTIAL AREA OF INVESTIGATION 1

In a few words, describe an area within the topic
that you would like to know more about:

_____

_____

_____

Explain why you are interested in this area of the
topic:

_____

_____

_____

Express your potential Area of Investigation as a
question or problem:

_____

_____

ODELL
EDUCATION

EXPLORING A TOPIC TOOL

Name _____

Topic _____

POTENTIAL AREA OF INVESTIGATION 2	POTENTIAL AREA OF INVESTIGATION 3	POTENTIAL AREA OF INVESTIGATION 4
In a few words, describe what you would like to know more about within the topic:	In a few words, describe what you would like to know more about within the topic:	In a few words, describe what you would like to know more about within the topic:
Explain why you are interested in this:	Explain why you are interested in this:	Explain why you are interested in this:
Express your potential area of investigation as a question or problem:	Express your potential area of investigation as a question or problem:	Express your potential area of investigation as a question or problem:

POTENTIAL SOURCES TOOL

Name _____ Topic _____

Area of Investigation _____

SOURCE	Title:		
No.		Location:	
	Author:	Text type:	Publication date:
General Content/Key Ideas/Personal Comments:			Connection to Inquiry Paths:
Accessibility/Interest: [ ] High [ ] Medium [ ] Low	Credibility: [ ] High [ ] Medium [ ] Low		Relevance/Richness: [ ] High [ ] Medium [ ] Low

SOURCE	Title:		
No.		Location:	
	Author:	Text type:	Publication date:
General Content/Key Ideas/Personal Comments:			Connection to Inquiry Paths:
Accessibility/Interest: [ ] High [ ] Medium [ ] Low	Credibility: [ ] High [ ] Medium [ ] Low		Relevance/Richness: [ ] High [ ] Medium [ ] Low

SOURCE	Title:		
No.		Location:	
	Author:	Text type:	Publication date:
General Content/Key Ideas/Personal Comments:			Connection to Inquiry Paths:
Accessibility/Interest: [ ] High [ ] Medium [ ] Low	Credibility: [ ] High [ ] Medium [ ] Low		Relevance/Richness: [ ] High [ ] Medium [ ] Low

POTENTIAL SOURCES TOOL

Name _____ **Topic** _____

Area of Investigation _____

SOURCE

No.	Title:		Location:	
	Author:		Text type:	Publication date:

General Content/Key Ideas/Personal Comments:

Connection to Inquiry Paths:

Accessibility/Interest: [ ] High [ ] Medium [ ] Low   **Credibility:** [ ] High [ ] Medium [ ] Low   **Relevance/Richness:** [ ] High [ ] Medium [ ] Low

---

SOURCE

No.	Title:		Location:	
	Author:		Text type:	Publication date:

General Content/Key Ideas/Personal Comments:

Connection to Inquiry Paths:

Accessibility/Interest: [ ] High [ ] Medium [ ] Low   **Credibility:** [ ] High [ ] Medium [ ] Low   **Relevance/Richness:** [ ] High [ ] Medium [ ] Low

---

SOURCE

No.	Title:		Location:	
	Author:		Text type:	Publication date:

General Content/Key Ideas/Personal Comments:

Connection to Inquiry Paths:

Accessibility/Interest: [ ] High [ ] Medium [ ] Low   **Credibility:** [ ] High [ ] Medium [ ] Low   **Relevance/Richness:** [ ] High [ ] Medium [ ] Low

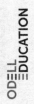

ODELL EDUCATION

POTENTIAL SOURCES TOOL

Name _____

Topic _____

Area of Investigation _____

SOURCE	Title:		Location:	
No.	Author:		Publication date:	

General Content/Key Ideas/Personal Comments:

Text type:

Connection to Inquiry Paths:

Accessibility/Interest: [ ] High [ ] Medium [ ] Low   Credibility: [ ] High [ ] Medium [ ] Low   Relevance/Richness: [ ] High [ ] Medium [ ] Low

SOURCE	Title:		Location:	
No.	Author:		Publication date:	

General Content/Key Ideas/Personal Comments:

Text type:

Connection to Inquiry Paths:

Accessibility/Interest: [ ] High [ ] Medium [ ] Low   Credibility: [ ] High [ ] Medium [ ] Low   Relevance/Richness: [ ] High [ ] Medium [ ] Low

SOURCE	Title:		Location:	
No.	Author:		Publication date:	

General Content/Key Ideas/Personal Comments:

Text type:

Connection to Inquiry Paths:

Accessibility/Interest: [ ] High [ ] Medium [ ] Low   Credibility: [ ] High [ ] Medium [ ] Low   Relevance/Richness: [ ] High [ ] Medium [ ] Low

ANALYZING DETAILS TOOL

Name _____ Text _____

Reading purpose:

A question I have about the text:

SEARCHING FOR DETAILS

I read the text closely and mark words and phrases that help me think about my question.

SELECTING DETAILS

I select words or phrases from my search that I think are the most important in thinking about my question.

Detail 1 (Ref.:)	Detail 2 (Ref.:)	Detail 3 (Ref.:)

ANALYZING DETAILS

I reread parts of the text and think about the meaning of the details and what they tell me about my question.

What I think about detail 1:	What I think about detail 2:	What I think about detail 3:

CONNECTING DETAILS

I compare the details and explain the connections I see among them.

How I connect the details:

ODELL EDUCATION

PART 2

GATHERING INFORMATION

Overview and Tools

OBJECTIVE:	You will learn how to conduct searches, assess and annotate sources, and keep an organized record of your findings. By the end of Part 2, you will have framed your inquiry and gathered your main body of research material.

MATERIALS:
- *Potential Sources Tool*
- *Assessing Sources Handout*
- *Taking Notes Tool*

- *Posing Inquiry Questions Handout*
- *Research Frame Tool*

COMMON SOURCES:
- *Common Sources 1 through 4*

- *Student-identified sources*

ACTIVITIES

1. PLANNING SEARCHES FOR INFORMATION
Your teacher works with you to determine how to organize your search and where to look for the information you need.

2. BUILDING AN INITIAL RESEARCH FRAME
You develop an initial plan to organize your research.

3. CONDUCTING SEARCHES FOR BACKGROUND SOURCES USING INQUIRY QUESTIONS AND PATHS
You use Inquiry Questions to help you look for sources that can help you better understand your topic.

4. ASSESSING SOURCES
Your teacher explains how to assess sources to determine their credibility and relevance to your Inquiry Questions.

5. MAKING AND RECORDING NOTES
Your teacher explains how to annotate sources and record key information and ideas as you conduct your research.

6. CONDUCTING SEARCHES INDEPENDENTLY
You use Inquiry Questions to conduct strategic searches for potential sources. You annotate promising sources and make and record notes for them.

7. REVIEWING AND REVISING THE RESEARCH FRAME
You reflect on how your research is going and make adjustments to your strategy.

ODELL
EDUCATION

RESEARCH FRAME TOOL

Name _ **Topic** _

Area of Investigation _

INQUIRY PATH	INQUIRY PATH	INQUIRY PATH
Reference: IP No.	Reference: IP No.	Reference: IP No.
Name this Inquiry Path in the form of a brief description or question:	Name this Inquiry Path in the form of a brief description or question:	Name this Inquiry Path in the form of a brief description or question:
List all the questions in this Inquiry Path:	List all the questions in this Inquiry Path:	List all the questions in this Inquiry Path:

ODELL EDUCATION

POTENTIAL SOURCES TOOL

Name _ _ _ _ _ _ _ _ _ _ _ _ _ Topic _ _ _ _ _ _ _ _ _ _ _ _

Area of Investigation _

SOURCE		Title:	Location:	
No.		Author:	Text type:	Publication date:
General Content/Key Ideas/Personal Comments:				Connection to Inquiry Paths:
Accessibility/Interest: [ ] High [ ] Medium [ ] Low	Credibility: [ ] High [ ] Medium [ ] Low		Relevance/Richness: [ ] High [ ] Medium [ ] Low	

SOURCE		Title:	Location:	
No.		Author:	Text type:	Publication date:
General Content/Key Ideas/Personal Comments:				Connection to Inquiry Paths:
Accessibility/Interest: [ ] High [ ] Medium [ ] Low	Credibility: [ ] High [ ] Medium [ ] Low		Relevance/Richness: [ ] High [ ] Medium [ ] Low	

SOURCE		Title:	Location:	
No.		Author:	Text type:	Publication date:
General Content/Key Ideas/Personal Comments:				Connection to Inquiry Paths:
Accessibility/Interest: [ ] High [ ] Medium [ ] Low	Credibility: [ ] High [ ] Medium [ ] Low		Relevance/Richness: [ ] High [ ] Medium [ ] Low	

TAKING NOTES TOOL

Name _

Source(s) _

Inquiry Question/Path _ _ _ _ _ _ _ _ _ _ _ _ _ _

REFERENCE	DETAILS	COMMENTS
Source no. and location in the source:	I record details, ideas, or information that I find in my sources that help me answer my Inquiry Questions:	I explain the reason why I think they are important and write personal comments:

TAKING NOTES TOOL

Name _

Source(s) _

Inquiry Question/Path _ _ _ _ _ _ _ _ _ _ _ _ _ _

REFERENCE	DETAILS	COMMENTS
Source no. and location in the source:	I record details, ideas, or information that I find in my sources that help me answer my Inquiry Questions:	I explain the reason why I think they are important and write personal comments:

ODELL
EDUCATION

TAKING NOTES TOOL

Name _

Source(s) _

Inquiry Question/Path _ _ _ _ _ _ _ _ _ _ _ _ _

REFERENCE	DETAILS	COMMENTS
Source no. and location in the source:	I record details, ideas, or information that I find in my sources that help me answer my Inquiry Questions:	I explain the reason why I think they are important and write personal comments:

TAKING NOTES TOOL

Name _ _ _ _ _ _ _ _ _ _ _ _ _ _ _ _ _ _ _

Source(s) _ _ _ _ _ _ _ _ _ _ _ _ _ _ _ _ _ _

Inquiry Question/Path _ _ _ _ _ _ _ _ _ _ _ _ _

REFERENCE	DETAILS	COMMENTS
Source no. and location in the source:	I record details, ideas, or information that I find in my sources that help me answer my Inquiry Questions:	I explain the reason why I think they are important and write personal comments:

ODELL
EDUCATION

TAKING NOTES TOOL

Name _ _ _ _ _ _ _ _ _ _ _ _ _ _ _ _ _ _ _

Source(s) _ _ _ _ _ _ _ _ _ _ _ _ _ _ _ _ _ _ _

Inquiry Question/Path _ _ _ _ _ _ _ _ _ _ _

REFERENCE	DETAILS	COMMENTS
Source no. and location in the source:	*I record details, ideas, or information that I find in my sources that help me answer my Inquiry Questions:*	*I explain the reason why I think they are important and write personal comments:*

TAKING NOTES TOOL

Name _

Source(s) _

Inquiry Question/Path _ _ _ _ _ _ _ _ _ _ _ _ _

REFERENCE	DETAILS	COMMENTS
Source no. and location in the source:	I record details, ideas, or information that I find in my sources that help me answer my Inquiry Questions:	I explain the reason why I think they are important and write personal comments:

ODELL EDUCATION

TAKING NOTES TOOL

Name _

Source(s) _

Inquiry Question/Path _ _ _ _ _ _ _ _ _ _ _ _ _

REFERENCE	DETAILS	COMMENTS
Source no. and location in the source:	I record details, ideas, or information that I find in my sources that help me answer my Inquiry Questions:	I explain the reason why I think they are important and write personal comments:

RESEARCH FRAME TOOL

Name _ _ _ _ _ _ _ _ _ _ _ _   **Topic** _ _ _ _ _ _ _ _ _ _ _ _ _ _ _ _ _ _

Area of Investigation _ _ _ _ _ _ _ _ _ _ _ _ _ _ _ _

INQUIRY PATH	INQUIRY PATH	INQUIRY PATH
Reference: IP No.	**Reference: IP No.**	**Reference: IP No.**
Name this Inquiry Path in the form of a brief description or question:	Name this Inquiry Path in the form of a brief description or question:	Name this Inquiry Path in the form of a brief description or question:
List all the questions in this Inquiry Path:	List all the questions in this Inquiry Path:	List all the questions in this Inquiry Path:

RESEARCH FRAME TOOL

Name -

Topic -

Area of Investigation -

INQUIRY PATH	INQUIRY PATH	INQUIRY PATH
Reference: IP No.	**Reference: IP No.**	**Reference: IP No.**
Name this Inquiry Path in the form of a brief description or question:	Name this Inquiry Path in the form of a brief description or question:	Name this Inquiry Path in the form of a brief description or question:
List all the questions in this Inquiry Path:	List all the questions in this Inquiry Path:	List all the questions in this Inquiry Path:

ODELL
EDUCATION

PART 3

DEEPENING UNDERSTANDING

Overview and Tools

OBJECTIVE:	You will read and analyze key sources closely to deepen your understanding and draw personal conclusions about your Area of Investigation. By the end of Part 3, you will have a series of evidence-based claims addressing each Inquiry Path of your research frame.

MATERIALS:
- *Research Frame Tool*
- *Assessing Sources Handout*
- *Forming EBC Research Tool*

- *Attending to Details Handout*
- *Writing EBC Handout*
- *Connecting Ideas Handout*

COMMON SOURCES:
- *Common Source 5*

- *Student-identified sources*

ACTIVITIES

1. SELECTING KEY SOURCES
Your teacher discusses how to identify the most relevant sources and helps you select key sources to analyze through close reading.

2. ANALYZING A SOURCE'S PERSPECTIVE
Your teacher explains how to analyze a source's perspective and relevance to your research, and you practice analyzing a source.

3. READING KEY SOURCES CLOSELY—FORMING CLAIMS
You use your Inquiry Questions to read key sources closely, analyzing them for content, perspective, and relevance.

4. WRITING EBCs ABOUT SOURCES
You develop evidence-based summaries and explanations of key sources using your notes and annotations.

QUESTIONING PATH TOOL

Name: _____   **Text:** _____

APPROACHING: *I determine my reading purposes and take note of key information about the text. I identify the LIPS domain(s) that will guide my initial reading.*

Purpose:

Key information:

LIPS domain(s):

QUESTIONING: *I use Guiding Questions to help me investigate the text (from the **Guiding Questions Handout**).*

1.

2.

ANALYZING: *I question further to connect and analyze the details I find (from the **Guiding Questions Handout**).*

1.

2.

DEEPENING: *I consider the questions of others.*

1.

2.

3.

EXTENDING: *I pose my own questions.*

1.

2.

ANALYZING DETAILS TOOL

Name _____ **Text** _____

Reading purpose:

A question I have about the text:

SEARCHING FOR DETAILS

I read the text closely and mark words and phrases that help me think about my question.

SELECTING DETAILS

I select words or phrases from my search that I think are the most important in thinking about my question.

Detail 1 (Ref.:)

Detail 2 (Ref.:)

Detail 3 (Ref.:)

ANALYZING DETAILS

I reread parts of the text and think about the meaning of the details and what they tell me about my question.

What I think about detail 1:

What I think about detail 2:

What I think about detail 3:

CONNECTING DETAILS

I compare the details and explain the connections I see among them.

How I connect the details:

ODELL EDUCATION

FORMING EVIDENCE-BASED CLAIMS RESEARCH TOOL

Name _____   Source(s) _____

Inquiry Question:

SEARCHING FOR DETAILS

I read the sources closely and mark words and phrases that help me answer my question.

SELECTING DETAILS

I select words or phrases from my search that I think are the most important for answering my question. I write the reference next to each detail.

Detail 1 (Ref.:)	Detail 2 (Ref.:)	Detail 3 (Ref.:)

ANALYZING AND CONNECTING DETAILS

I reread parts of the texts and think about the meaning of the details and what they tell me about my question. Then I compare the details and explain the connections I see among them.

What I think about the details and how I connect them:

MAKING A CLAIM

I state a conclusion I have come to and can support with evidence from the texts after reading them closely.

My claim that answers my Inquiry Question:

ODELL
EDUCATION

FORMING EVIDENCE-BASED CLAIMS RESEARCH TOOL

Name _____ Source(s) _____

Inquiry Question:

SEARCHING FOR DETAILS

I read the sources closely and mark words and phrases that help me answer my question.

SELECTING DETAILS

I select words or phrases from my search that I think are the most important for answering my question. I write the reference next to each detail.

Detail 1 (Ref.:)	Detail 2 (Ref.:)	Detail 3 (Ref.:)

ANALYZING AND CONNECTING DETAILS

I reread parts of the texts and think about the meaning of the details and what they tell me about my question. Then I compare the details and explain the connections I see among them.

What I think about the details and how I connect them:

MAKING A CLAIM

I state a conclusion I have come to and can support with evidence from the texts after reading them closely.

My claim that answers my Inquiry Question:

FORMING EVIDENCE-BASED CLAIMS RESEARCH TOOL

Name _ _ _ _ _ _ _ _ _ _ _ _ _ _ _ _ **Source(s)** _ _ _ _ _ _ _ _ _ _ _ _ _ _ _

Inquiry Question:

SEARCHING FOR DETAILS

I read the sources closely and mark words and phrases that help me answer my question.

SELECTING DETAILS

I select words or phrases from my search that I think are the most important for answering my question. I write the reference next to each detail.

Detail 1 (Ref.:)	Detail 2 (Ref.:)	Detail 3 (Ref.:)

ANALYZING AND CONNECTING DETAILS

I reread parts of the texts and think about the meaning of the details and what they tell me about my question. Then I compare the details and explain the connections I see among them.

What I think about the details and how I connect them:

MAKING A CLAIM

I state a conclusion I have come to and can support with evidence from the texts after reading them closely.

My claim that answers my Inquiry Question:

ODELL
EDUCATION

PART 4

FINALIZING INQUIRY

Overview and Tools

OBJECTIVE:	You will analyze and evaluate your material with respect to your Inquiry Questions and refine and complete your research. By the end of Part 4, you will have an analyzed body of research addressing your Inquiry Questions. You will be ready to develop your final perspective on the topic and communicate it to others.

MATERIALS:
- *Research Frame Tool*
- *Forming EBC Research Tool*
- *Organizing EBC Research Tool*
- *Connecting Ideas Handout*
- *Research Evaluation Tool*

ACTIVITIES

1. ADDRESSING INQUIRY PATHS
You review your notes and analysis for the sources that address one of your Inquiry Paths.

2. ORGANIZING EVIDENCE
You review and organize your research and analysis. You think about how you will address all the Inquiry Paths of your research frame.

3. EVALUATING RESEARCH
You review and discuss your research frames and researched materials to determine whether they are relevant, make sense, and will fully support your researched perspective.

4. REFINING AND EXTENDING INQUIRY
You refine and extend your research based on teacher and peer feedback.

ODELL
EDUCATION

ORGANIZING EVIDENCE-BASED CLAIMS
RESEARCH TOOL (2 POINTS)

Name _ _ _ _ _ _ _ _ _ _ _ _ _ _ Inquiry Path _ _ _ _ _ _ _ _ _ _ _ _ _ _ _ _ _ _

CLAIM:

Point 1

A	Supporting Evidence	B	Supporting Evidence
(Reference:)		(Reference:)	
C	Supporting Evidence	D	Supporting Evidence
(Reference:)		(Reference:)	

Point 2

A	Supporting Evidence	B	Supporting Evidence
(Reference:)		(Reference:)	
C	Supporting Evidence	D	Supporting Evidence
(Reference:)		(Reference:)	

ODELL EDUCATION

ORGANIZING EVIDENCE-BASED CLAIMS
RESEARCH TOOL (3 POINTS)

Name _ _ _ _ _ _ _ _ _ _ _ _ _ _ Inquiry Path _ _ _ _ _ _ _ _ _ _

CLAIM:

Point 1

	Supporting Evidence
A	Supporting Evidence
(Reference:	)
B	Supporting Evidence
(Reference:	)
C	Supporting Evidence
(Reference:	)

Point 2

	Supporting Evidence
A	Supporting Evidence
(Reference:	)
B	Supporting Evidence
(Reference:	)
C	Supporting Evidence
(Reference:	)

Point 3

	Supporting Evidence
A	Supporting Evidence
(Reference:	)
B	Supporting Evidence
(Reference:	)
C	Supporting Evidence
(Reference:	)

ODELL EDUCATION

ORGANIZING EVIDENCE-BASED CLAIMS
RESEARCH TOOL (2 POINTS)

Name _

Inquiry Path _

CLAIM:

Point 1

Point 2

A   Supporting Evidence

B   Supporting Evidence

(Reference:)

C   Supporting Evidence

D   Supporting Evidence

(Reference:)

A   Supporting Evidence

B   Supporting Evidence

(Reference:)

C   Supporting Evidence

D   Supporting Evidence

(Reference:)

ODELL EDUCATION

ORGANIZING EVIDENCE-BASED CLAIMS
RESEARCH TOOL (3 POINTS)

Name _____

- - - - - Inquiry Path -

CLAIM:

Point 1	Point 2	Point 3
A Supporting Evidence	**A** Supporting Evidence	**A** Supporting Evidence
(Reference:)	(Reference:)	(Reference:)
B Supporting Evidence	**B** Supporting Evidence	**B** Supporting Evidence
(Reference:)	(Reference:)	(Reference:)
C Supporting Evidence	**C** Supporting Evidence	**C** Supporting Evidence
(Reference:)	(Reference:)	(Reference:)

ODELL EDUCATION

ORGANIZING EVIDENCE-BASED CLAIMS
RESEARCH TOOL (2 POINTS)

Name _ **Inquiry Path** _ _ _ _ _ _ _ _ _ _ _ _ _ _ _ _ _

CLAIM:

Point 1

A Supporting Evidence

B Supporting Evidence

(Reference:)

C Supporting Evidence

D Supporting Evidence

(Reference:)

Point 2

A Supporting Evidence

B Supporting Evidence

(Reference:)

C Supporting Evidence

D Supporting Evidence

(Reference:)

ORGANIZING EVIDENCE-BASED CLAIMS
RESEARCH TOOL (3 POINTS)

Name

Inquiry Path

CLAIM:

Point 1	Point 2	Point 3
A Supporting Evidence	**A** Supporting Evidence	**A** Supporting Evidence
(Reference:)	(Reference:)	(Reference:)
B Supporting Evidence	**B** Supporting Evidence	**B** Supporting Evidence
(Reference:)	(Reference:)	(Reference:)
C Supporting Evidence	**C** Supporting Evidence	**C** Supporting Evidence
(Reference:)	(Reference:)	(Reference:)

FORMING EVIDENCE-BASED CLAIMS RESEARCH TOOL

Name _____ Source(s) _____

Inquiry Question:

SEARCHING FOR DETAILS	I read the sources closely and mark words and phrases that help me answer my question.

SELECTING DETAILS I select words or phrases from my search that I think are the most important for answering my question. I write the reference next to each detail.	Detail 1 (Ref.:)	Detail 2 (Ref.:)	Detail 3 (Ref.:)

ANALYZING AND CONNECTING DETAILS I reread parts of the texts and think about the meaning of the details and what they tell me about my question. Then I compare the details and explain the connections I see among them.	What I think about the details and how I connect them:

MAKING A CLAIM I state a conclusion I have come to and can support with evidence from the texts after reading them closely.	My claim that answers my Inquiry Question:

ODELL
EDUCATION

PART 1 RESEARCH EVALUATION CRITERIA CHECKLIST

Name _____   Area of Investigation _____   Date ____

RESEARCH EVALUATION CRITERIA CHECKLIST		√	COMMENTS
I. ADEQUACY AND SUFFICIENCY OF RESEARCH *The researcher's investigation follows the research frame and the information gathered is sufficient.*	**Adequacy of the research:** The researcher's investigation is based on the Research Frame and the claims and information presented link directly to the Inquiry Questions.	☐	
	Sufficiency of the answers: The answers formulated by the researcher based on his or her investigation are sufficient to cover the scope of each Inquiry Question.	☐	
	Adequacy of the scope and focus of the research: No Inquiry Questions or Paths of the research seem irrelevant with respect to the research frame.	☐	
II. CREDIBILITY AND RICHNESS OF SOURCES *The sources gathered by the researcher are credible and rich.*	**Credibility of sources:** The sources gathered by the researcher are credible.	☐	
	Richness of sources: The researcher found a reasonable amount of rich sources that provide important information that is relevant to the inquiry.	☐	
III. RANGE OF PERSPECTIVES *The researcher has considered a wide range of perspectives.*	**Richness of perspectives:** The researcher has considered and explored multiple perspectives.	☐	
	Sufficiency of perspectives: No important perspective has been ignored.	☐	
	Balance among perspectives: There is no overreliance on any one source or perspective.	☐	
IV. COHERENCE OF THE PERSPECTIVE *The evidence-based claims drawn from the analysis of the sources are coherent, sound, and supported.*	**Coherence of evidence-based claims:** The evidence-based claims drawn from the analysis of the sources are coherent with respect to the research frame.	☐	
	Soundness of evidence-based claims: The evidence-based claim demonstrates knowledge of and sound thinking about the area of investigation.	☐	
	Support for evidence-based claims: The evidence-based claims are supported by quotations and examples from the texts.	☐	

ODELL EDUCATION

PART 2 PEER EVALUATION OF RESEARCH

Presenter: _ _ _ _ _ _ _ _ _ _ _ _ _ **Reviewer:** _ _ _ _ _ _ _ _ _ _ _ _ _

Work in small groups to evaluate each other's research. Rotate roles in your group.

AS A PRESENTER:

- **Present your Area of Investigation and Research Frame.** Describe the general scope of your research and explain why you are interested in this area.

- **Summarize from your written claims** for each of your answers to the Inquiry Paths. Make sure you reference evidence from sources to support your claims.

- **Present two key sources.** Explain why you think they are key, summarize their content and explain your analysis of these sources to your peers. Show your peers and comment on your annotations, notes, and EBCs about these sources.

- Make sure you **give your peers the opportunity to ask you questions** during the entire presentation.

- **Take notes** on a Revising Research tool to determine actions you may take to revise your research based on your peers review.

AS A REVIEWER:

- **Listen** carefully to the presentation. **Ask clarifying questions** to the presenter when necessary.

- Using the table below, **make comments and suggestions** about the presentation answering the guiding questions.

GUIDING QUESTIONS	COMMENTS AND SUGGESTIONS
What have you learned about the presenter's area of investigation?	
What was interesting to you in the presentation?	
What new information does the presenter need to find to more fully address existing or new Inquiry Paths?	
What was not clear to you in the presentation?	
What would you like to know more about the presenter's area of investigation?	
Do you have any other comment or suggestions that you think would help the presenter improve his/her work?	

ODELL
EDUCATION

PART 3 REVISING RESEARCH

Presenter: ------------------------------------ **Reviewer:** -----------------------------

Review the feedback on your Research and think about ways you should revise your work. For each action you choose, explain what specific steps you are planning to take.

GUIDING QUESTIONS	MY NOTES, COMMENTS, AND FUTURE STEPS
What adjustments and additions do I need to make to my Research Frame?	
Are there sources lacking in credibility that I need to replace?	
What new information do I need to find to more fully address existing or new Inquiry Paths?	
What missing perspectives do I need to research?	
Are there any parts of my research I should discard?	
Other:	

RESEARCH FRAME TOOL

Name _____ **Topic** _____

Area of Investigation _____

INQUIRY PATH	INQUIRY PATH	INQUIRY PATH
Reference: IP No.	**Reference: IP No.**	**Reference: IP No.**
Name this Inquiry Path in the form of a brief description or question:	Name this Inquiry Path in the form of a brief description or question:	Name this Inquiry Path in the form of a brief description or question:
List all the questions in this Inquiry Path:	List all the questions in this Inquiry Path:	List all the questions in this Inquiry Path:

POTENTIAL SOURCES TOOL

Name _____

Topic _____

Area of Investigation _____

SOURCE	Title:	Location:
No.	Author:	Text type:
		Publication date:
General Content/Key Ideas/Personal Comments:		Connection to Inquiry Paths:
Accessibility/Interest: [ ] High [ ] Medium [ ] Low	Credibility: [ ] High [ ] Medium [ ] Low	Relevance/Richness: [ ] High [ ] Medium [ ] Low

SOURCE	Title:	Location:
No.	Author:	Text type:
		Publication date:
General Content/Key Ideas/Personal Comments:		Connection to Inquiry Paths:
Accessibility/Interest: [ ] High [ ] Medium [ ] Low	Credibility: [ ] High [ ] Medium [ ] Low	Relevance/Richness: [ ] High [ ] Medium [ ] Low

SOURCE	Title:	Location:
No.	Author:	Text type:
		Publication date:
General Content/Key Ideas/Personal Comments:		Connection to Inquiry Paths:
Accessibility/Interest: [ ] High [ ] Medium [ ] Low	Credibility: [ ] High [ ] Medium [ ] Low	Relevance/Richness: [ ] High [ ] Medium [ ] Low

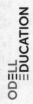

ODELL EDUCATION

POTENTIAL SOURCES TOOL

Name _ _ _ _ _ _ _ _ _ _ _ _ _ _ **Topic** _ _ _ _ _ _ _ _ _ _ _ _ _ _

Area of Investigation _ _ _ _ _ _ _ _ _ _

SOURCE	**Title:**		**Location:**	
No.	**Author:**		**Text type:**	**Publication date:**
General Content/Key Ideas/Personal Comments:				Connection to Inquiry Paths:
Accessibility/Interest: [ ] High [ ] Medium [ ] Low		**Credibility:** [ ] High [ ] Medium [ ] Low		**Relevance/Richness:** [ ] High [ ] Medium [ ] Low

SOURCE	**Title:**		**Location:**	
No.	**Author:**		**Text type:**	**Publication date:**
General Content/Key Ideas/Personal Comments:				Connection to Inquiry Paths:
Accessibility/Interest: [ ] High [ ] Medium [ ] Low		**Credibility:** [ ] High [ ] Medium [ ] Low		**Relevance/Richness:** [ ] High [ ] Medium [ ] Low

SOURCE	**Title:**		**Location:**	
No.	**Author:**		**Text type:**	**Publication date:**
General Content/Key Ideas/Personal Comments:				Connection to Inquiry Paths:
Accessibility/Interest: [ ] High [ ] Medium [ ] Low		**Credibility:** [ ] High [ ] Medium [ ] Low		**Relevance/Richness:** [ ] High [ ] Medium [ ] Low

TAKING NOTES TOOL

Name _

Source(s) _ _ _ _ _ _ _ _ _ _ _ _ _ _ _ _ _ _ _

Inquiry Question/Path _ _ _ _ _ _ _ _ _ _

REFERENCE	DETAILS	COMMENTS
Source no. and location in the source:	I record details, ideas, or information that I find in my sources that help me answer my Inquiry Questions:	I explain the reason why I think they are important and write personal comments:

ODELL
EDUCATION

TAKING NOTES TOOL

Name _ _ _ _ _ _ _ _ _ _ _ _ _ _ _ _ _ _

Source(s) _ _ _ _ _ _ _ _ _ _ _ _ _ _ _ _ _

Inquiry Question/Path _ _ _ _ _ _ _ _ _ _

REFERENCE	DETAILS	COMMENTS
Source no. and location in the source:	I record details, ideas, or information that I find in my sources that help me answer my Inquiry Questions:	I explain the reason why I think they are important and write personal comments:

TAKING NOTES TOOL

Name _ _ _ _ _ _ _ _ _ _ _ _ _ _ _ _ _ _ _

Source(s) _ _ _ _ _ _ _ _ _ _ _ _ _ _ _ _ _

Inquiry Question/Path _ _ _ _ _ _ _ _ _ _ _

REFERENCE	DETAILS	COMMENTS
Source no. and location in the source:	I record details, ideas, or information that I find in my sources that help me answer my Inquiry Questions:	I explain the reason why I think they are important and write personal comments:

ODELL EDUCATION

TAKING NOTES TOOL

Name _ _ _ _ _ _ _ _ _ _ _ _ _ _ _ _ _ _ _

Source(s) _ _ _ _ _ _ _ _ _ _ _ _ _ _ _ _ _ _

Inquiry Question/Path _ _ _ _ _ _ _ _ _ _ _ _

REFERENCE	DETAILS	COMMENTS
Source no. and location in the source:	*I record details, ideas, or information that I find in my sources that help me answer my Inquiry Questions:*	*I explain the reason why I think they are important and write personal comments:*

TAKING NOTES TOOL

Name _

Source(s) _

Inquiry Question/Path _ _ _ _ _ _ _ _ _ _ _ _ _ _ _

REFERENCE	DETAILS	COMMENTS
Source no. and location in the source:	I record details, ideas, or information that I find in my sources that help me answer my Inquiry Questions:	I explain the reason why I think they are important and write personal comments:

ODELL
EDUCATION

TAKING NOTES TOOL

Name _

Source(s) _

Inquiry Question/Path _ _ _ _ _ _ _ _ _ _ _ _ _

REFERENCE	DETAILS	COMMENTS
Source no. and location in the source:	I record details, ideas, or information that I find in my sources that help me answer my Inquiry Questions:	I explain the reason why I think they are important and write personal comments:

ORGANIZING EVIDENCE-BASED CLAIMS
RESEARCH TOOL (2 POINTS)

Name _____   Inquiry Path _ _ _ _ _ _ _ _ _ _ _ _

CLAIM:

Point 1

		Point 2	
A Supporting Evidence	**B** Supporting Evidence	**A** Supporting Evidence	**B** Supporting Evidence
(Reference:)	(Reference:)	(Reference:)	(Reference:)
C Supporting Evidence	**D** Supporting Evidence	**C** Supporting Evidence	**D** Supporting Evidence
(Reference:)	(Reference:)	(Reference:)	(Reference:)

ORGANIZING EVIDENCE-BASED CLAIMS
RESEARCH TOOL (3 POINTS)

Name _____

Inquiry Path _____

CLAIM: _____

Point 1

Point 2

Point 3

A Supporting Evidence	A Supporting Evidence	A Supporting Evidence
(Reference:)	(Reference:)	(Reference:)
B Supporting Evidence	B Supporting Evidence	B Supporting Evidence
(Reference:)	(Reference:)	(Reference:)
C Supporting Evidence	C Supporting Evidence	C Supporting Evidence
(Reference:)	(Reference:)	(Reference:)

ORGANIZING EVIDENCE-BASED CLAIMS
RESEARCH TOOL (2 POINTS)

Name _____   Inquiry Path _ _ _ _ _ _ _ _ _ _ _ _ _ _

CLAIM:

Point 1

A	Supporting Evidence	B	Supporting Evidence

(Reference:)   (Reference:)

C	Supporting Evidence	D	Supporting Evidence

(Reference:)   (Reference:)

Point 2

A	Supporting Evidence	B	Supporting Evidence

(Reference:)   (Reference:)

C	Supporting Evidence	D	Supporting Evidence

(Reference:)   (Reference:)

ORGANIZING EVIDENCE-BASED CLAIMS
RESEARCH TOOL (3 POINTS)

Name _____

Inquiry Path _____

CLAIM: _____

Point 1

A Supporting Evidence

(Reference:)

B Supporting Evidence

(Reference:)

C Supporting Evidence

(Reference:)

Point 2

A Supporting Evidence

(Reference:)

B Supporting Evidence

(Reference:)

C Supporting Evidence

(Reference:)

Point 3

A Supporting Evidence

(Reference:)

B Supporting Evidence

(Reference:)

C Supporting Evidence

(Reference:)

ODELL
EDUCATION

FORMING EVIDENCE-BASED CLAIMS RESEARCH TOOL

Name _____   Source(s) _____

Inquiry Question:

SEARCHING FOR DETAILS

I read the sources closely and mark words and phrases that help me answer my question.

Detail 1 (Ref.:)	Detail 2 (Ref.:)	Detail 3 (Ref.:)

SELECTING DETAILS

I select words or phrases from my search that I think are the most important for answering my question. I write the reference next to each detail.

ANALYZING AND CONNECTING DETAILS

What I think about the details and how I connect them:

I reread parts of the texts and think about the meaning of the details and what they tell me about my question. Then I compare the details and explain the connections I see among them.

MAKING A CLAIM

My claim that answers my Inquiry Question:

I state a conclusion I have come to and can support with evidence from the texts after reading them closely.

PART 5

DEVELOPING AND COMMUNICATING AN EVIDENCE-BASED PERSPECTIVE

Overview and Tools

OBJECTIVE:	You will organize your research and tools to help you write a reflective research narrative on the topic and inquiry experience. You might also express your research-based perspective in a final project such as a multimedia presentation or academic paper.

MATERIALS:
- *Research Frame Tool*
- *Potential Sources Tool*
- *Organizing EBC Research Tool*

- *Connecting Ideas Handout*
- *Writing EBC Handout*
- *RDU Final Writing Task Handout*

ACTIVITIES

1. REVIEWING RESEARCH PORTFOLIOS
You review and organize your research portfolio in preparation for communicating your evidence-based perspectives through a reflective research narrative.

2. COMMUNICATING AN EVIDENCE-BASED PERSPECTIVE
You write a reflective research narrative explaining your experience researching your topic and the understanding you have developed.

3. WRITING A BIBLIOGRAPHY
You use your Potential Sources Tools to write a bibliography of your sources.

4. COMMUNICATING A FINAL EVIDENCE-BASED PRODUCT (OPTIONAL)
You organize your evidence and research-based claims into a communication plan or final product that addresses your purposes for research.

STUDENT RESEARCHING TO DEEPEN UNDERSTANDING LITERACY SKILLS AND HABITS CHECKLIST

	RESEARCH LITERACY SKILLS AND ACADEMIC HABITS	✔	EVIDENCE Demonstrating the SKILLS AND HABITS
READING	1. **Identifying Relationships:** Notices important connections among details, ideas, and texts		
	2. **Making Inferences:** Draws sound conclusions from examining a text closely		
	3. **Summarizing:** Correctly explains what a text says about a topic		
	4. **Questioning:** Develops questions and lines of inquiry that lead to important ideas		
THINKING	5. **Recognizing Perspective:** Identifies and explains the author's view of the text's topic		
	6. **Evaluating Information:** Assesses the relevance and credibility of information in sources		
	7. **Forming Claims:** States a meaningful conclusion that is well supported by evidence from sources		
	8. **Using Evidence:** Uses well-chosen details from sources to explain and support claims; accurately paraphrases or quotes		
	9. **Presenting Details:** Describes and explains details that are important in the story of the research process		
	10. **Organizing Ideas:** Organizes the narrative and its claims, supporting ideas, and evidence in a logical order		
	11. **Publishing:** Uses effective formatting and citations when paraphrasing, quoting, and listing sources		
ACADEMIC HABITS	12. **Reflecting Critically:** Uses research concepts and terms to discuss and evaluate learning		
	13. **Generating Ideas:** Generates and develops ideas, perspectives, products, and solutions to problems.		
	14. **Organizing Work:** Maintains materials so that they can be used effectively and efficiently		
	15. **Completing Tasks:** Finishes short and extended tasks by established deadlines		
	16. **Understanding Purpose and Process:** Understands why and how a task should be accomplished		
	General comments:		

AREA EVALUATION CHECKLIST

Date   **Name**   **Area of Investigation**

AREA EVALUATION CHECKLIST	√	COMMENTS
I. COHERENCE OF AREA *What is the Area of Investigation?* The researcher can speak and write about the Area of Investigation in a way that makes sense to others and is clearly understood.		
II. SCOPE OF AREA *What do I need to know to gain an understanding of the Area of Investigation?* The questions necessary to investigate for gaining an understanding require more than a quick review of easily accessed sources. The questions are reasonable enough so that the researcher is likely to find credible sources that address the issue in the time allotted for research.		
III. RELEVANCE OF AREA *How is this Area of Investigation related to a larger topic?* The Area of Investigation is relevant to the larger topic.		
IV. INTEREST IN AREA *Why are you interested in this Area of Investigation?* The researcher is able to communicate genuine interest in the Area of Investigation. Gaining an understanding of the area would be valuable for the student.		

In one or two sentences express the potential Area of Investigation in the form of a problem or overarching question:

....

....

....

UNIT 5

BUILDING
EVIDENCE-BASED
ARGUMENTS

DEVELOPING CORE LITERACY
PROFICIENCIES

GRADE 9

"What is the virtue of a proportional
response?"

ODELL
EDUCATION

GOAL

In this unit you will develop your proficiency as a presenter of reasoned arguments. You will learn how to do the following:

1. Understand the background and key aspects of an important issue.
2. Look at various viewpoints on the issue.
3. Read the arguments of others closely and thoughtfully.
4. Develop your own view of the issue and take a stand about it.
5. Make and prove your case by using sound evidence and reasoning to support it.
6. Improve your writing so that others will clearly understand and appreciate your evidence-based argument—and think about the case you have made for it.

TOPIC

The topic area and texts focus on terrorism. More specifically, you will read texts that explore what is meant when we use the word *terrorism* and what makes a violent event "terrorism" or a "an act of terror." You will also read about the events leading up to 9/11, examine and analyze the responses to the attacks, and investigate the relationship between terrorism and war. Terrorism, and policy related to terrorism, is a complex topic with many possible perspectives and positions—not a simple pro and con arena for debate—which enables you to approach and study the issue from many possible angles.

ACTIVITIES

You will begin the unit learning about terrorism in general—how it is defined as well as historical terrorist events. As you begin to understand the issue, you will explore the various perspectives on terrorism in the United States. You will then read and analyze a few arguments. After analyzing arguments, you will develop your own position on the issue. Using your notes, you will plan an argument to defend your position. The unit finishes with a collaborative process you will use with your classmates to help you write and revise your final argumentative essay.

Developing Core Literacy Proficiencies

BUILDING EVIDENCE-BASED ARGUMENTS LITERACY TOOLBOX

In *Building Evidence-Based Arguments*, you will continue to build your "literacy toolbox" by learning how to use the following handouts, tools and checklists organized in your Student Edition.

⬛ HANDOUTS AND MODEL ARGUMENTS

To support your work with the texts and the tools, you will be able to use the following informational handouts. You may also use handouts from previous Core Proficiencies units:

Guiding Questions Handout

from the *Reading Closely* unit

Connecting Ideas Handout

from the *Research* unit

Evidence-Based Arguments Final Writing Task Handout

The handout gives you a detailed breakdown of the final argumentative essay.

Evidence-Based Arguments Terms

This handout defines the terms used in the unit to talk about and analyze arguments.

Model Arguments

These examples present familiar situations about which people take different positions. You can use these models to practice analyzing arguments.

⬛ TOOLS

In addition to using the handouts, you will learn how to use the following tools. You may also use tools from previous Developing Core Literacy Proficiencies units:

Questioning Path Tool

from the *Reading Closely* unit

Forming Evidence-Based Claims Tool

from the *Making Evidence-Based Claims* unit

Organizing Evidence-Based Claims Tool

from the *Making Evidence-Based Claims* unit

Delineating Arguments Tool

This tool helps you identify and analyze components of an argument. You can use it to analyze other people's arguments or to help you develop your own.

Evaluating Arguments Tool

This tool helps you evaluate eight characteristics of an argument (some you have seen in the ***Delineating Arguments Tool***): the argument's issue, perspective, credibility and bias, position or thesis, claims, evidence, reasoning and logic, and conclusions. You can also use this tool to rate how convincing the argument is overall.

 # CHECKLIST

You will also use this checklist throughout the unit to support peer- and self-review:

Building Evidence-Based Arguments Skills and Habits Checklist

This checklist presents and briefly describes the literacy skills and habits you will be working on during the unit. You can use it to remind you of what you are trying to learn; to reflect on what you have done when reading, discussing, or writing; or to give feedback to other students. Your teacher may use it to let you know about your areas of strength and areas in which you need to improve.

BUILDING EVIDENCE-BASED ARGUMENTS UNIT TEXT

The following table lists the unit texts (organized by numbered text sets) that are used in the activities you will experience as you learn about argumentation. You will read some, but not all, of these texts, depending on decisions your teacher and students in your class make. Additional texts you can read to deepen your understanding are indicated with an "AT."

These texts are accessible on the web for free without any login information, membership requirements, or purchase. Your teacher may provide you with copies of the texts you will read, or you may need to do an Internet search to find them. Because of the ever-changing nature of website addresses, links are not provided. You can locate these texts through web searches using the information provided. To find some of the texts, you may need to use online database portals (e.g., EBSCO, Gale) that are available to teachers and students through your state or district library systems.

NO.	TITLE	AUTHOR	DATE	SOURCE/ PUBLISHER
Text Set 1: Background Informational Texts				
1.1	"What Is terrorism?"	Laura Beth Nielsen	4/17/2013	Al Jazeera—English
1.2	"Terrorists or Freedom Fighters: What's the Difference?"	John Bolt	11/14/2001	Acton Institute
1.3	"Militant Extremists in the United States"	Jonathan Masters	2/7/2011	Council on Foreign Relations
Text Set 2: Additional Background Informational Texts				
2.1	Major Terrorism Cases: Past and Present	FBI	NA	FBI.gov
2.2	September 11 Attacks Timeline	National September 11 Memorial and Museum	NA	9/11memorial.org
2.3	Events of 9/11	History.com	NA	History.com
AT	"Title 18: Crimes and Criminal Procedure; Part 1—Crimes; Chapter 113B—Terrorism"	Cornell Law	NA	*Cornell Law*
AT	"A Brief History of Terrorism in the United States"	Brian Resnick	4/16/2013	*National Journal*
AT	USS *Cole* Bombing Fast Facts	CNN Library	9/18/2013	CNN
AT	The History of Terrorism	Amy Zalman	NA	About.com

Text Set 3: Political Cartoons			
3.1	"Political Cartoons: The Human Aspect of Modern Conflict"	Various	NA	College of Education at the University of Texas—Austin
Text Set 4: Seminal Arguments				
4.1	"Authorization for Use of Military Force"	Public Law 107—40	9/18/2001	107th Congress gpo.gov, fas.org
4.2	George W. Bush's Address to the Nation on September 11, 2001 (text)	President Bush	9/11/2001	Salem Press
4.2	"George W. Bush's Address to the Nation on September 11, 2001" (video)	President Bush	9/11/2001	CNN/YouTube.com
4.3	"A Place of Peace: For a 9/11 Victim's Widow, Revenge Is Not the Answer"	Lauren Frohne	9/4/2011	*Boston Globe*
AT	Osama bin Laden's Declaration of Jihad against Americans	Osama bin Laden	1996	Salem Press
AT	9/11 Paul Wolfowitz Interview PBS *News Hour* with Jim Lehrer	Paul Wolfowitz	9/14/2001	PBS.org— NewsHour with Jim Lehrer (transcript)/ YouTube.com (video)
AT	"U.S. Response to Terrorism: A Strategic Analysis of the Afghanistan" "Campaign	Valentina Taddeo	Summer 2010	*Journal of Strategic Security* (http:// scholarcommons. usf.edu)
Text Set 5: Additional Arguments				
5.1	Our War on Terrorism	Howard Zinn	11/2004	Progressive.org
5.2	"Obama's Speech on Drone Policy"	President Obama	5/23/2013	*New York Times*
5.3	Remarks by President Obama on the death of Osama bin Laden	President Obama	5/2/2011	Whitehouse.gov
5.4	"Why Drones Work: The Case for Washington's Weapon of Choice"	Daniel L. Byman	2013	Brookings.edu
AT	"Terrorism Can Only Be Defeated by Education, Tony Blair Tells the UN"	NA	11/22/2013	*UN News* (news article and video)

BUILDING EVIDENCE-BASED ARGUMENTS

DEVELOPING CORE LITERACY PROFICIENCIES

GRADE 9

Literacy Toolbox

ODELL
EDUCATION

EVIDENCE-BASED ARGUMENTS TERMS

ISSUE	An important aspect of human society for which there are many different opinions about what to think or do; many issues can be framed as a problem-based question
RELATIONSHIP TO ISSUE	A person's particular personal involvement with an issue, given his or her experience, education, occupation, socioeconomic-geographical status, interests, or other characteristics
PERSPECTIVE	How someone understands and views an issue based on his or her current relationship to it and analysis of the issue
POSITION	Someone's stance on what to do or think about a clearly defined issue based on his or her perspective and understanding of it; when writing an argumentative essay, one's position may be expressed as a thesis
THESIS	Another word for *position* sometimes used when writing an argument to support it
IMPLICATIONS	The practical and logical consequences of a position that has been supported by evidence-based argumentation
PREMISES	The claims of an argument that are linked together logically using evidence and reasoning to support a position or thesis
EVIDENCE	The topical and textual facts, events, and ideas from which the claims of an argument arise and which are cited to support the argument's position
REASONING	The logical relationships among ideas, including claims, premises, and evidence
CHAIN OF REASONING	The logical relationships linking the premises of an argument that lead to the demonstration and support of a position
CLAIM	A personal conclusion about a text, topic, event, or idea
EVIDENCE-BASED CLAIM	A personal conclusion that arises from and is supported by textual and topical evidence

ODELL EDUCATION

CONNECTING IDEAS

USING TRANSITIONAL WORDS AND PHRASES

Transitional words and phrases create links between your ideas when you are speaking and writing. They help your audience understand the logic of your thoughts. When using transitional words, make sure that they are the right match for what you want to express. And remember, transition words work best when they are connecting two or more strong ideas that are clearly stated. Here is a list of transitional words and phrases that you can use for different purposes.

ADD RELATED INFORMATION	GIVE AN EXAMPLE OR ILLUSTRATE AN IDEA	MAKE SURE YOUR THINKING IS CLEARLY UNDERSTOOD	COMPARE IDEAS OR SHOW HOW IDEAS ARE SIMILAR	CONTRAST IDEAS OR SHOW HOW THEY ARE DIFFERENT
• furthermore • moreover • too • also • again • in addition • next • further • finally • and, or, nor	• to illustrate • to demonstrate • specifically • for instance • as an illustration • for example	• that is to say • in other words • to explain • i.e., (that is) • to clarify • to rephrase it • to put it another way	• in the same way • by the same token • similarly • in like manner • likewise • in similar fashion	• nevertheless • but • however • otherwise • on the contrary • in contrast • on the other hand

EXPLAIN HOW ONE THING CAUSES ANOTHER	EXPLAIN THE EFFECT OR RESULT OF SOMETHING	EXPLAIN YOUR PURPOSE	LIST RELATED INFORMATION	QUALIFY SOMETHING
• because • since • on account of • for that reason	• therefore • consequently • accordingly • thus • hence • as a result	• in order that • so that • to that end, to this end • for this purpose • for this reason	• First, second, third . . . • First, then, also, finally	• almost • nearly • probably • never • always • frequently • perhaps • maybe • although

BUILDING EVIDENCE-BASED ARGUMENTS—FINAL WRITING TASK

In this unit, you have been developing your skills as a presenter of reasoned arguments. You have learned to do the following things:

- Understand the background and key aspects of an important issue
- Look at various viewpoints on the issue
- Read the arguments of others closely and thoughtfully
- Develop your own view of the issue and take a position on it
- Make and prove your case by using sound evidence and reasoning to support it
- Improve your thinking and writing so that others will clearly understand and appreciate your evidence-based argument—and think about the case you have made for it

Your final writing assignment—the development of an evidence-based argumentative essay—will provide you with opportunities to use all of these related skills and to demonstrate your proficiency and growth in building evidence-based arguments. The assignment will also represent your final work in the Developing Core Literacy Proficiencies sequence and should demonstrate all that you have learned as a reader, thinker, and writer this year.

FINAL ASSIGNMENT

Developing, Writing, and Revising an Evidence-Based Argumentative Essay

Having read a collection of informational texts and arguments related to the unit's issue, you will develop a supported position on the issue. You will then plan, draft, and revise a multiparagraph essay that makes a case for your position. To do this, you will do the following:

1. Review the texts you have read, the tools you have completed, and the claims you have formed throughout the unit to determine the position you will take on the issue.

2. Write a paragraph that clearly states and explains your position—and the support you have found for it.

3. Read or reread arguments related to your position, looking for evidence you might use to support your argument.

4. Read or reread arguments that take an opposed or different position and think about how you might respond to these arguments.

5. Use a **Delineating Arguments Tool** to plan a multiparagraph essay that presents a series of claims, supported by evidence, to develop an argument in favor of your position.

ODELL
EDUCATION

FINAL WRITING TASK (Continued)

FINAL ASSIGNMENTS (Continued)

6. Draft a multiparagraph essay that explains, develops, and supports your argumentative position—keeping in mind these criteria for this final writing assignment. Your essay should accomplish the following:

   ⇒ Present a convincing argument that comes from your understanding of the issue and a clear perspective and position.

   ⇒ Organize a set of claims in an order that explains and supports your position.

   ⇒ Use relevant and trustworthy evidence to support all claims and your overall position.

   ⇒ Represent the best thinking and writing you can do.

7. Use a collaborative process with other students to review and improve your draft in key areas:

   ⇒ The information and ideas that make up your argument

   ⇒ The organization (unity and logical sequence) of your argument

   ⇒ Your selection, use, and integration of supporting evidence (quotations, facts, statistics, references to other arguments, etc.)

   ⇒ The clarity of your writing—in areas identified by your teacher

8. Reflect on how well you have used literacy skills and academic habits throughout the unit and in developing your final written argument.

SKILLS AND HABITS TO BE DEMONSTRATED

As you become an expert on your issue and develop your evidence-based position and argument, think about demonstrating the Literacy Skills and Academic Habits you have been working on to the best of your ability. Your teacher will evaluate your work and determine your grade based on how well you are able to do the following things:

Read

Recognize Perspective: Identify and explain each author's view of the unit's issue.

Evaluate Information: Assess the relevance and credibility of information in texts about the issue.

Delineate Arguments: Identify and analyze the claims, evidence, and reasoning of arguments related to the issue.

DEVELOP ACADEMIC HABITS

Remain Open to New Ideas: Ask questions of others rather than arguing for your own ideas or opinions.

Qualify Your Views: Explain and change your ideas in response to thinking from others.

Revise: Rethink your position and refine your writing based on feedback from others.

Reflect Critically: Discuss and evaluate your learning, using the criteria that describe the literacy skills and academic habits you have been developing.

FINAL WRITING TASK (Continued)

DEVELOP ACADEMIC HABITS (Continued)

Write

Form Claims: State meaningful positions and conclusions that are well supported by evidence from texts you have examined.

Use Evidence: Use well-chosen details from the texts to support your position and claims. Accurately paraphrase or quote what the authors say in the texts.

Use Logic: Argue for your position through a logical sequence of related claims, and supporting evidence.

Organize Ideas: Organize your argument, supporting claims, and evidence in an order that makes sense to others.

Use Language: Write clearly so others can understand your position, claims, and supporting ideas.

Use Conventions: Correctly use sentence elements, punctuation, and spelling to produce clear writing.

Publish: Correctly use, format, and cite textual evidence to support your argument.

NOTE

These skills and habits are also listed on the *Student EBA Literacy Skills and Academic Habits Checklist*, which you can use to assess your work and the work of other students.

ODELL
EDUCATION

PART 1

UNDERSTANDING THE NATURE OF AN ISSUE

Overview and Tools

"What does it mean when we say something is 'terrorism' and why does it matter?"

OBJECTIVE:	You will apply your close-reading skills to understand a complex societal issue.

MATERIALS:
- *Guiding Questions Handout*
- *Questioning Path Tool*
- *Forming EBC Tool*
- *Organizing EBC Tool*
- *EBA Terms*

TEXTS:

Text Set 1: Background Informational Texts
- *1.1 "What Is terrorism?" Laura Beth Nielsen*
- *1.2 "Terrorists or Freedom Fighters: What's the Difference?" John Bolt*
- *1.3 "Militant Extremists in the United States" Jonathan Masters*

Text Set 2: Additional Background Informational Texts
- *2.1 Major Terrorism Cases: Past and Present, FBI*
- *2.2 September 11 Attacks Timeline, National September 11 Memorial and Museum,*
- *2.3 Events of 9/11, History.com*

ACTIVITIES

1. INTRODUCING THE UNIT
Your teacher presents an overview of the unit and its societal issue.

2. EXPLORING THE ISSUE
You read and analyze a background text to develop an initial understanding of the issue.

3. DEEPENING UNDERSTANDING OF THE ISSUE
You read and analyze an additional background text to deepen your understanding of the issue.

4. QUESTIONING TO REFINE UNDERSTANDING
You develop text-dependent questions to guide your reading and expand your knowledge of the issue.

5. WRITING AN EBC ABOUT THE NATURE OF THE ISSUE
You write a multipart EBC about the nature of the issue.

QUESTIONING PATH TOOL

Text 1.1—"What Is Terrorism?"

APPROACHING:
I determine my reading purposes and take note of key information about the text. I identify the LIPS domain(s) that will guide my initial reading.

QUESTIONING: *I use Guiding Questions to help me investigate the text (from the **Guiding Questions Handout**).*

ANALYZING: *I question further to connect and analyze the details I find (from the **Guiding Questions Handout**).*

1. How might I summarize the main ideas of the text and the key supporting details?

2. How do the text's main ideas relate to what I already know, think, or have read?

3. In what way are ideas, events, and claims linked together in the text?

DEEPENING: *I consider the questions of others.*

4. Throughout the article, the author asks several questions. Why does the author do this? How do the questions develop the author's point of view about the complexity of terrorism?

5. Toward the end of the article the author asks, "What work is the word 'terrorism' doing in these conversations?" How does the author use the word *work* in the context of this question?

EXTENDING: *I pose my own questions.*

6. What evidence does this text provide that builds my understanding of the issue of terrorism?

ODELL EDUCATION

QUESTIONING PATH TOOL

Text 1.2—"Terrorists or Freedom Fighters: What's the Difference?"

APPROACHING: *I determine my reading purposes and take note of key information about the text. I identify the LIPS domain(s) that will guide my initial reading.*

QUESTIONING: *I use Guiding Questions to help me investigate the text (from the Guiding Questions Handout).*

ANALYZING: *I question further to connect and analyze the details I find (from the Guiding Questions Handout).*

1. How might I summarize the main ideas of the text and the key supporting details?

2. How does the author's choice of words reveal his purposes and perspective?

3. What evidence supports the claims in the text, and what is left uncertain or unsupported?

DEEPENING: *I consider the questions of others.*

4. The author uses the word *perception* to explain the difference between a terrorist and freedom fighter. What does he mean by "perception" and how does this contrast with a "metaphysical difference"?

5. How does the author use two of the seven deadly sins (greed and envy) to characterize terrorists and freedom fighters? How does he use one of the sins to ultimately categorize those who carried out the attacks of 9/11?

EXTENDING: *I pose my own questions.*

6. What evidence does this text provide that builds my understanding of the issue of terrorism?

QUESTIONING PATH TOOL

Text 1.3— "Militant Extremists in the United States"

APPROACHING:
I determine my reading purposes and take note of key information about the text. I identify the LIPS domain(s) that will guide my initial reading.

QUESTIONING: *I use Guiding Questions to help me investigate the text (from the **Guiding Questions Handout**).*

ANALYZING: *I question further to connect and analyze the details I find (from the **Guiding Questions Handout**).*

1. How might I summarize the main ideas of the text and the key supporting details?

2. In what ways are ideas, events, and claims linked together in the text?

DEEPENING: *I consider the questions of others.*

3. The author uses the words *terrorist* and *extremist* throughout the article. What distinctions, if any, are drawn between the two concepts?

4. According to the article, what are some of the outcomes of this new era of facing terrorism?

EXTENDING: *I pose my own questions.*

5. What evidence does this text provide that builds my understanding of the issue of terrorism?

ODELL
EDUCATION

FORMING EVIDENCE-BASED CLAIMS TOOL (EBA)

Name _____

Text _____

A question I have about the text:

_____

SEARCHING FOR DETAILS

I read the text closely and mark words and phrases that help me answer my question.

SELECTING DETAILS

I select words or phrases from my search that I think are the most important for answering my question. I write the reference next to each detail.

Detail 1 (Ref.:)	Detail 2 (Ref.:)	Detail 3 (Ref.:)

ANALYZING DETAILS

I reread parts of the texts and think about the meaning of the details and what they tell me about my question. Then I compare the details and explain the connections I see among them.

What I think about detail 1:

What I think about detail 2:

What I think about detail 3:

CONNECTING DETAILS

I compare the details and explain the connections I see among them.

How I connect the details:

MAKING A CLAIM

I state a conclusion I have come to and can support with evidence from the text after reading it closely.

My claim about the text:

ODELL
EDUCATION

FORMING EVIDENCE-BASED CLAIMS TOOL (EBA)

Name _____

Text _ _ _ _ _ _ _ _ _ _ _ _ _ _ _ _ _ _

A question I have about the text:

SEARCHING FOR DETAILS

I read the text closely and mark words and phrases that help me answer my question.

SELECTING DETAILS

I select words or phrases from my search that I think are the most important for answering my question. I write the reference next to each detail.

Detail 1 (Ref.:)	Detail 2 (Ref.:)	Detail 3 (Ref.:)

ANALYZING DETAILS

I reread parts of the texts and think about the meaning of the details and what they tell me about my question. Then I compare the details and explain the connections I see among them.

What I think about detail 1:	What I think about detail 2:	What I think about detail 3:

CONNECTING DETAILS

I compare the details and explain the connections I see among them.

How I connect the details:

MAKING A CLAIM

I state a conclusion I have come to and can support with evidence from the text after reading it closely.

My claim about the text:

ODELL
EDUCATION

QUESTIONING PATH TOOL

Text 2.1—"Major Terrorism Cases: Past and Present"

APPROACHING:
I determine my reading purposes and take note of key information about the text. I identify the LIPS domain(s) that will guide my initial reading.

QUESTIONING: *I use Guiding Questions to help me investigate the text (from the **Guiding Questions Handout**).*

ANALYZING: *I question further to connect and analyze the details I find (from the **Guiding Questions Handout**).*

1. How might I summarize the main ideas of the text and the key supporting details?

2. How does the text's language influence my understanding of important ideas or themes?

DEEPENING: *I consider the questions of others.*

3. How does the FBI develop their point of view or perspective in their descriptions of the various terrorist attacks?

EXTENDING: *I pose my own questions.*

4. What evidence does this text provide that builds my understanding of the issue of terrorism?

QUESTIONING PATH TOOL

Text 2.2—"9/11: Timeline of Events"

APPROACHING: *I determine my reading purposes and take note of key information about the text. I identify the LIPS domain(s) that will guide my initial reading.*

QUESTIONING: *I use Guiding Questions to help me investigate the text (from the **Guiding Questions Handout**).*

ANALYZING: *I question further to connect and analyze the details I find (from the **Guiding Questions Handout**).*

1. How might I summarize the main ideas of the text and the key supporting details?

2. In what ways are ideas, events, and claims linked together in the text?

DEEPENING: *I consider the questions of others.*

3. How do the images and information presented in the time line fit the description of terrorism that you are familiar with or have read about in this unit so far?

EXTENDING: *I pose my own questions.*

4. What evidence does this text provide that builds my understanding of the issue of terrorism?

ODELL EDUCATION

QUESTIONING PATH TOOL

Text 2.3—"September 11 Attacks Timeline"

APPROACHING:
I determine my reading purposes and take note of key information about the text. I identify the LIPS domain(s) that will guide my initial reading.

QUESTIONING: *I use Guiding Questions to help me investigate the text (from the **Guiding Questions Handout**).*

ANALYZING: *I question further to connect and analyze the details I find (from the **Guiding Questions Handout**).*

1. How might I summarize the main ideas of the text and the key supporting details?

2. In what ways are ideas, events, and claims linked together in the text?

DEEPENING: *I consider the questions of others.*

3. How do the images and information presented in the time line fit the description of 9/11 or terrorism that you are familiar with or have read about in this unit so far?

EXTENDING: *I pose my own questions.*

4. What evidence does this text provide that builds my understanding of the issue of terrorism?

FORMING EVIDENCE-BASED CLAIMS TOOL (EBA)

Name _____

Text _____

A question I have about the text:

SEARCHING FOR DETAILS

I read the text closely and mark words and phrases that help me answer my question.

Detail 1 (Ref.:)	Detail 2 (Ref.:)	Detail 3 (Ref.:)

SELECTING DETAILS

I select words or phrases from my search that I think are the most important for answering my question. I write the reference next to each detail.

ANALYZING DETAILS

I reread parts of the texts and think about the meaning of the details and what they tell me about my question. Then I compare the details and explain the connections I see among them.

What I think about detail 1:	What I think about detail 2:	What I think about detail 3:

CONNECTING DETAILS

I compare the details and explain the connections I see among them.

How I connect the details:

MAKING A CLAIM

I state a conclusion I have come to and can support with evidence from the text after reading it closely.

My claim about the text:

ODELL
EDUCATION

FORMING EVIDENCE-BASED CLAIMS TOOL (EBA)

Name _____   Text _____

A question I have about the text:

SEARCHING FOR DETAILS — I read the text closely and mark words and phrases that help me answer my question.

SELECTING DETAILS
I select words or phrases from my search that I think are the most important for answering my question. I write the reference next to each detail.

Detail 1 (Ref.:)	Detail 2 (Ref.:)	Detail 3 (Ref.:)

ANALYZING DETAILS
I reread parts of the texts and think about the meaning of the details and what they tell me about my question. Then I compare the details and explain the connections I see among them.

What I think about detail 1:	What I think about detail 2:	What I think about detail 3:

CONNECTING DETAILS
I compare the details and explain the connections I see among them.

How I connect the details:

MAKING A CLAIM
I state a conclusion I have come to and can support with evidence from the text after reading it closely.

My claim about the text:

ODELL
EDUCATION

FORMING EVIDENCE-BASED CLAIMS TOOL (EBA)

Name _____

Text _____

A question I have about the text:

SEARCHING FOR DETAILS — I read the text closely and mark words and phrases that help me answer my question.

SELECTING DETAILS

I select words or phrases from my search that I think are the <u>most</u> important for answering my question. I write the <u>reference</u> next to each detail.

Detail 1 (Ref.:)	Detail 2 (Ref.:)	Detail 3 (Ref.:)

ANALYZING DETAILS

I reread parts of the texts and think about the meaning of the details and what they tell me about my question. Then I compare the details and explain <u>the connections</u> I see among them.

What I think about detail 1:	What I think about detail 2:	What I think about detail 3:

CONNECTING DETAILS

I compare the details and explain <u>the connections</u> I see among them.

How I connect the details:

MAKING A CLAIM

I state a conclusion I have come to and can support with <u>evidence</u> from the text after reading it closely.

My claim about the text:

ODELL EDUCATION

QUESTIONING PATH TOOL

Name: _____ **Text:** _____

APPROACHING: *I determine my reading purposes and take note of key information about the text. I identify the LIPS domain(s) that will guide my initial reading.*

Purpose:

Key information:

LIPS domain(s):

QUESTIONING: *I use Guiding Questions to help me investigate the text (from the **Guiding Questions Handout**).*

1.

2.

ANALYZING: *I question further to connect and analyze the details I find (from the **Guiding Questions Handout**).*

1.

2.

DEEPENING: *I consider the questions of others.*

1.

2.

3.

EXTENDING: *I pose my own questions.*

1.

2.

QUESTIONING PATH TOOL

Name: _____ **Text:** _____

APPROACHING: *I determine my reading purposes and take note of key information about the text. I identify the LIPS domain(s) that will guide my initial reading.*	Purpose: Key information: LIPS domain(s):
QUESTIONING: *I use Guiding Questions to help me investigate the text (from the **Guiding Questions Handout**).*	1. 2.
ANALYZING: *I question further to connect and analyze the details I find (from the **Guiding Questions Handout**).*	1. 2.
DEEPENING: *I consider the questions of others.*	1. 2. 3.
EXTENDING: *I pose my own questions.*	1. 2.

ODELL EDUCATION

ORGANIZING EVIDENCE-BASED CLAIMS TOOL (2 POINTS)

Name _ _ _ _ _ _ _ _ _ _ _ _ _ _ _ _ _

Text _ _ _ _ _ _ _ _ _ _ _ _

CLAIM:

Point 1

A Supporting Evidence

(Reference:)

B Supporting Evidence

(Reference:)

C Supporting Evidence

(Reference:)

D Supporting Evidence

(Reference:)

Point 2

A Supporting Evidence

(Reference:)

B Supporting Evidence

(Reference:)

C Supporting Evidence

(Reference:)

D Supporting Evidence

(Reference:)

ODELL
EDUCATION

ORGANIZING EVIDENCE-BASED CLAIMS TOOL (3 POINTS)

Name _ _ _ _ _ _ _ _ _ _ Text _ _ _ _ _ _ _ _ _ _ _ _ _ _

CLAIM:

Point 1

	Supporting Evidence
A	Supporting Evidence
(Reference:	)
B	Supporting Evidence
(Reference:	)
C	Supporting Evidence
(Reference:	)

Point 2

	Supporting Evidence
A	Supporting Evidence
(Reference:	)
B	Supporting Evidence
(Reference:	)
C	Supporting Evidence
(Reference:	)

Point 3

	Supporting Evidence
A	Supporting Evidence
(Reference:	)
B	Supporting Evidence
(Reference:	)
C	Supporting Evidence
(Reference:	)

ORGANIZING EVIDENCE-BASED CLAIMS TOOL (2 POINTS)

Name _ Text _ _ _ _ _ _ _ _ _ _ _ _ _ _ _ _

CLAIM:

Point 1

A Supporting Evidence	B Supporting Evidence
(Reference:)	(Reference:)
C Supporting Evidence	D Supporting Evidence
(Reference:)	(Reference:)

Point 2

A Supporting Evidence	B Supporting Evidence
(Reference:)	(Reference:)
C Supporting Evidence	D Supporting Evidence
(Reference:)	(Reference:)

ODELL EDUCATION

ORGANIZING EVIDENCE-BASED CLAIMS TOOL (3 POINTS)

Name _ _ _ _ _ _ _ _ _ _ _ _   Text _

CLAIM:

Point 1

A	Supporting Evidence

(Reference:)

B	Supporting Evidence

(Reference:)

C	Supporting Evidence

(Reference:)

Point 2

A	Supporting Evidence

(Reference:)

B	Supporting Evidence

(Reference:)

C	Supporting Evidence

(Reference:)

Point 3

A	Supporting Evidence

(Reference:)

B	Supporting Evidence

(Reference:)

C	Supporting Evidence

(Reference:)

PART 2

ANALYZING ARGUMENTS

Overview and Tools

"They [terrorists] are usually clever enough to cloak their motives by hijacking the popular will of an oppressed people, but their wrath is not appeased when they acquire what they say they want."

OBJECTIVE:	You will delineate and analyze different parts of arguments.

MATERIALS:
- *Guiding Questions Handout*
- *Forming EBC Tool*
- *Delineating Arguments Tool*

- *Model Arguments*
- *EBA Terms*

OPTIONAL:
- *Questioning Path Tool*

- *Organizing EBC Tool*

TEXTS:

Text Set 3: Political Cartoons
- *3.1 "Political Cartoons: The Human Aspect of Modern Conflict," College of Education at The University of Texas*

Text Set 4: Seminal Arguments
- *4.1 "Authorization for Use of Military Force," Public Law 107—40*
- *4.2 George W. Bush's Address to the Nation on September 11, 2001 (text), President Bush*
- *4.2 "George W. Bush's Address to the Nation on September 11, 2001" (video), President Bush*
- *4.3 "A Place of Peace: For a 9/11 Victim's Widow, Revenge Is Not the Answer," Lauren Frohne*

Text Set 5: Additional Arguments
- *5.1 Our War on Terrorism, Howard Zinn*
- *5.2 "Obama's Speech on Drone Policy," President Obama*
- *5.3 Remarks by President Obama on the death of Osama bin Laden, President Obama*
- *5.4 "Why Drones Work: The Case for Washington's Weapon of Choice," Daniel L. Byman*

ACTIVITIES

1. UNDERSTANDING ARGUMENTATIVE POSITION
Your teacher uses the unit's issue to discuss what an argumentative position is.

2. IDENTIFYING ELEMENTS OF AN ARGUMENT
Your teacher introduces and the class explores the different parts of argumentation using model arguments.

3. DELINEATING ARGUMENTS
In teams, you read and delineate arguments and write an evidence-based claim about one author's argument.

4. UNDERSTANDING PERSPECTIVE
Your teacher discusses what perspective is and how it relates to argumentation.

5. DELINEATING AND COMPARING ARGUMENTS
You analyze and compare perspectives in argumentative texts.

6. DELINEATING ADDITIONAL ARGUMENTS
As needed, you read and analyze more arguments related to the unit's issue.

7. WRITING TO ANALYZE ARGUMENTS
You write a short essay analyzing an argument.

ODELL
EDUCATION

QUESTIONING PATH TOOL

Name: _____ **Text:** _____

APPROACHING: *I determine my reading purposes and take note of key information about the text. I identify the LIPS domain(s) that will guide my initial reading.*	Purpose: Key information: LIPS domain(s):

QUESTIONING: *I use Guiding Questions to help me investigate the text (from the* **Guiding Questions Handout***).*	1. 2.

ANALYZING: *I question further to connect and analyze the details I find (from the* **Guiding Questions Handout***).*	1. 2.

DEEPENING: *I consider the questions of others.*	1. 2. 3.

EXTENDING: *I pose my own questions.*	1. 2.

QUESTIONING PATH TOOL

Name: _____ **Text:** _____

APPROACHING: *I determine my reading purposes and take note of key information about the text. I identify the LIPS domain(s) that will guide my initial reading.*	Purpose: Key information: LIPS domain(s):

QUESTIONING: *I use Guiding Questions to help me investigate the text (from the **Guiding Questions Handout**).*

1.

2.

ANALYZING: *I question further to connect and analyze the details I find (from the **Guiding Questions Handout**).*

1.

2.

DEEPENING: *I consider the questions of others.*

1.

2.

3.

EXTENDING: *I pose my own questions.*

1.

2.

ODELL EDUCATION

DELINEATING ARGUMENTS TOOL

Name ---------------- **Topic** ------------------

ISSUE

PERSPECTIVE

POSITION

PREMISE/CLAIM 1
Supporting evidence:

PREMISE/CLAIM 2
Supporting evidence:

PREMISE/CLAIM 3
Supporting evidence:

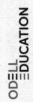

ODELL EDUCATION

QUESTIONING PATH TOOL

Text 4.1—"Authorization for Use of Military Force," 107th Congress

APPROACHING:
I determine my reading purposes and take note of key information about the text. I identify the LIPS domain(s) that will guide my initial reading.

QUESTIONING: *I use Guiding Questions to help me investigate the text (from the **Guiding Questions Handout**).*

ANALYZING: *I question further to connect and analyze the details I find (from the **Guiding Questions Handout**).*

1. What evidence supports the claims in the text, and what is left uncertain or unsupported?

2. How does the author's choice of words reveal his purposes and perspective?

3. In what ways are ideas, events, and claims linked together in the text?

DEEPENING: *I consider the questions of others.*

4. Which sentences or paragraphs best communicate the position of 107th Congress?

5. What powers does the law give to President Bush?

6. What reasons does the Congress provide for giving President Bush authorization to use the United States Armed Forces?

EXTENDING: *I pose my own questions.*

7. What argumentative premises and evidence does this text provide that influence your understanding of or perspective on the issue and problem of terrorism?

ODELL EDUCATION

QUESTIONING PATH TOOL

Text 4.2—"George W. Bush's Address to the Nation on September 11, 2001"

APPROACHING: *I determine my reading purposes and take note of key information about the text. I identify the LIPS domain(s) that will guide my initial reading.*

QUESTIONING: *I use Guiding Questions to help me investigate the text (from the Guiding Questions Handout).*

ANALYZING: *I question further to connect and analyze the details I find (from the Guiding Questions Handout).*

1. How does the author's perspective influence his presentation of ideas, themes, or arguments?

2. How does the author's choice of words reveal his purposes and perspective?

DEEPENING: *I consider the questions of others.*

3. How does President Bush use rhetoric (such as religious language and metaphors) in his speech? How does his rhetoric further develop his purpose?

4. President Bush establishes a series of claims in favor of his position. How does one of these claims relate to his overall argument, and what specific evidence does he provide to support the claim?

EXTENDING: *I pose my own questions.*

5. What argumentative premises and evidence does this text provide that influence your understanding of or perspective on the issue and problem of terrorism?

QUESTIONING PATH TOOL

Text 4.3—"A Place of Peace: For a 9/11 Victim's Widow, Revenge Is Not the Answer"

APPROACHING: *I determine my reading purposes and take note of key information about the text. I identify the LIPS domain(s) that will guide my initial reading.*

QUESTIONING: *I use Guiding Questions to help me investigate the text (from the **Guiding Questions Handout**).*

ANALYZING: *I question further to connect and analyze the details I find (from the **Guiding Questions Handout**).*

1. How does the author's choice of words reveal her purposes and perspective?

2. How does the author's perspective influence her presentation of ideas, themes, or arguments?

DEEPENING: *I consider the questions of others.*

3. What is Leblanc's perspective on the response to the attacks of 9/11? How does her perspective help shape her position? How does her perspective differ from that of President Bush's?

4. How does Leblanc use language to convey her position?

5. Leblanc talks about a "frightening patriotism" that followed 9/11. How does she describe this idea? How does this sentiment fit into her overall argument?

EXTENDING: *I pose my own questions.*

6. What argumentative premises and evidence does this text provide that influence your understanding of or perspective on the issue and problem of terrorism?

ODELL EDUCATION

DELINEATING ARGUMENTS TOOL

Name _____   Topic _____

ISSUE	

PERSPECTIVE	

POSITION	

PREMISE/CLAIM 1
Supporting evidence:

PREMISE/CLAIM 2
Supporting evidence:

PREMISE/CLAIM 3
Supporting evidence:

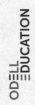
ODELL EDUCATION

ORGANIZING EVIDENCE-BASED CLAIMS TOOL (2 POINTS)

Name _____   Text _____

CLAIM:

Point 1

A Supporting Evidence	B Supporting Evidence
(Reference:)	(Reference:)
C Supporting Evidence	D Supporting Evidence
(Reference:)	(Reference:)

Point 2

A Supporting Evidence	B Supporting Evidence
(Reference:)	(Reference:)
C Supporting Evidence	D Supporting Evidence
(Reference:)	(Reference:)

ORGANIZING EVIDENCE-BASED CLAIMS TOOL (3 POINTS)

Name _ _ _ _ _ _ _ _ _ _ _ _ Text _ _ _ _ _ _ _ _ _ _ _ _

CLAIM:

Point 1

Point 2

Point 3

A	Supporting Evidence	A	Supporting Evidence	A	Supporting Evidence
(Reference:	)	(Reference:	)	(Reference:	)
B	Supporting Evidence	B	Supporting Evidence	B	Supporting Evidence
(Reference:	)	(Reference:	)	(Reference:	)
C	Supporting Evidence	C	Supporting Evidence	C	Supporting Evidence
(Reference:	)	(Reference:	)	(Reference:	)

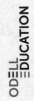

PART 3

EVALUATING ARGUMENTS AND DEVELOPING A POSITION

Overview and Tools

"Terrorist attacks can shake the foundations of our biggest buildings, but they cannot touch the foundation of America."

OBJECTIVE:	You will evaluate arguments, determine which arguments you find most convincing, and synthesize what you have learned so far to establish your own position.

MATERIALS:
- *Forming EBC Tool*
- *Delineating Arguments Tool*
- *Organizing EBC Tool*
- *Student EBA Literacy Skills and Academic Habits Checklist*
- *Evaluating Arguments Tool*
- *EBA Terms*

TEXT SET:

Text Set 3: Political Cartoons
- *3.1 "Political Cartoons: The Human Aspect of Modern Conflict", College of Education at The University of Texas*

Text Set 4: Seminal Arguments
- *4.1 "Authorization for Use of Military Force", Public Law 107—40*
- *4.2 George W. Bush's Address to the Nation on September 11, 2001 (text), President Bush*
- *4.2 "George W. Bush's Address to the Nation on September 11, 2001" (video), President Bush*
- *4.3 "A Place of Peace: For a 9/11 Victim's Widow, Revenge Is Not the Answer", Lauren Frohne*

Text Set 5: Additional Arguments
- *5.1 Our War on Terrorism, Howard Zinn*
- *5.2 "Obama's Speech on Drone Policy", President Obama*
- *5.3 Remarks by President Obama on the death of Osama bin Laden, President Obama*
- *5.4 "Why Drones Work: The Case for Washington's Weapon of Choice", Daniel L. Byman*

ACTIVITIES

1. EVALUATING ARGUMENTS
You review and evaluate arguments based on your own developing perspective on the issue.

2. DEVELOPING A PERSPECTIVE AND POSITION
You synthesize what you have learned about the issue and arguments, and work on developing your perspective and position on the issue.

3. DEEPENING UNDERSTANDING
If needed, you research more to help develop and support your position.

ODELL
EDUCATION

4. USING OTHERS' ARGUMENTS TO SUPPORT A POSITION

You identify an argument that supports your position and write an evidence-based claim about why the argument is convincing or makes sense to you.

5. RESPONDING TO OPPOSING ARGUMENTS

You identify an argument that is against your position and write an evidence-based claim that:

⇒ recognizes the argument's position

⇒ points out its limitations

⇒ refutes its claims

⇒ or refutes it as invalid, illogical, or unsupported.

EVALUATING ARGUMENTS TOOL

As you read and delineate the argument, think about each of the **elements** and their **guiding evaluation questions**. Rate each element as

– a **questionable** part or weakness of the argument ✔ a reasonable or **acceptable** part of the argument + a **strength** of the argument

ELEMENTS	EVALUATING AN ARGUMENT: GUIDING QUESTIONS	?	✔	+	TEXT-BASED OBSERVATIONS
Issue	• How clearly is the issue presented and explained? • How accurate and current is the explanation of the issue?				
Perspective	• What is the author's relationship to the issue? What is the purpose for the argument? • What is the author's viewpoint or attitude about the issue? How reasonable is this perspective?				
Credibility and Bias	• What are the author's background and credentials relative to the issue? • Does the author have a bias that affect the argument's perspective or interferes with its reasoning? • Does the author use inflammatory language or make highly biased claims?				
Position/ Thesis	• How clearly is the author's position presented and explained? • How well is the position or thesis connected to the claims and evidence of the argument?				
Claims	• How clearly are the argument's claims explained and connected to the position? • Are the claims supported with evidence? • How well are the claims linked together as the premises of the argument?				
Evidence	• Does the supporting evidence come from a range of credible sources? Is it believable? • Is there enough evidence to make the argument convincing?				
Reasoning and Logic	• Are the claims and premises clearly and consistently connected to the position? • Are the connections among the position, premises, evidence, and conclusions of the argument clear and logical?				
Conclusions	• How logical and reasonable are the conclusions drawn by the author? • How well do the the argument's conclusions or suggestions address the issue and align with the position?				
Convincing Argument	• How do the author's overall perspective and position on the issue compare with others? With my own? • Does the argument make sense to me? Do I agree with its claims? Am I convinced?				
Comments:					

EVALUATING ARGUMENTS TOOL

As you read and delineate the argument, think about each of the **elements** and their **guiding evaluation questions**. Rate each element as
– a **questionable** part or weakness of the argument   ✔ a reasonable or **acceptable** part of the argument   + a **strength** of the argument

ELEMENTS	EVALUATING AN ARGUMENT: GUIDING QUESTIONS	?	✔	+	TEXT-BASED OBSERVATIONS
Issue	• How clearly is the issue presented and explained? • How accurate and current is the explanation of the issue?				
Perspective	• What is the author's relationship to the issue? What is the purpose for the argument? • What is the author's viewpoint or attitude about the issue? How reasonable is this perspective?				
Credibility and Bias	• What are the author's background and credentials relative to the issue? • Does the author have a bias that affect the argument's perspective or interferes with its reasoning? • Does the author use inflammatory language or make highly biased claims?				
Position/ Thesis	• How clearly is the author's position presented and explained? • How well is the position or thesis connected to the claims and evidence of the argument?				
Claims	• How clearly are the argument's claims explained and connected to the position? • Are the claims supported with evidence? • How well are the claims linked together as the premises of the argument?				
Evidence	• Does the supporting evidence come from a range of credible sources? Is it believable? • Is there enough evidence to make the argument convincing?				
Reasoning and Logic	• Are the cliams and premises clearly and consistently connected to the position? • Are the connections among the position, premises, evidence, and conclusions of the argument clear and logical?				
Conclusions	• How logical and reasonable are the conclusions drawn by the author? • How well do the the argument's conclusions or suggestions address the issue and align with the position?				
Convincing Argument	• How do the author's overall perspective and position on the issue compare with others? With my own? • Does the argument make sense to me? Do I agree with its claims? Am I convinced?				

Comments:

ODELL EDUCATION

EVALUATING ARGUMENTS TOOL

As you read and delineate the argument, think about each of the **elements** and their **guiding evaluation questions**. Rate each element as

− a **questionable** part or weakness of the argument ✔ a reasonable or **acceptable** part of the argument + a **strength** of the argument

ELEMENTS	EVALUATING AN ARGUMENT: GUIDING QUESTIONS	?	✔	+	TEXT-BASED OBSERVATIONS
Issue	• How clearly is the issue presented and explained? • How accurate and current is the explanation of the issue?				
Perspective	• What is the author's relationship to the issue? What is the purpose for the argument? • What is the author's viewpoint or attitude about the issue? How reasonable is this perspective?				
Credibility and Bias	• What are the author's background and credentials relative to the issue? • Does the author have a bias that affect the argument's perspective or interferes with its reasoning? • Does the author use inflammatory language or make highly biased claims?				
Position/ Thesis	• How clearly is the author's position presented and explained? • How well is the position or thesis connected to the claims and evidence of the argument?				
Claims	• How clearly are the argument's claims explained and connected to the position? • Are the claims supported with evidence? • How well are the claims linked together as the premises of the argument?				
Evidence	• Does the supporting evidence come from a range of credible sources? Is it believable? • Is there enough evidence to make the argument convincing?				
Reasoning and Logic	• Are the cliams and premises clearly and consistently connected to the position? • Are the connections among the position, premises, evidence, and conclusions of the argument clear and logical?				
Conclusions	• How logical and reasonable are the conclusions drawn by the author? • How well do the the argument's conclusions or suggestions address the issue and align with the position?				
Convincing Argument	• How do the author's overall perspective and position on the issue compare with others? With my own? • Does the argument make sense to me? Do I agree with its claims? Am I convinced?				

Comments:

ORGANIZING EVIDENCE-BASED CLAIMS TOOL (2 POINTS)

Name _ _ _ _ _ _ _ _ _ _ _ _ _ _ _ _ _ _   Text _

CLAIM:

Point 1

A	Supporting Evidence	B	Supporting Evidence

(Reference:)   (Reference:)

C	Supporting Evidence	D	Supporting Evidence

(Reference:)   (Reference:)

Point 2

A	Supporting Evidence	B	Supporting Evidence

(Reference:)   (Reference:)

C	Supporting Evidence	D	Supporting Evidence

(Reference:)   (Reference:)

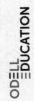

ORGANIZING EVIDENCE-BASED CLAIMS TOOL (3 POINTS)

Name _ _ _ _ _ _ _ _ _ _ _ _ _ Text _ _ _ _ _ _ _ _ _ _ _ _ _ _ _

CLAIM:

Point 1

A   Supporting Evidence

(Reference:)

B   Supporting Evidence

(Reference:)

C   Supporting Evidence

(Reference:)

Point 2

A   Supporting Evidence

(Reference:)

B   Supporting Evidence

(Reference:)

C   Supporting Evidence

(Reference:)

Point 3

A   Supporting Evidence

(Reference:)

B   Supporting Evidence

(Reference:)

C   Supporting Evidence

(Reference:)

ODELL EDUCATION

DELINEATING ARGUMENTS TOOL

Name ----------------------------- **Topic** -----------------------------

ISSUE	

PERSPECTIVE	

POSITION	

PREMISE/CLAIM 1	
Supporting evidence:	

PREMISE/CLAIM 2	
Supporting evidence:	

PREMISE/CLAIM 3	
Supporting evidence:	

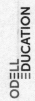

DELINEATING ARGUMENTS TOOL

Name _____

Topic _____

ISSUE	

PERSPECTIVE	

POSITION	

PREMISE/CLAIM 1	
	Supporting evidence:

PREMISE/CLAIM 2	
	Supporting evidence:

PREMISE/CLAIM 3	
	Supporting evidence:

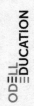
ODELL EDUCATION

EVALUATING ARGUMENTS TOOL

As you read and delineate the argument, think about each of the **elements** and their **guiding evaluation questions.** Rate each element as

– **a questionable** part or weakness of the argument ✔ a reasonable or **acceptable** part of the argument + **a strength** of the argument

ELEMENTS	EVALUATING AN ARGUMENT: GUIDING QUESTIONS	?	✔	+	TEXT-BASED OBSERVATIONS
Issue	• How clearly is the issue presented and explained? • How accurate and current is the explanation of the issue?				
Perspective	• What is the author's relationship to the issue? What is the purpose for the argument? • What is the author's viewpoint or attitude about the issue? How reasonable is this perspective?				
Credibility and Bias	• What are the author's background and credentials relative to the issue? • Does the author have a bias that affect the argument's perspective or interferes with its reasoning? • Does the author use inflammatory language or make highly biased claims?				
Position/ Thesis	• How clearly is the author's position presented and explained? • How well is the position or thesis connected to the claims and evidence of the argument?				
Claims	• How clearly are the argument's claims explained and connected to the position? • Are the claims supported with evidence? • How well are the claims linked together as the premises of the argument?				
Evidence	• Does the supporting evidence come from a range of credible sources? Is it believable? • Is there enough evidence to make the argument convincing?				
Reasoning and Logic	• Are the claims and premises clearly and consistently connected to the position? • Are the connections among the position, premises, evidence, and conclusions of the argument clear and logical?				
Conclusions	• How logical and reasonable are the conclusions drawn by the author? • How well do the the argument's conclusions or suggestions address the issue and align with the position?				
Convincing Argument	• How do the author's overall perspective and position on the issue compare with others? With my own? • Does the argument make sense to me? Do I agree with its claims? Am I convinced?				
Comments:					

PART 4

ORGANIZING AN EVIDENCE-BASED ARGUMENT

Overview and Tools

"There's no doubt that al Qaeda will continue to pursue attacks against us. We must—and we will—remain vigilant at home and abroad."

OBJECTIVE: You will write claims and sequence them to create a coherent, logical argument.

MATERIALS:
- *Guiding Questions Handout*
- *Forming EBC Tool*
- *Organizing EBC Tool*
- *Delineating Arguments Tool*
- *EBA Terms*

 ACTIVITIES

1. IDENTIFYING SUPPORTING EVIDENCE
You review your notes, tools, and previously written claims to figure out what you will use as evidence to develop and support your position.

2. DEVELOPING AND SEQUENCING CLAIMS AS PREMISES OF THE ARGUMENT
You review the claims you have previously written (and maybe write new claims) to figure out how you will use them as premises to develop your argument. You think about a potential sequence for your claims.

3. ORGANIZING EVIDENCE TO SUPPORT CLAIMS
You list and sequence your claims. You then organize and cite sources for the evidence you will use to explain and support each claim.

4. REVIEWING A PLAN FOR WRITING AN ARGUMENT
You review and revise your plans to make sure that they are clear, strategically sequenced, well reasoned, and supported by enough evidence.

ORGANIZING EVIDENCE-BASED CLAIMS TOOL (2 POINTS)

Name _ _ _ _ _ _ _ _ _ _ Text _ _ _ _ _ _ _ _ _ _

CLAIM:

Point 1

A	Supporting Evidence	B	Supporting Evidence
(Reference:)		(Reference:)	

C	Supporting Evidence	D	Supporting Evidence
(Reference:)		(Reference:)	

Point 2

A	Supporting Evidence	B	Supporting Evidence
(Reference:)		(Reference:)	

C	Supporting Evidence	D	Supporting Evidence
(Reference:)		(Reference:)	

ODELL EDUCATION

ORGANIZING EVIDENCE-BASED CLAIMS TOOL (3 POINTS)

Name _ _ _ _ _ _ _ _ _ _ _ _ _ _ _ _ _ _ _ Text _ _ _ _ _ _ _ _ _ _ _ _ _ _

CLAIM:

Point 1			Point 2		Point 3	
A	Supporting Evidence		A	Supporting Evidence	A	Supporting Evidence
(Reference: _____)			(Reference: _____)		(Reference: _____)	
B	Supporting Evidence		B	Supporting Evidence	B	Supporting Evidence
(Reference: _____)			(Reference: _____)		(Reference: _____)	
C	Supporting Evidence		C	Supporting Evidence	C	Supporting Evidence
(Reference: _____)			(Reference: _____)		(Reference: _____)	

DELINEATING ARGUMENTS TOOL

Name _____ Topic _____

ISSUE	

PERSPECTIVE	

POSITION	

PREMISE/CLAIM 1	PREMISE/CLAIM 2	PREMISE/CLAIM 3
Supporting evidence:	Supporting evidence:	Supporting evidence:

PART 5

DEVELOPING WRITING THROUGH A COLLABORATIVE PROCESS

Overview and Tools

"For students, writing is a key means of asserting and defending claims, showing what they know about a subject, and conveying what they have experienced, imagined, thought, and felt."

CCSS ELA Literacy Standards, p. 41

OBJECTIVE:	You will work with your classmates to improve your writing and write an argumentative essay.

MATERIALS:
- *Student EBA Literacy Skills and Academic Habits Checklist*
- *Connecting Ideas Handout*
- *Organizing EBC Tool*
- *EBA Terms*

ACTIVITIES

1. STRENGTHENING WRITING COLLABORATIVELY: PRINCIPLES AND PROCESSES
You learn and practice how to use criteria and Guiding Questions while working with your classmates to improve your writing and begin drafting your essay.

2. FOCUS ON CONTENT: INFORMATION AND IDEAS
You write, discuss, and revise with a focus on expressing your overall ideas with necessary information.

3. FOCUS ON ORGANIZATION: UNITY, COHERENCE, AND LOGICAL SEQUENCE
You write, discuss, and revise with a focus on the unity, coherence, and logic of your initial draft.

4. FOCUS ON SUPPORT: INTEGRATING AND CITING EVIDENCE
You write, discuss, and revise with a focus on your selection and use of evidence.

5. ADDITIONAL ROUNDS OF FOCUSED REVIEW AND REVISION
You write, discuss, and revise with a focus on additional issues of clarity, grammar, or publication, as determined by your teacher.

ORGANIZING EVIDENCE-BASED CLAIMS TOOL (2 POINTS)

Name _____   Text _ _ _ _ _ _ _ _ _ _ _ _ _ _

CLAIM:

Point 1

A	Supporting Evidence	B	Supporting Evidence

(Reference:)

C	Supporting Evidence	D	Supporting Evidence

(Reference:)

Point 2

A	Supporting Evidence	B	Supporting Evidence

(Reference:)

C	Supporting Evidence	D	Supporting Evidence

(Reference:)

ODELL EDUCATION

ORGANIZING EVIDENCE-BASED CLAIMS TOOL (3 POINTS)

Name _____   Text _____

CLAIM:

Point 1

A	Supporting Evidence

(Reference:)

B	Supporting Evidence

(Reference:)

C	Supporting Evidence

(Reference:)

Point 2

A	Supporting Evidence

(Reference:)

B	Supporting Evidence

(Reference:)

C	Supporting Evidence

(Reference:)

Point 3

A	Supporting Evidence

(Reference:)

B	Supporting Evidence

(Reference:)

C	Supporting Evidence

(Reference:)

ODELL
EDUCATION

DELINEATING ARGUMENTS TOOL

Name _____ Topic _____

ISSUE	

PERSPECTIVE	

POSITION	

PREMISE/CLAIM 1	PREMISE/CLAIM 2	PREMISE/CLAIM 3
Supporting evidence:	**Supporting evidence:**	**Supporting evidence:**

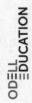

BUILDING EVIDENCE-BASED ARGUMENTS LITERACY SKILLS AND ACADEMIC HABITS RUBRIC

Name _____ **Text** _____

NE: Not enough evidence to make a rating

1—**Emerging:** needs improvement

2—**Developing:** shows progress

3—**Becoming Proficient:** demonstrates skills

4—**Excelling:** exceeds expectations

+—**Growth:** evidence of growth within the unit or task

I. READING SKILLS CRITERIA	NE	1	2	3	4	+
1. **Recognizes Perspective:** Uses textual details to recognize authors' perspectives on a topic						
2. **Delineates Argumentation:** Identifies and analyzes the components and accuracy of claims, evidence, and reasoning in explanations and arguments						
3. **Evaluates Information:** Assesses the relevance and credibility of information, ideas, evidence, and logic presented in texts						
II. DEVELOPING AN EVIDENCE-BASED POSITION: SKILLS AND HABITS CRITERIA	NE	1	2	3	4	+
1. **Remains Open:** Adopts a stance of inquiry—asking questions to learn more—rather than arguing for entrenched positions						
2. **Qualifies Views:** Modifies and further justifies ideas in response to thinking from others						
3. **Revises:** Rethinks and refines work based on teacher-, peer-, and self-review processes						
4. **Reflects Critically:** Uses literacy terminology and concepts to reflect on, discuss, and evaluate personal and peer literacy development						
III. EVIDENCE-BASED WRITING CRITERIA	NE	1	2	3	4	+
1. **Forms Claims:** Establishes and presents a clear and defensible position that is supported by a series of valid premises and set in the context of the topic						
2. **Uses Evidence:** Presents a comprehensive view of the issue by providing textual evidence to support claims and using sufficient and accurate quotations, paraphrases, and references						
3. **Uses Language:** Selects and combines words that precisely communicate ideas, generate appropriate tone, and evoke intended responses from an audience						

ODELL EDUCATION

EBA SKILLS AND HABITS RUBRIC (Continued)

	NE	1	2	3	4	+
4. **Uses Logic:** Establishes and supports a position through a logical sequence of related premises and supporting evidence						
5. **Organizes Ideas:** Sequences sentences and paragraphs to establish a coherent, logical, and unified argument						
6. **Uses Conventions:** Uses effective sentence structure, grammar, punctuation, and spelling to express ideas and achieve writing purposes						
7. **Publishes:** Uses effective formatting and citations to present ideas						
IV. FINAL ASSIGNMENT CRITERIA	**NE**	**1**	**2**	**3**	**4**	**+**
1. Presents a convincing argument that stems from an understanding of the issue, a reasoned perspective, and a clear, defensible position						
2. Organizes a set of evidence-based claims in a logical sequence that explains and supports the thesis of the argument						
3. Uses and cites relevant and credible (trustworthy) evidence to support all claims, counterarguments, and the overall position						
4. Revises essay based on teacher and peer feedback						
SUMMARY EVALUATION		**1**	**2**	**3**	**4**	

Comments:

1. Explanation of ratings—**evidence** found (or not found) in the work:

2. Strengths and **areas of growth** observed in the work:

3. Areas for improvement in future work:

BUILDING EVIDENCE-BASED ARGUMENTS LITERACY SKILLS AND ACADEMIC HABITS CHECKLIST

	EVIDENCE-BASED ARGUMENTATION LITERACY SKILLS AND ACADEMIC HABITS	✔	EVIDENCE Demonstrating the SKILLS AND HABITS
READING	1. **Recognizing Perspective:** Identifies and explains the author's view of the text's topic		
	2. **Evaluating Information:** Assesses the relevance and credibility of information in texts		
	3. **Delineating Argumentation:** Identifies and analyzes the claims, evidence, and reasoning in arguments		
ACADEMIC HABITS	4. **Remaining Open:** Asks questions of others rather than arguing for a personal idea or opinion		
	5. **Qualifying Views:** Explains and changes ideas in response to thinking from others		
	6. **Revising:** Rethinks ideas and refines work based on feedback from others		
	7. **Reflecting Critically:** Uses literacy concepts to discuss and evaluate personal and peer learning		
WRITING SKILLS	8. **Forming Claims:** States a meaningful position that is well supported by evidence from texts		
	9. **Using Evidence:** Uses well-chosen details from texts to explain and support claims; accurately paraphrases or quotes		
	10. **Using Logic:** Supports a position through a logical sequence of related claims, premises, and supporting evidence		
	11. **Organizing Ideas:** Organizes claims, supporting ideas, and evidence in a logical order		
	12. **Using Language:** Writes clearly so others can understand claims and ideas		
	13. **Using Conventions:** Correctly uses sentence elements, punctuation, and spelling to produce clear writing		
	14. **Publishing:** Correctly uses, formats, and cites textual evidence to support claims		
	General comments:		

ODELL EDUCATION

DELINEATING ARGUMENTS: CASE STUDY

Friending a Teacher

Mr. Higgins is a twenty-three-year-old social studies teacher at Thunder Ridge Middle School. Over the weekend, he received a friend request on Facebook from Derek, who is one of his students. Derek is a B student who is generally quiet in class. Mr. Higgins has never had a problem with Derek, but he also hasn't interacted with Derek much, either inside or out of class. In order to keep his school life separate from his personal life, Mr. Higgins decided

when he took the job at Thunder Ridge that he would not accept a friend request from any of his students. When Derek's parents hear that Mr. Higgins did not accept Derek's request, they scheduled a meeting with Mr. Higgins to demand that he accept the request. They are worried that Mr. Higgins will damage Derek's confidence in school if he continues to reject their son's request.

DEREK

Derek considers himself a technically savvy student. He thinks that social media are fascinating and he is an avid user of Facebook. One of the reasons he likes Facebook is that it gives teachers and students a way to get to know one another outside of class. Derek sent the request to Mr. Higgins in order to include Facebook as part of the learning environment at Thunder Ridge.

At the meeting, Derek explains why he thinks Mr. Higgins should accept his request:

Look, Mr. Higgins. Everyone is on Facebook these days. You should know this because you have a profile and even with your privacy settings I can tell you use it a lot. If you are using Facebook, you should be a good Facebook citizen and accept requests from people. It's just part of the deal. And it's not a big deal. There's no harm in being friends with students. If you post something, you're okay sharing it, so why not let me learn a bit more about you? I mean, I'll find out anyway when I Google you, so it's not like there are a lot of secrets to find. What really makes me mad about rejecting my friend request is that you aren't treating me fairly. I never do anything wrong in class, so there is no reason to reject my request.

MR. HIGGINS

Mr. Higgins is a popular teacher at Thunder Ridge. He is well known for creating new ways to bring technology to the classroom. Most of the students at Thunder

Ridge follow him on Twitter. He doesn't hold Derek's request against him, but Mr. Higgins decided before he started his job that accepting friend requests from any student wouldn't be a good idea.

Mr. Higgins explains his decision to Derek:

Even though online platforms are changing the way students and teachers interact, there need to be boundaries. Facebook is a personal space and if I accept your request, I am worried that you'll forget that I am your teacher. There is a further problem to keep in mind. If I accept your request, I am obligated to accept a request from any student. Even if I had a guarantee that you would handle being friends on Facebook appropriately, I cannot be sure about this with everyone, so I don't want to be in a position in which others can accuse me of playing favorites based on what friend requests I accept. And I'd like to ask you, Derek, if you are friends with your parents on Facebook? I'm guessing that you are probably like most of your classmates who don't want to be friends with their parents because they want to keep their social lives private. My Facebook account is no different. It is a place for me to have a life that is separate from my job as your teacher.

OTHER PERSPECTIVES

Derek's parents, Derek's classmates, Mr. Higgins's colleagues

DELINEATING ARGUMENTS: CASE STUDY

School Conflict

ISSUE

Recently, a student came to school wearing a T-shirt with a provocative graphic on it and what some people viewed as misogynistic lyrics from a popular rap artist. A teacher who was offended by the shirt referred the student to the office, where the assistant principal told him to go home, change the shirt, and never wear it to school again. When the student refused to do so, he was suspended for insubordination. In protest, a large group of sympathetic students produced and wore T-shirts that read, "Life's a b——…… when you lose your right to free speech."

When asked to stop wearing the shirts, these students also refused to do so. Faced with the dilemma of what to do, the school administration is proposing changes to school policy and a dress code that prohibits clothing with any words, logos, graphics, or designer labels. Those opposed to the code claim that it essentially requires students to wear a school "uniform."

At a school board meeting, students and staff present arguments about the proposed policy change.

PERSPECTIVES

HIGH SCHOOL STUDENT

The junior class president, a male, has been one of the leaders of the T-shirt protest group. He sees the issue as a symbolic one and is opposed to policies and actions that deny students' rights. His parents, among the more affluent families in the school district, are active members of the American Civil Liberties Union (ACLU), and supported the production of the protesters' T-shirts.

He presents the following argument:

Any restriction on student dress violates students' basic rights. Once a student clothing choice is prohibited because it is considered "offensive," a precedent is set for limiting free speech in all areas of school life.

Americans, including American high school students, are guaranteed the right to free speech by the US Constitution. The First Amendment in the Bill of Rights states, "Congress shall make no law… abridging the freedom of speech…"

Public schools are agencies of government, and therefore are expected to follow the law as established in the Constitution and Bill of Rights. The US Supreme Court has upheld the free speech rights of students. In a case similar to this one, Justice Abe Fortas wrote, "First Amendment rights, applied in light of the special characteristics of the school environment, are available to teachers and students…"

The school's argument to support banning the shirt was flawed. School officials said that the lyrics on the shirt were "offensive" and therefore "disruptive" to the school environment. As our protest T-shirts showed, however, there are many meanings for the word in question, most of which are not offensive to anyone. It is defined in the dictionary as meaning: "a female dog," "a difficult situation," or "a querulous, nagging complaint."

The protesters' T-shirts, which they were asked to remove, used the word to represent the "difficult situation" that will result if students' rights to free speech are not respected. The school administration has shown in a number of specific instances that it is more concerned with controlling student behavior than guaranteeing student rights. An example would be last spring in the student government elections, when posters making fun of some school rules were taken down.

In conclusion, restrictions on student dress violate students' basic rights. The school overstepped its bounds when it used an interpretation of the words on the shirt to argue that the shirt was offensive. The school's proposal of a more restrictive dress code will create a "difficult situation" in which students' rights may continue to be lost. Therefore, the wearing of such shirts should be allowed and the dress code should remain nonrestrictive so that we don't set a precedent that limits free speech in all areas of school life.

School Conflict (Continued)

HIGH SCHOOL PRINCIPAL

The high school principal, a woman, is concerned about disruptions in school resulting from the wearing of clothing that may be offensive to some students and staff members. Although she was personally offended by the words on the T-shirt, she has also tried to listen to and reason with the protesting students, to little avail. Regarding student dress in general, she is concerned that many of her students lack the money to afford the designer label clothing worn by some of her more affluent students and the class distinctions that result based mostly on student dress.

She presents the following argument:

The offensive T-shirt, and the student's refusal to remove it, put school administrators in a difficult, no-win situation. When the assistant principal asked the student to go home and change his shirt, he was making a "reasonable request," as defined in the school's Code of Conduct. When the student refused, the administrator had no choice but to suspend him for "insubordination."

The school has over 1,500 students and 100 staff members. Many staff members and a number of female students found the shirt's message and graphic to be offensive. In situations such as this one, the school administration must ensure that the school environment is not disrupted. Administrators often have to prioritize the "good of many" over the preferences of a few.

When the referring teacher and a group of students who accompanied her came to the office, they testified that they were "deeply offended" by how the shirt depicted women. They demanded that the student be sent home to change, and said they could not remain in class with him if he wore the shirt. In cases such as this, conflict often results. Our job is to prevent this sort of disruptive conflict.

Disruptive situations such as this incident can be prevented by a more uniform dress code. Shirts without any logos, graphics, or designer labels can not offend anyone and will not be seen as expressions of style, economic status (or free speech, for that matter). A more uniform dress code will help remove distinctions of class and lead to a more unified school community.

In conclusion, and because having to decide what is acceptable or offensive and what is not is a "slippery slope," the school administration therefore proposes a stricter dress code, clearly describing what is acceptable, uniform dress — with no words, logos, or graphics visible. In so doing, we can reduce the wearing of offensive clothing, disruptive interpersonal conflict, and class distinctions in our high school.

DELINEATING ARGUMENTS: CASE STUDY

Course Scheduling Conflict

ISSUE

It is spring and a eighth grader named Nicole is choosing classes for her ninth grade year. She is an excellent, well-rounded student with dreams of attending an Ivy League University. As they review the possible courses she can take next year, she and her parents discover that dance class and honors math will be given at the same time.

Nicole has shown real talent in math and her teacher would like her to enroll in ninth grade honors math class. Nicole has been studying dance since she was 3 and wants to continue dancing in high school and perhaps beyond. The school's dance instructor used to be professional dancer and believes that if Nicole keeps studying, she may win a college scholarship for dance.

The guidance counselor has met with Nicole to explain the options. He always tries to allow students to select at least one course that they are really interested in taking. He has decided to hold a meeting with Nicole and her parents to make a decision. At the meeting, both Nicole and her parents present their positions.

PERSPECTIVES

NICOLE'S PARENTS

Nicole's parents have supported her participation in dance class since she was a young girl. They believe the extracurricular activities are important and want her to continue doing them. However, they believe the opportunity to take ninth grade honors math cannot be passed up because it will prepare her for upper level classes in high school and beyond. They consider taking this honors math class to be more important for providing her with those opportunities than taking the dance class.

They present the following argument:

We believe that being asked to take the honors math class presents an opportunity that cannot passed up—regardless of other courses that Nicole may want to take.

The honors math class will prepare Nicole to take upper level math classes like calculus in high school. Taking calculus in high school will allow her to earn college credit and start college in an advanced math course, thus, lowering the number of courses she has to take in college.

To get into a good college or university, students usually need to do well on the ACT or the SAT. There are other important components of college applications, but strong SAT/ACT match scores will show Nicole's academic talent.

Also, many high-paying careers require a strong background in math and science. You need to be an innovator and have strong reasoning and problem-solving skills in today's job market. Nicole can develop these skills in higher-level math classes.

In conclusion, if Nicole wants to attend an Ivy League school and have the opportunity to get a good job, she needs to develop her abilities in the honors math class. It is difficult to give up on dance for a year, but perhaps we can find another way to take dance class the following year. The opportunities the math class will provide her over the course of her life are limitless and are more important than one year of dance class.

NICOLE

Nicole wants to attend an Ivy League school and is committed to working hard to get good grades, participating in extracurricular activities, and volunteering to help boost her resume. She loves to dance because she has been doing it since she was very young, her best friends are all dancers, and she knows that to be considered for an Ivy League school, you have to have more than just good grades and test scores. She wants to take the honors math course, but not if it means giving up on her dance class which she believes is just as important.

Course Scheduling Conflict (Continued)

She presents the following argument:

Dance is not easy. It takes a lot of training to do it well. Dancers practice steps thousands of times to become good at them. This type of dedication is something that dance has taught me and something I know will be required in Ivy League schools. I know it is not an academic course, but the skills of persistence, perfection, and passion I am learning through dance will be transferable to school.

Participating in extra-curricular activities like dance is very important in the college applications. I know that schools expect you to be well rounded. This means participating in non-academic activities inside and outside of school. My dance career will look very nice on my resume when I am applying to school.

I am still a kid. I know I have ambitious goals and want to go to college and have a good career. But, I'm 12 years old and dance is who I am. Shouldn't I be able to still have fun, socialize with my friends, and follow my passions? Isn't that what most adults do? I already get straight As, volunteer, and have become an exceptional dancer. What is wrong with the path I'm on?

So, I would not be the person that I am without dance. I want to take the honors math course but not if it means missing a year of dance class with my dance teacher and friends. I do know the importance of developing my math skills and preparing for college admissions examinations, but I also cannot consider my life without dance in it right now.

OTHER PERSPECTIVES:

Guidance Counselor, Dance Instructor, Nicole's older sibling, Nicole's friend

DELINEATING ARGUMENTS: CASE STUDY

Tweeting about a Pop Quiz

ISSUE

Justin has Spanish class during first period. When the bell rings Monday morning, the teacher announces that there will be a pop quiz. Justin studied over the weekend, so he's confident he did well on the quiz. His friend Mark, however, told Justin on the ride to school that he didn't study at all. Mark has Spanish with the same teacher during third period. Justin decides to Tweet a warning to Mark about the pop quiz so that Mark will have second period to study. Mark sees the Tweet and he studies during his history class.

His grade on the pop quiz is much higher than his average grade for the course, so the teacher becomes suspicious. The teacher eventually finds out that Justin Tweeted a warning to Mark about the quiz. The teacher calls a meeting with Justin and the school principal to inform Justin that the Tweet was cheating and he will be penalized as such. Justin argues that the Tweet isn't cheating and he shouldn't be punished for letting Mark know about the quiz.

PERSPECTIVES

THE TEACHER

The teacher has been at the school for more than twenty years. During that time, she has earned a reputation as a hard but fair grader. She has been nominated for teacher of the year several times. She has a policy in her class that cell phones are not allowed to be on.

The teacher explains why she considers the Tweet to be cheating:

When I decide to give a pop quiz, I want to evaluate whether my students are keeping up with the ideas and homework in my course. These quizzes need to be surprises in order to evaluate students' commitment to my course. I don't announce these quizzes ahead of time because this will just encourage students to study at the last minute. This doesn't provide the insight I want into students' performance. Because Justin sent that message to his friend, there was an opportunity for his friend and anyone else who heard about this message to prepare for the quiz. This is an unfair advantage and the grades for the third-period quizzes will almost certainly be higher. This isn't fair to my first-period students. In addition to undermining my quiz, Justin has also created extra work for me. I'll have to redo the quiz at another surprise point in the course. I am going to have to deal with complaints from students who did well on the quiz but will have to take a replacement.

JUSTIN

Justin is a good student. His GPA is a 3.7 and he takes a couple of AP courses. He is also involved in the speech and debate team and the chess club. He glazes hams for extra money on the weekend. He and Mark have been friends for five years, though they aren't best friends. Mark moved to Justin's street so they often see one another over the weekend. Justin knows that Mark struggles with school.

Justin defends his decision to Tweet with the following statement:

Sending a Tweet isn't cheating because I didn't tell Mark or anyone else who saw the Tweet what was on the quiz. I just said that we had a quiz so they might have a quiz. I had no idea if the teacher was going to have a quiz for the third-period class. I can't read her mind. What I did isn't different from the other students who told their friends about the quiz in person. Besides, couldn't Mark have thought there might be a quiz even if he hadn't seen the Tweet? At the end of the day, Mark studied and did well, so I don't see what the problem is. It doesn't matter what I Tweeted or what he thought. What matters is that he spent time preparing for the quiz and he earned his grade.

OTHER PERSPECTIVES

Other students, the principal, the teacher's colleagues

ODELL EDUCATION

NOTES

Developing Core Literacy Proficiencies